# Mayors and Schools

# Mayors and Schools
## *Minority Voices and Democratic Tensions in Urban Education*

Stefanie Chambers

Temple University Press
PHILADELPHIA

*For Donna, Joseph, and Owen*

**Stefanie Chambers** is Assistant Professor of Political Science at Trinity College in Hartford, Connecticut. She has written widely on urban education reform, racial and ethnic politics, and urban public policy.

**Temple University Press**
1601 North Broad Street
Philadelphia PA 19122
*www.temple.edu/tempress*

∞ The paper used in this publication meets the requirements of the American National Standard for Information Sciences—Permanence of Paper for Printed Library Materials, ANSI Z39.48–1992

Library of Congress Cataloging-in-Publication Data

Chambers, Stefanie.
    Mayors and schools: minority voices and democratic tensions in urban education/Stefanie Chambers.
        p.   cm.
    Includes bibliographical references and index.
    ISBN 1-59213-468-8 (cloth : alk. paper) — ISBN 1-59213-469-6 (pbk. : alk. paper)
        1. Education, Urban—United States—Case studies.   2. Minorities—Education—United States—Case studies.   3. Educational change—United States—Case studies.   I. Title.
LC5131.C385 2006
370.9173′2–dc22                                        2005056893

2  4  6  8  9  7  5  3  1

# Contents

# Acknowledgments

When I reflect on my personal and professional accomplishments, I feel compelled to offer my gratitude publicly to a very special person: my mother. As my first and most important role model, she has influenced me like no other. Her work ethic inspired me to be a diligent student, and her perseverance continues to motivate me to take on tough challenges and see them to completion. Her commitment to education and equality has profoundly influenced my research. I also offer my heartfelt thanks to my loving husband and our delightful son, who are my most devoted supporters and are the people who made the largest sacrifices as I wrote this book. My family was gracious enough to try to understand the importance of my work and the countless hours I spent doing fieldwork, writing, revising, and editing. Despite my divided attention, they found joy in the time we spent together. It is to them that I dedicate this book.

The successful completion of this project was made possible only through the support and guidance of many caring and talented professionals. It has been a fulfilling yet arduous process, and although I am extremely proud of having my work published, I realize that I could not have done it alone. First, I thank Professor William E. Nelson Jr. for his role as the chair of my dissertation committee at The Ohio State University and for his continued encouragement as I expanded my research. Professor Nelson's constant faith in this project gave me the energy to continue working through the hard times that inevitably occurred. His research skills, dedication to community activism, and support for the professional and personal development of his students have provided the model to which I aspire in my own career. In addition, the interviews I conducted for this project would not have been possible without his willingness to contact his friends and associates in Chicago and Cleveland on my behalf.

I would also like to thank Professor Katherine Tate at the University of California–Irvine. As my postgraduate advisor, Katherine has been a valued mentor and a trusted friend. I am especially grateful for her assistance in developing a theoretical framework for this project. Her friendship and advice have been a great source of support at the most challenging times.

Professor Janet Boles, my undergraduate advisor and mentor at Marquette University, has also played an important role in my career decisions ever since my undergraduate years. I am also grateful to Wilbur Rich at Wellesley College. Wilbur's willingness to collaborate with me on my Cleveland research opened doors for me in Cleveland and in the profession that would have otherwise been out of reach. Parts of our chapter from *Mayors in the Middle* (Henig and Rich, 2004) appear in Chapter 4 of this book.

I would also like to acknowledge the tremendous assistance that I received from several of my colleagues at Trinity College. As a junior faculty member, I am fortunate to work in an environment with such outstanding and supportive scholars. Jack Dougherty, Diana Evans, and Jerry Watts were always willing to discuss my research and offer their valuable feedback. Each read countless versions of the manuscript and provided incredibly helpful suggestions. They gave more of their time and energy than was fair to ask. The book is much better than it would otherwise have been without their selfless support and keen observations. I would also like to thank Mark Franklin for his methodological assistance as I finished this project. During the proofreading process, Barb Chapman, Jack Dougherty, Margo Perkins, and Barbara Sicherman offered their keen eyes, for which I am very grateful.

A number of Trinity students assisted me with various parts of this project. I am grateful for their willingness to search for articles and books, transcribe my interviews, and work on my bibliography and index. I would like to acknowledge the work of Russell Fugett, Rachel Gravel, Sarah Gomez, Melissa Marlett, Saki Mori, Elizabeth Reichert, Alex Spurrier, Shannon Stormont, Alicia Whilby, Jennifer Williams, and Kathryn O'Leary.

I would also like to offer my deepest gratitude to each of the Chicago and Cleveland residents who took time away from their busy schedules and sat for my interviews. I have done my best to allow their voices to be heard in this book. The deep commitment many of these people share for the children in the Chicago and Cleveland public schools fueled my work and gave me the enthusiasm to complete this project.

Finally, I would like to thank Alex Holzman and Peter Wissoker at Temple University Press for their interest and help with the publication process. I am also grateful to the anonymous reviewers who provided helpful recommendations for improving the book. This research was supported by a grant from the American Political Science Association's Small Research Expense Grant, a Trinity College One-Year Research Expense Grant, and a Madison Scott Grant from The Ohio State University.

An earlier version of Chapter 5, "Urban Education Reform and Minority Political Empowerment," was published in *Political Science Quarterly*, Winter 2002–2003, 117(4), 643–665. An earlier version of Chapter 4, "Cleveland: Takeovers and Makeovers Are Not the Same," appeared in *Mayors in the Middle: Politics, Race, and Mayoral Control of Urban Schools* (Jeffrey R. Henig and Wilbur Rich, eds., Princeton University Press, Princeton, NJ, 2004).

# 1 INTRODUCTION

# 1 School Reform in Two American Cities

*In an era when students, teachers and principals are being held responsible for upgrading their performance, the schools desperately need someone at the top who is responsible to the electorate for the performance of the entire system. That person should be the mayor.*
"Mayoral Control" 2000

*I'm really quite pessimistic that the mayor will be able to address the underlying fundamental problem, which is how to improve the test scores and the educational capacities of low-income minority children.*
Paul Peterson, Harvard University, in Stanfield 1997

Since the 1983 publication of the federal report *A Nation at Risk* (National Commission on Excellence in Education 1983), improving the nation's system of urban education remains at the top of the public agenda. The quest for solutions to America's ailing public schools has attracted the attention of parents, politicians, and business leaders as well as scholars and policy analysts (see Gittell 1998; Stone 1996, 1998; Bryk et al. 1998; A. G. Hess 1991, 1995; Katznelson and Weir 1985). The public has traditionally blamed school boards for failing public school systems. Boards have been criticized as financially undisciplined, corrupt, unresponsive, and unaccountable to the communities they serve and to the government. Altering the governance structure of urban schools has gained momentum across the country as a method of reversing some of the alarming trends in urban education. The increasing popularity of this trend raises the question of whether changes to the governance structure of urban schools will improve educational opportunities for the largely minority students who rely on these schools for their educational and economic futures.

There are numerous reforms aimed at improving public education currently under way in American cities. Philadelphia, for example, has turned over management of twenty schools to the private company Edison Schools. Milwaukee led the trend in the use of publicly funded educational vouchers for private and parochial schools. Some states have taken over the administration of local school systems. Other school districts are tinkering with decentralized control of the schools. Still other cities have focused on strong local centralization, believing such a structure is the key to improving student performance. In these cities, independent school boards are eliminated and replaced with mayor-appointed boards, typically without any legislative checks by the city council.

This new model of school governance is the focus of this book. Not surprisingly, mayoral control of the schools has ignited controversy. Advocates of mayoral control contend that mayors are able to centralize public school services, making schools more cost-effective. In fact, many of the cities with mayors at the top of the educational hierarchy have achieved balanced school budgets, a feat previously considered unobtainable for big cities with growing populations of poor people and decomposing fiscal structures. Advocates also contend that, because democratically elected mayors are accountable to the entire city, the use of mayor-appointed boards eliminates the petty politics often associated with elected boards (Henig and Rich 2004; Kirst 2002).

In contrast, critics argue that appointed boards take power away from poor, working class, and predominantly minority residents who rely on the public schools. Some critics also argue that although some mayors may make wise appointments, others facing the multiple pressures and challenges of urban governance may not. In addition, because urban schools serve a low-income, majority-minority population, critics argue that when school boards are under mayoral control, those with the least power are further distanced from influencing the policies that have an impact on the educational opportunities of their children (Stone 2004).

We face many crises in American urban education, but one of the most serious is the underlying tension between two potentially competing values: participatory democracy versus higher measurable student achievement. On the one hand, America has historically valued public schooling as a method of cultivating democratic citizenship. On the other hand, as demonstrated in the report *A Nation at Risk*, in recent decades America has placed increasing pressure on public schools to raise standardized test scores in the name of international economic competition. This tension most directly affects racial minorities, who have become the numerical majority in many urban areas. After decades of educational neglect, African American and Latino citizens have mobilized to achieve both of these goals: gaining a greater voice in urban politics and reducing the racial "achievement gap" in student performance.

The twin goals of participatory democracy and higher student achievement matter a great deal to all Americans. But, how should we respond if we discover that an urban school reform favors one of these goals over the other? This book examines the shift toward centralized mayoral control of big-city school systems in Chicago and Cleveland and considers its consequences for these competing American values. This study reveals that the centralization of urban school governance reduces minority participation in democratic politics, even when the mayor is Black. At the same time, preliminary evidence suggests that minority students' standardized test scores may increase under mayoral control. If the evidence continues to pull us in different directions, then how should we respond? How do we evaluate an urban school reform that exacerbates the tension between the competing values of participatory democracy and higher student achievement? These questions are addressed in the final chapter of the book.

The problem of sustaining the promise of public education for poor and minority communities is one confronting all big American cities. In my investigation of the politics of urban school reform, I chose to focus on two cities: Chicago and Cleveland. Like other urban school systems, the public school systems in these cities have experienced numerous problems caused by fiscal difficulties, deteriorating physical facilities, low student achievement, and administrative mismanagement. Low public confidence in the school board led Mayors Richard M. Daley of Chicago and Michael White of Cleveland to execute takeovers of their school boards to establish direct accountability to the city government. Chicago led the pattern of mayoral control of school systems when, in 1995, the Illinois state legislature granted Mayor Daley control of the Chicago schools. Following Chicago's reform in 1995, the Ohio state legislature gave Mayor White control of the Cleveland schools. Unlike mayoral control in Chicago, Cleveland's model followed a brief period of state control of the schools and management by a school board that was elected by the people. On gaining control of the school system, Cleveland's mayor replaced the elected school board with an appointed one in 1998. An important component of Cleveland's model of mayoral control is that an occupationally and socially diverse nominating committee plays a central role in selecting board members. In 2002, Cleveland voters were given the option of maintaining or rejecting mayoral control. The Illinois legislature included no such measure for Chicago residents. In both cities, the reforms gave the mayors broad oversight of school district finances as well as the ability to hire (and fire) the board's chief executive officer or superintendent.

The reforms undertaken in Chicago and Cleveland raise three important questions. The first relates to whether mayoral control has improved urban education. Has student achievement improved under mayoral control of the schools? We live in an era in which test scores, despite the controversies surrounding them, are emphasized as the primary measure of student achievement; and these scores have become an important political matter. Understanding the effects on student performance of the mayoral control governance structure is a timely issue.

To some, centralizing control of school bureaucracies holds the promise of turning around troubled school systems. Essentially, placing mayors at the top of the educational hierarchy holds the promise of creating more consistency, stability, and efficiency for the school system. On the other hand, some analysts believe that the financial crises faced by cities are the overwhelming factor behind the failure of urban school systems. Altering the governance structure of the schools, therefore, would not in and of itself necessarily remedy the immediate crises that affect urban public school students. Many of the problems associated with urban education are rooted in social, political, and economic inequalities that extend beyond the educational realm (Stone 2004). Residential segregation and the fact that urban schools rely on a declining tax base are contributing factors to the problems faced by urban schools. When examining urban school reform, we must ask whether a particular reform has actually targeted the root causes of the urban education crisis, or whether it has merely addressed the symptoms of the problem.

A second question is whether racial minorities in urban school systems have gained or lost power from the centralization of power in the hands of mayors. Current school reform efforts are pursued during an era when minority groups have won considerable influence in big-city governments. Scholars have demonstrated that Black and Latino political mobilization during the late 1960s and 1970s led to greater minority office holding and ultimately increased governmental responsiveness to the minority community's needs (Browning, Marshall, and Tabb 1984, 1997; Button 1989; Karnig and Welch 1980). As Wilbur Rich (1996) demonstrated, Black activism in many rust-belt cities during the 1960s and 1970s resulted not only in more minority representation in municipal governments, but also in minority administrative control of school boards and educational policy by the 1980s.

The fact that minority groups play a more critical role in governing cities appears to have complicated the analysis of school reform efforts. In cities such as Baltimore, as documented by Marion Orr (1999), minority control of the school bureaucracy coincided with a declining economy, White flight to the suburbs, and reduction in federal aid to cities. Because of the reciprocal relationship among economic crises, politics, and public education in postindustrial cities, performance improvements among students have not been evident. This is not to say that the symbolic implications of minority incorporation in educational decision making are inconsequential. Rather, as minorities gained increased influence, their efforts to improve schools were hampered by the political and economic realities of urban America.

Alongside these two empirical questions stands a third and broader policy question: What should we do if the dual values of minority incorporation and rising student achievement pull us in different directions? There are obvious moral reasons for caring that minorities have a voice in policymaking. At the extreme, exclusion of the people served by the schools from the decision making that affects their children seems unfair. Beyond this, there is a broader political and social reason. Even when benevolent Whites dominate educational policy decision making, excluding minorities' voices and

exclusion, disabled

personal expertise with the schools places students at a disadvantage. Because minorities are at the heart of urban education, excluding them means that the people with the deepest understanding of the local schools are silenced. Even if community members are under-educated, their firsthand experiences with the schools offers valuable input on the experiences of their children in the schools. This is input that can help the schools more effectively teach children in homes and communities that face multiple social and economic challenges.

Therefore, even if we see some evidence of improvements in student performance after a school reform is implemented, ignoring the level of minority incorporation in the policy process misses a component of urban school reform that can also have an impact on outcomes. Furthermore, Meier and England (1984) found that Black membership on school boards leads to more equitable educational opportunities for Black students. Thus, if decisions are made at the top of the hierarchy without the inclusion of the minority residents served by the system, then educational policy may be less responsive to minority interests. I argue that minority incorporation is essential if we want to have a system in which those on the receiving end of public education have a voice in the policy process. Although improvements in student performance are important and are a measure of the overall health of the school system, if the minority community plays a limited role in the education of their children, then the system lacks an important component of urban education.

## Conceptual Framework: Evaluating Urban School Reforms

In their book Politics, Markets, and America's Schools (1990), John Chubb and Terry Moe critique public education and efforts to reform it. According to the authors, public schools are democratically run, yet these very institutions of democratic control undermine school autonomy and effectiveness (23). They argue that entrenched interest groups, such as unions, school boards, superintendents, administrators, and professionals, participate in the democratic process in education and are resistant to institutional change. From this critique, Chubb and Moe make the case for a market-based approach to public education. Attention to their work has centered primarily on their strong case for school choice. They "turn away from government" as a solution to the identified problem and support a market-based system reliant on consumer choice (Henig and Rich 2004).

There are three major political variables that Chubb and Moe largely overlook in their analysis of public education. The first and foremost omission is race. The second variable, which is very much correlated with race, is class. Third, they downplay the role of state dynamics in the distribution of resources for urban schools. All of these variables represent important arenas of conflict in urban education.

Regarding the important issues of race and class, Chubb and Moe's critique of American schools draws all of its examples of schools that fail to foster student performance improvements from urban schools. Although they mention suburban and private schools in their book, they argue that these are the schools that avoid the democracy trap to which the downfall of public education is attributed. These schools have more autonomy, and there is far less democratic competition, making them generally more successful. Chubb and Moe raise the following questions to develop their argument that too much democracy is the root of failing public (urban) schools:

> What is the relationship between democratic control and the organization of schools? Is it possible that there is something inherent in America's traditional institutions of democratic governance that systematically creates and nurtures the kinds of schools that no one really wants? (25)

Although the "schools that no one really wants" are clearly urban schools, Chubb and Moe overlook that many suburban public schools remain highly desirable, which calls into question their implication that there is something inherently flawed in the democratic control of American schools.

I argue that these questions misdiagnose the problems of urban schools. Missing from their analysis is the recognition that race or class plays a role in the politics of urban education. It is well known that urban schools in the United States are majority-minority and serve lower-class students. To downplay these facts is to overlook a significant pattern of inequality in public education. Rather than acknowledging the race and class patterns of inequality in urban and suburban education, they simply claim that suburban schools are more autonomous and have less democratic competition among stakeholders for control over resources, making them more effective. In addition, the competition that urban schools experience, particularly for resources, is different from what we typically see in suburban schools, which have fewer minorities and more access to resources. The authors also ignore the fact that it is common to see racial and class conflicts within urban education. For example, it would not be uncommon to see minority parents and teachers at odds with majority White groups such as unions, school boards, business groups, or even local foundations over the shape of school reform.

The third arena of conflict that Chubb and Moe overlook is the role that the state plays in urban education. Although they do recommend that states play more of a role in public education in their market-driven prescription for reform (225), they do not address how state policies constrain urban schools. It is common knowledge that reliance on property taxes for education places urban schools at a disadvantage because of their typically low tax base. Together with reductions in federal spending on education, urban schools are highly dependent on state resources. However, competition for these resources is fierce. In most state governments, White suburban and rural interests typically dominate minority urban interests. In sum, racial politics inside city school districts is happening simultaneously within the political struggle for resources at the state level. These arenas of conflict are both ignored by Chubb and Moe, and I argue that these omissions lead to their misdirected criticism of democratic control of urban education.

By contrast, Marion Orr's book, *Black Social Capital* (1999), makes it abundantly clear that race and economics played a critical role in Baltimore's urban school reforms during the 1980s and 1990s. In explaining what can cause a school reform to fail or succeed, Orr argues that both racial factors and financial resources matter. Orr develops his own theoretical framework to evaluate urban school reform in part by building on Robert Putnam's theory of social capital. According to Putnam, social capital represents the "features of social organization, such as trust, norms, and networks, that can improve the efficiency of society by facilitating coordinated actions," (Putnam in Orr 1999, 3). Orr argues that this definition does not capture Baltimore's experience with school reform, particularly because it does not include the challenges of working across racial lines. He explains:

> A major flaw in the social capital argument is that it does not consider the difficulty in transferring intragroup to intergroup social capital. To appreciate the importance of social capital, especially in many of America's central cities, it is necessary to consider it within the context of intergroup competition and the distrusts built up over the years of racial divisions and black subordination. (10)

To improve the social capital theory, Orr distinguishes between two new dimensions of social capital: intragroup (Black) and intergroup (Black-White). By doing so, Orr develops a model of urban school reform that places race at the center of the policy arena. Black social capital is defined as "the interpersonal and institutional forms within the African-American community" (8) that create political cohesion within that group. The second dimension, intergroup social capital, requires interracial coalitions (10), which Orr refers to as the "cross-sector formations of mutual trust and networks that bridge the black-white divide, especially at the elite level of sociopolitical organization" (8). In his Baltimore case study, Orr concludes that Black social capital is considerable, but school reform cannot succeed without forging intergroup social capital, which he finds lacking.

Orr examines the history of Baltimore to show how racial segregation and a culture of White supremacy contributed to the high level of Black social capital in the city, yet intergroup social capital remains a more challenging reality. One of the main reasons for this is that racial mistrust runs through public policy. The facts that the city's school administration is predominantly Black and that those who control the key to resources (business leaders, state legislators, foundations) are predominantly White present hurdles for intergroup social capital formation. Orr shows that, even with strong Black social capital, the fiscal realities of public education and the racial dynamics of the policy arena complicate urban school reform. At the root of Orr's study is the idea that to understand the challenges of reforming our urban schools, we must acknowledge the challenges associated with building cooperative arrangements between groups who control different sectors of urban education.

The void in Chubb and Moe's research in terms of race and state dynamics is directly filled by Orr's work. Orr convincingly argues that race is a necessary variable in understanding urban school reform and its connections to resources in the broader political arena; Chubb and Moe largely ignore both. By contrast with those authors, Orr does not argue that too much democracy is the reason urban school reforms fail. Rather, he sees the challenges of building intergroup social capital and the fiscal dependency of urban schools as leading factors in the challenges of urban school reform.

My work builds on the conflict between the work of Chubb and Moe and that of Marion Orr. In contrast to Chubb and Moe's critique of a high degree of democratic control of the schools, I examine the possibility that democratic incorporation in educational policy, particularly of the minority community, is critical to a successful school system. I argue that democratic participation can empower minorities and make public education more effective. I also find great merit in Orr's argument for the importance of Black and Black-White social capital in urban school reform. His argument is persuasive that without resources, which are often controlled by Whites, urban school reform may be an elusive goal.

However, although Orr examines a series of school reforms in one urban system, my study takes a different approach. I examine changes in the governance structures of two urban school systems: Chicago and Cleveland (During the period of study, Chicago's mayor was White, and Cleveland's was Black). The other divergence from Orr's research is that my work emphasizes the evaluation of student achievement outcomes as a key political variable in urban school debates, something Orr's study did not fully consider. This type of examination is timely as there is an increasing emphasis on evaluation tools such as test scores to measure the success of a school system.[1] In the end, my study confronts the important question of how the twin goals of participatory democracy and student achievement are affected by mayoral control of the schools in Chicago and Cleveland. I argue that even with improvements in student performance, we cannot overlook the importance of minority incorporation in urban education if we hope to have successful urban schools.

## A Tale of Two Cities: Chicago and Cleveland

This book systematically examines school reform in two U.S. cities: Chicago and Cleveland. These cities were selected because each has been in the forefront of the trend in mayoral control and because, like many other cities, they serve a majority-minority population. Because I am interested in understanding the structural changes in school boards in these cities, I examine school governance structures from 1965 through 2002. I selected this period because it was one of growing influence of minorities in urban governments and urban educational policy (W. C. Rich 1996).

Although the total Black and Latino population of Chicago and Cleveland is approximately 60 percent, the student minority percentage is higher in both cities (87 percent in Chicago and 80 percent in Cleveland). The cities differ significantly in size. Chicago is the third-largest school system in the nation; Cleveland is more typical of a midsize city. Together, they offer a model on which many large and midsize cities can reflect when considering mayoral control of their troubled schools. Although Cleveland modeled its mayoral control structure on the Chicago plan, there are differences in the details. In addition, the two cities contrast nicely on various political dimensions even though the demographics (with the exception of size) and economic profiles of the two cities are roughly similar.

Both of the mayors initially granted control were Democrats, but each came to power through different ethnic and racial coalitions. Since 1967, Cleveland's Black community has generally been able to elect mayors from its own racial group.[2] By contrast, Chicago elected its first Black mayor, Harold Washington, in 1983 in a racially divided election (Grimshaw 1992; Pinderhughes 1987). Since Washington's untimely death in 1987, Chicago's Black electorate has played a less-decisive role in mayoral elections.

Prior to the institution of mayoral control, Chicago's school board selection process involved the community, and Cleveland's school board was directly elected. Both of these earlier models incorporated the community and were arguably more democratic than the mayoral control models. These models of school board selection provide interesting contrasts to mayoral control models.

Both cities previously experimented with other school governance reforms such as decentralization of control to parents or local schools. Chicago undertook a major effort to decentralize control from the central school administration to local schools and community members in 1988. This legislation included provisions by which parents essentially managed each public school. But, in 1995, the Illinois legislature reversed course by centralizing control of Chicago's schools to the mayor, and the decision-making authority of parents was significantly reduced. The Cleveland schools experimented with limited decentralization in the 1990s and had a stint under state receivership, a form of school governance reform to which state governments have increasingly resorted. In contrast to Chicago, Cleveland's elected school board was stripped of power in 1998, when the state took control of the schools. However, just three years later, the state turned control of the schools over to the mayor, much to the frustration of many parents, the teachers' union, and the local National Association for the Advancement of Colored People (NAACP). One of the most common arguments against mayoral control of schools in Cleveland was that it stripped residents of their right to a democratically elected school board. Although supporters of these various governance reforms claim that there are benefits to each plan, a thorough evaluation of governance reform is necessary to determine whether these governance changes actually improved the educational and economic opportunities for the students served and the degree to which the community is incorporated in educational policymaking.

Although this study discusses state control of the Cleveland schools and decentralization in Cleveland and Chicago, primary emphasis is placed on mayoral control of the schools as a method of governance reform. This reform is gaining popularity nationwide, and it is crucial to understand its impact. The effects of recentralizing educational power must be examined if we hope to understand the impact of mayoral control of the schools on community inclusion in educational policy and overall student improvement.

## Methodology

To determine the impact of mayoral control on urban education, I examine the impact of this reform on both minority incorporation and student achievement. Two variables assess minority incorporation: school system responsiveness to minority concerns and administrators' perceptions of their accountability when making educational policy decisions. Looking at minority incorporation through these two variables allows assessment of community satisfaction with mayoral control and examination of the other end of the spectrum, the extent to which administrators believe they are accountable to the community they serve. Together, these variables provide a clearer lens than either variable alone.

To evaluate student achievement under mayoral control, I draw on various measures of student performance, including test scores, attendance rates, and graduation figures. These measurements provide a more comprehensive evaluation of student achievement than just examining test scores.

Together, measurement of responsiveness, accountability, and student performance by these variables allows systematic evaluation of the changes in school governance structures, specifically the manner in which school board members are selected and the level of parental involvement in educational policy decisions. For both cities, I describe the details of their respective mayoral control governance structures, including how school board members are chosen and whether the mayor has complete autonomy in the appointment process. Differences in the details of the governance structure could influence outcomes; thus, it is important to examine them carefully.

A unique component of this study is the use of in-depth interviews conducted with non-elites and elites in Chicago and Cleveland between 1998 and 2002. During my research visits to Chicago between 1998 and 1999, I conducted forty-six formal in-depth interviews.[3] I began with an initial list of possible respondents supplied by scholars with expertise on Chicago politics.[4] As the interviews progressed, I added names to the list based on suggestions I received from the interviewees. This research methodology allowed conducting interviews with a broad range of community activists, parents, elected and appointed officials, school board members, school administrators, and academicians in Chicago. I used the same strategy in Cleveland.[5] Between 2000 and 2002, I conducted thirty-seven in-depth interviews with Cleveland community activists, parents, elected and appointed officials, school board members, school administrators, and academicians.[6]

Interviews in both cities were recorded unless the respondent objected. In those cases, I took detailed notes during the interview. Interviews generally lasted between one and three hours. Several shorter interviews were also conducted by telephone and either recorded or summarized through written notes. Direct quotations appear and are used to strengthen my analysis by allowing the voices of those active in the struggle to improve urban education to be heard directly. As I promised my subjects, I use pseudonyms to maintain the anonymity of the respondents. Names are attributed to the quotations of prominent administrators or elected officials only when identification is required to understand the context of their comments and when doing so did not violate my promise of anonymity. My research methodology also included an extensive examination of special reports, books, and newspaper articles. I engaged in participant observation during my visits to the two cities. I attended school board meetings, community organizational meetings, and other events to which my respondents were kind enough to invite me.

## Importance of Studying Urban School Reform

As a political scientist, my interests are rooted in the minority empowerment literature (Browning, Marshall, and Tabb 1984, 1997; Bobo and Gilliam 1990; Eisinger 1982). Although this body of research emphasizes mayors and city councils as the principal policy actors, I explore the school board as a third important policy actor in cities. Further, this study attempts to bridge the gap between the educational policy literature and the minority empowerment literature. Although several notable contributions have been made in this area (Henig and Rich 2004; Henig et al. 1999; Mirel 1999; Orr 1999; Portz, Stein, and Jones 1999; Portz 1996; Meier and Stewart 1991), this study offers a unique evaluation of governance reform and its impact on minorities.

Although my research is motivated by a concern over educational policy and what Kozol (1991) has correctly labeled the "savagely unequal" educational opportunities provided for our urban youth, my findings also speak to a number of important ongoing controversies in urban politics. First addressed is the long-standing and broad question of community power—Who governs urban America? (Dahl 1961; Hunter 1953)—by extending the issue to minority groups. Specifically examined is the extent minorities influence public school policy in cities. This is an important consideration in light of the school reform movement and the rapid pace by which new policies have been adopted, including citywide voucher plans or "choice" programs, as well as the new court-sanctioned retreat of urban districts from their decades-long goal of racial integration. Are minority interests represented in these reforms? Who now directs school policy? Does the reconcentration of power over urban education in the hands of the mayor expand or restrict the political influence of the poor and minorities?

Second, my research enters the debate regarding whether politics matters in urban governments. Does the governance structure of a school system affect its responsiveness to the community? Does the governance structure of a school system affect its ability to improve educational outcomes? Do school boards perform better when directed by the mayor or when the community is more directly involved in educational policymaking? To some, school board politics might seem inconsequential. However, if this is so, then why have so many mayors, most recently Michael Bloomberg of New York and Antonio Villaraigosa of Los Angeles, sought control of their city schools? Certainly, we must consider the financial condition of school districts. As scholars have demonstrated, by providing large budgets, direct employment, and public contracts, school districts are essential to urban economies (W. C. Rich 1996; Pinderhughes 1987; Peterson 1981; Herrick 1971). Both the Chicago and Cleveland public schools oversee billion-dollar budgets annually, provide thousands of jobs, and continue to sell bonds, all of which have a significant impact on the city's economic vitality.

Those who favor school boards appointed solely by mayors contend that mayoral control provides better fiscal management and more efficient services. Those who believe that political control of school systems and city government makes little difference in the larger distribution and redistribution of political goods, including education, may be correct in a broader sense. But, it is clear that an investigation of the impact of altering the governance structure of an urban school district is necessary. We must understand whether changing the governance structure gets to the heart of the problems that relegate largely poor and minority students to a position of educational inferiority.

In the end, fixing the predicament of urban schools may be beyond the reach of school boards, superintendents, and even mayors. The large disparities in urban and suburban educational systems as measured by student test performance, dropout rates, truancy figures, and college attendance rates might necessitate a more comprehensive reform of the political economy to lift urban schools to the level of their suburban counterparts. School boards may be unfairly targeted for blame for the problems that require urban-suburban, state, and federal cooperation. In addition, although mayors seeking quick political boosts to aid in reelection may turn to mayoral control, it may not be the way to elevate urban schools.

This study of minority power amid the movement to centralize school governance may also yield important insights related to other educational governance reforms in other cities, such as vouchers, privatization, and charter schools. In particular, centralization may reduce minority influence over educational policymaking in cities where they were previously well represented. The fact that centralization has emerged as a new reform trend begs for analysis to determine its public policy implications and ultimate effect on minority students.

School reform is pursued at a time when the Great Society welfare state has been greatly discredited, resulting in a diminished federal role in urban affairs. This is most apparent when looking at the 1996 welfare reform legislation and the general trend in government devolution of federal programs to the state and local levels. The direction of these reforms is in many ways consistent with what is occurring in education: a growing reallocation of the burden of education from the state to the local level. Passing responsibility to city hall is a relatively new trend that has taken hold because of the "new breed" of mayors, who are seen as pragmatic, comfortable with private sector cooperation, and less idealistic than many of their counterparts in the 1960s and 1970s (Henig and Rich 2004; Kirst and Buckley 2000).

## Plan of the Book

Following this introductory section, Section II, The Politics of School Reform and Minority Political Empowerment, provides a brief historical overview of urban education reform and the position of minorities in educational reform. The three chapters in this section address major trends in urban education from the 1960s onward, with special emphasis on reforms that have taken place in Chicago and Cleveland.

After providing the necessary background on urban school reform in Cleveland and Chicago, Section III, Measuring Success in Education Reform, focuses on the influence of mayoral control on urban education. The three chapters in this section examine the three variables that are the focus of this study: responsiveness to the community, administrative accountability, and overall educational improvement under mayoral control in both Chicago and Cleveland.

Chapter 5 examines the extent to which school boards are responsive to different segments of the community under the different governance structures. I consider whether board members act as "delegates" for their constituents or as "trustees" who rely on their personal judgments to determine which policies are best for the school system. The social and political backgrounds of appointed and elected school board members are compared to draw conclusions about descriptive and substantive aspects of representation. The examination of responsiveness centers on whom community and minority groups look to for school change.

My approach to the study of responsiveness to minority involvement stems from Browning, Marshall, and Tabb's (1984) notion that minority group mobilization at the local level can lead to incorporation in city governance and ultimately to governmental responsiveness to minority residents' concerns. This notion of responsiveness is also influenced by Berry, Portney, and Thomson's (1993) contention that revitalizing urban democracy requires citizen participation to ensure governmental responsiveness to the preferences of citizens.

I view the involvement of the minority community in educational policymaking as an important aspect of democracy in urban America. The minority community is emphasized because the Chicago and Cleveland public schools educate a student body that is predominantly Black and Latino. Responsiveness has been operationalized in this study as the ability of the administration to meet the vocalized concerns of the community.

Chapter 6 examines whether school board members are accountable to different interests when operating under different governance structures. *Responsiveness* is defined as the set of actors and institutions to which community and minority groups look for school change. In contrast, *accountability* is assessed in terms of the individuals and groups included by board members in school policy decisions. Whom do members represent in their voting and policymaking patterns: the community, municipal politicians, interest groups, business organizations? Interviews with past and present school board members, chief executive officers, and the former mayor of Cleveland provide valuable information regarding whom policymakers consider themselves accountable when the school board is appointed solely by the mayor as compared to board appointments that involve the community and the city council or when the board is elected.

Ester Fuchs (1992) and Martin Shefter (1985) found not only that interest groups exerted more influence over policy in cities marked by weak and fragmented leadership, but also that the degree to which interest groups dominated city politics contributed to the city's fiscal instability. Boards elected or selected with a high level of community involvement may cast votes that cater to too many special interests, including teachers' unions, leading the district down the road to fiscal insolvency. For example, the high degree of decentralization in Chicago following the 1988 legislation and the election of school boards in Cleveland prior to 1998 may have involved too many access points for organized interests to exercise their influence over the school board. Furthermore, the political clout of organized interests in cities may be greater than that of minority residents, making minority involvement less important than perhaps anticipated.

Student performance under different reform initiatives is examined in Chapter 7 by assessing various measures of achievement to evaluate whether a city's school governance structure is related to that performance. Student performance is considered first based on student test scores on citywide tests over time. In addition, the aggregate changes on these tests are compared to long-term results on the federally sponsored National Assessment of Educational Progress to determine whether scores in the cities kept pace with changes seen nationally. Although gauging changes in student performance also includes an evaluation of student attendance statistics and high school graduation rates, a content analysis of national news stories on mayoral control in these cities is also included because it provides a useful assessment of the mainstream interpretation of mayoral control and student performance since the governance shift.

The final section of the book, Resolving Tensions in Urban Education, addresses the troubling question of how we should respond when two competing values—greater minority incorporation in educational policymaking and improved student performance—pull us in different directions. When weighing their merits, democracy deserves the highest priority. Therefore, evaluations of the success of urban education should emphasize democratic participation in terms of minority incorporation as well as how well the schools are preparing future citizens for a life of inclusion in the policymaking process. In addition to resolving the tension between minority incorporation and student performance, my recommendations are intended to offer a new lens for evaluating the success of all urban education reform efforts, not just mayoral control.

# II THE POLITICS OF SCHOOL REFORM AND MINORITY POLITICAL EMPOWERMENT

# 2 Big-City Mayors and the Politics of School Reform

*no guarantee of a pay off*

As part of an age-old cyclical tradition of casting out old political structures and policies and adopting the new (F. M. Hess 1998; Tyack and Cuban 1995), some big-city mayors are seeking to reform urban education by centralizing control of school systems. The innovative component of these new urban education reforms is in conferring greater authority and control over school systems to mayors. In many ways, mayor-centered reforms may be seen as a new reform model that incorporates aspects of past reforms while offering a new twist.

At the same time that mayor-centered reforms reflect some aspects of the past, they are also a departure from the past. Current interest on the part of big-city mayors to assume control of their school systems is unrivaled in the history of American education reform. However, these entrepreneurial mayors also face the reality that education is both a redistributive and an economic public good. In the redistributive sense, mayors may not want to invest in it because it is not guaranteed to pay off electorally, politically, or economically. On the economic side, mayors must demonstrate a commitment to improving public education if they wish to maintain an urban middle class and promote business growth. The new group of mayors leading this reform movement is characterized as more pragmatic, technocratic, less partisan, and less beholden to racial, ethnic, and public employee constituencies. They also have stronger corporate ties than their more populist predecessors did.

As Jeffrey Henig and Wilbur Rich (2004) explain, decision makers in the various branches of government at the federal and state levels appear to have faith in devolving powers to these new mayors. Why have mayors stepped into the politics of education reform now? What are the political motivations behind this educational reform?

Why does mayoral control of school systems incite such controversy? These are the main questions of this chapter.

Mayoral control reflects the perspective of early twentieth century administrative progressives who believed that elected school boards are by nature plagued by corruption. Progressives campaigned against ward-based, partisan school boards, arguing that they should be replaced with a more efficient method of centralized professional management (Tyack and Cuban 1995, 18). In many large cities, progressives passed legislation that opposed local political machines by installing nonpartisan school boards at the helm of autonomous school districts (Henig and Rich 2004; Tyack 1974). Yet, by the 1960s interest grew in some urban communities to reverse the progressive era's centralized hierarchy and replace it with decentralized decision making designed to enhance local community control of educational policymaking (Henig and Rich 2004, 6).

Reflecting the cyclical nature of urban school reform, mayoral control represents a more recent move toward recentralizing educational policymaking. In an untraditional sense, it also reflects devolution of power from the state to the city because, in many instances, state legislatures granted mayors control of their failing schools. Several state legislatures have recently thrown up their hands in frustration after years of bailing out struggling urban school districts. In addition, the federal government has increasingly taken a hands-off approach to education, with the important exception of the Bush administration's 2002 *No Child Left Behind* legislation. This legislation establishes standards that all public schools must meet to avoid serious consequences, such as allowing students to attend different schools and other financial penalties.

Mayoral control is especially controversial at a time when the racial composition of cities has changed from predominantly White to predominantly African American and Latino. In theory, mayoral control increases accountability because one elected official is responsible for the schools rather than numerous school board members and a superintendent who are likely beholden to specific constituencies. Some argue, however, that minority communities are stripped of their power when mayors assume control of the schools because fewer opportunities are available to address their concerns when power is more hierarchical. In addition, if mayors are more responsive to their electoral coalition when making educational policy decisions and if minorities in the city are not part of that electoral coalition, then it is likely that minorities will feel that their concerns are ignored as a consequence of mayoral control. Interestingly, in many of the cities that are operating under some form of mayoral control, the reform is perceived as a "White" initiative, even in cities where the mayor is Black (Henig and Rich 2004).

## Decentralization and Centralization: Contrasting Structures

The term *decentralization* simply means "the break-up and distribution of power from a central government authority . . . the transfer of school policymaking authority from the federal to state level, or the transfer of decision-making authority from the state level to districts or schools."[1] Decentralization is a broad term that has come to mean different things to different groups. For some, decentralized control is synonymous with the debate over voucher programs or the creation of individual charter schools because greater control is allocated to the school system to create educational alternatives for students through these nontraditional programs.

Others use the term to denote site-based management, the most common interpretation of decentralization. Site-based management means that each individual school in a district becomes responsible for decision making, budget management, and educational improvement. In this model, higher forms of government continue to serve the purpose of supervision, quality control, and data research collection. Those who support this model maintain that state and federal policymakers are out of tune with local variations, beliefs, and innovations (Wirt and Kirst 1972, 49). They charge the government with stifling progress with an overabundance of bureaucracy. They believe that educational decisions are better made and implemented by those closest to the schools. Some believe that it will lead to a greater sense of ownership by those directly involved in education, specifically teachers, principals, and parents who would design the focus, methods, and curricula of their schools.

Decentralization has been experimented with nationally. New York City attempted to decentralize schools but fell on myriad problems, especially union opposition to experimental districts created to set the stage for greater decentralization and community control (Gittell 1998). The first experiment with democratic localism occurred in 1967 because of the efforts of African American parents frustrated with their lack of influence in the schooling of their children in Ocean-Hill Brownsville. These parents wanted control over local Black schools and claimed that the professionals had failed them in educating their children, and that they deserved a chance to reform the schools themselves (Levin 1968, 4–8). The three demonstration districts were dissolved within a year, and the systemwide decentralization that was put in place in 1969 offered only limited opportunities for community involvement (Gittell 1998).

In 1979, Dade County, Florida, experimented earliest with site-based management. Community control was in theory designed to establish several new community-based school boards of lay members. In addition, it was supposed to give schools and teachers more freedom to introduce progressive methods and to give parents and other interested community members a chance to influence education. At this time, many conservative pundits praised the release of states and localities from centralized control. Some liberal activists began endorsing decentralization and site-based management as the only viable alternative for educational improvement.

Amid rampant criticism of the deplorable state of public schools, Chicago became the epicenter of this decentralization movement in 1988 when then Secretary of Education William Bennett named the Chicago schools the "worst in the nation." Hoping to reverse the low test scores and high dropout rates, Chicago turned to a collective power model in the form of eleven member local school councils for each of Chicago's 595 schools. These councils included parents, teachers, administrators, and other community members because "much of the problem, it was believed, was with the increasingly centralized, increasingly unwieldy school bureaucracy, which was trying to keep track of hundreds of schools, thousands of teachers, and hundreds of thousands of students" (Presser 1991).

Decentralization critics cite the many failures to decentralize power and note that the shift "does not necessarily translate into a more equal distribution of power . . . or into better school performance. Data suggests that the changes may have increased internal tensions and conflicts within schools" (King 1998). The critics also have research on their side. The Department of Education published a report citing that "decentralization makes for waste and inefficiency; it has not improved education; it has encouraged political corruption and mismanagement of funds, and has not corrected racial imbalance" (Shapiro 1986). Other critics believe that "decentralization is a simplistic approach to a problem that is deep and complex, an approach that has succeeded only in transferring power from one group that lacks facilities, funds and educational insight to many groups who lack the same things. . . . Local autonomy in school, as in governmental affairs, inevitably will lead toward politics, corruption, and inefficiency" (Shapiro 1986).

Advocates of decentralization defend these dismal reports by explaining that "improving school performance may be an unrealistic expectation for a governance reform that alters the balance of power within educational systems toward schools" (Wohlstetter, Smyer, and Mohrman 1994). These advocates believe that decentralization can lead to four "intermediate" outcomes that will eventually lead toward the ultimate goal of turning around low-performing students and schools: increased efficiency in use of resources and personnel; increased professionalism of teachers; implementation of curriculum reform; and increased community engagement (Drury and Levin 1994). Decentralization supporters also argue that students are best served if their programs are responsive to the unique character of each community and thereby each school. They consider centralized school bureaucracies with broad general policies and procedures unqualified to deal satisfactorily with divergent local needs. It is argued that decentralization empowers those closest to its effects and therefore guarantees its success.

Many believe decentralization might become a reality under President George W. Bush, who has proposed, as one of his four basic reforms, the removal of federal regulations on individual schools and school districts in exchange for accountability through improved test results ("Education President" 2001). There has always been an ideological turf battle between the right, who see increased competition and accountability as rational ways to minimize the gap between rich and poor, and those on the left, who fear these policies will only exacerbate educational disparities. Thus, many depict decentralization reforms as "conservative methods that can achieve liberal goals" ("Education President" 2001). Although community control was initially supported by liberals, decentralization is now viewed as a conservative solution. Supporters acknowledge the flaws of past decentralization efforts but contend that it has the potential to succeed if it is instituted genuinely by people truly interested in educational progress and quality. They believe that through a decentralized system, schools will get the power and responsibility to choose what type of institution to become by setting their own goals and selecting the methods to achieve them. Decentralization has many supporters and, like school choice, creates strange bedfellows in a way that links conservative Republicans and alienated minority groups.

## The Shift to Mayors

Big-city mayors are enjoying unprecedented power and influence over educational policy. By having the freedom to set local policy initiatives, mayors are "no longer poor dependents of the federal government" ("City Politics" 1999) but are now more than ever on the front line of educational innovation, authority, and vision. Many observers are excited by the prospect of mayors taking over struggling school systems because it cuts down on the bureaucracy, makes the system more fiscally responsible, creates clear accountability, sets education as a top priority of the city, and unites communities under a uniform plan for improving education. Mayors are increasingly involved because they see education as a key component in social mobility. Moreover, improving education is a way to lure the middle class back to the cities and is an integral mechanism for developing a strong workforce, an essential component of maintaining a healthy economy. Those who support mayoral control often label traditional school boards as highly politicized, strangled by red tape, and impeded by divergent opinions. Frustrated by these hurdles and the subsequent poor performance of schools, mayors in Chicago, Cleveland, Boston, Detroit, New York, and Washington, DC, have taken control of the reins of education.

In addition to the increased visibility caused by mayoral takeovers of schools is the intensified public attention given to the deplorable state of urban education. With high concentrations of poverty and a limited tax base, many urban educational systems are seemingly caught between the proverbial rock and a hard place with no way of helping themselves. William Boyd, a professor of education at Penn State University, noted, "Urban school districts are in crisis. They've become almost ungovernable, and it's no wonder the mayors are thinking about taking over these districts. . . . Mayoral takeovers are not a silver bullet, they may not be a panacea, but they might be a step in the right direction. People are willing to take a chance because what they're looking at now is so unattractive" (Heaney 1999).

This is not the first time that mayors have attempted to step in and fix the education systems in their cities. In the 1970s, the mayors of Detroit and New York failed in their bids to gain power to reverse the poor state of schools. Michael Kirst reported that, "It didn't last, because they began to be accused of not being able to raise achievement scores and improve the schools, so the mayors backed out on the basis that this was a no-win ball game" (Stanfield 1997). Thus, for a long time, "Mayors didn't want to go anywhere near the school system. . . . It was somebody else's problem" (Flint 1999a).

Today, given this history, many question why mayors would risk their credibility and political futures on such a potentially disastrous move. In many instances, mayors were sparked into action by the fiscal or managerial messes in their local school systems. Only then did they realize the scope of what administering education entails. "In all these cases, money was never far below the surface," explains John F. Jennings, director of the Center for National Education Policy, an education think tank (Stanfield 1997). Because school districts are financed separately from city budgets, the transfer of school budgets to city hall has allowed mayors to assume control of budgets that were formerly out of their reach.

Of the cities that adopted mayoral control of their schools in the 1990s, Boston was the initial educational renegade, leading the forefront of mayoral control of schools as a means of accountability, improvement, and innovation. In 1992, Mayor Flynn (1982–93) assumed full responsibility for the city's troubled school system, a move supported by 70 percent of the city's residents. Mayoral control gave Mayor Thomas Menino (1993–present) the power to appoint seven people to the board from a list provided by a nominating committee (Portz 2004, 100). Regarding this bold and potentially disastrous move, Menino stated, "As mayors, we take the blame for everything, no matter what happens.... The big thing is [that] somebody is now accountable for the system" (Stanfield 1997).

Under Menino's guidance, Boston took a much more moderate, incremental approach in which the board, although appointed by the mayor, appointed the superintendent and senior staff. Boston's approach more closely follows traditional school district characteristics than Chicago or Cleveland. The Boston district has approached improving student performance by trying to lay a foundation that will improve chances for success. Policy changes included redesigning the curriculum to focus on literacy, building new schools, ending social promotion, establishing afterschool programs, investing in teacher training, and integrating technology. According to Ellen Guiney, head of the Boston Plan for Excellence, "It's not just kid learning, but adult learning that has to go on. It's going to take six, seven, eight years to turn an urban school district around" (Stanfield 1997). Although test scores have improved only slightly, she believes the district's "accomplishments are very solid" (Stanfield 1997).

This is contrasted by some who mark Boston's educational reform as "painfully slow" (Flint 1999b). Menino has certainly made education a top priority in Boston, but the movement lacks the high-profile visibility that Chicago has enjoyed. As Menino states, "We don't do a good job of selling what we do, it sounds bad when you say it, but what we really need is more cheerleaders." Many sympathize with Menino's uphill battle. Michael McCormack, a former city councilor, states, "I don't know how you get the middle class back—Black or White. They just view the suburban or parochial schools as a better education. Plus, I think people are still fighting the battles of the 1970s, when division over busing twisted views of Boston schools" (Flint 1999b). In 1996, 53 percent of voters chose to continue with mayoral control of the schools, while 23 percent voted in favor of a return to an elected structure. However, 23 percent of the ballots were unmarked, indicating that a large minority did not know which was the right course to take in this reform initiative (Portz 2004, 106). As Portz found, the election results were racially divided, with Blacks voting for a return to an elected board, and Whites voting in favor of mayoral control.

Chicago undeniably has experimented the most aggressively and visibly with mayoral control. In 1995, the Illinois state legislature handed control to Mayor Richard M. Daley after the 1988 experiment with decentralization failed to turn the system around in terms of student achievement or financial stability. State Senator Arthur Berman, the ranking Democrat on the Illinois Senate's Education Committee, remembers, "That's an awesome responsibility for one person: Daley. The Republicans wanted him to drown in this" (Stanfield 1997). Others downplay the political toll that failure could have had on Daley. G. Alfred Hess Jr., executive director of the Chicago Panel on School Policy has stated, "We're talking big potential benefits with little downside risk for the mayor. If he fails, it's not going to be his voters, the ones he relies on for re-election, who are hurt. They don't use the public schools. But if he succeeds, this will relieve a great deal of financial pressure, and it would be a real feather in his cap in state and national influence. Plus, I think—most Chicagoans think he really does care. He's angered and embarrassed by these terrible schools blocking upward mobility for their students [more than 80 percent of whom are African American and Hispanic]" (Vitullo-Martin 1996). Daley welcomed the chance, saying, "Mayors can't afford not to get involved in school reform. . . . [Schools are] critical to the economic development of our cities. It's the mayor's duty to improve urban education as a way to attract business and retain middle class residents. . . . [Otherwise] people will leave your city" (Stanfield 1997).

Critics worry about the autonomous power that lies in the hands of a single person. "The mayor is entering a potentially dangerous time when he can choose to use his power to improve the city or abuse his power because he has no competition or balance of power," U.S. Representative Jesse Jackson Jr. has stated (Spielman 1996). Daley has responded by saying, "Everybody questions me and keeps me on my toes. Block Club organizations keep me on my toes, community organizations, religious leaders, citizens. I get letters. I get e-mail. I get all types of ideas and criticism" (Spielman 1996).

Cleveland presents an interesting route to mayoral control. In 1995, the state took over the school system because of problematic leadership, poor student performance, and budgetary chaos. Then, spurred by a coalition of Cleveland churches, prominent business executives, and community activists to take over, Mayor Michael White took the leadership reins of the failing school system in fall 1998 from the Ohio legislature. The legislation gave Mayor White the power to appoint a nine-member school board from a slate of eighteen candidates selected by a panel of parents, educators, business leaders, and the superintendent, known as the chief executive officer (CEO), whom the mayor had authority to appoint and fire as in Chicago.[2]

The opponents of mayoral control included some members of the elected school board, the Cleveland National Association for the Advancement of Colored People (NAACP), and the teachers' union. Meryl T. Johnson, spokeswoman for the union, stated that "the bill takes away the public's right to vote for school officials and disrespects the parents of our children.... Putting the mayor in charge is not going to cause them to learn" (Spielman 1996). One parent who opposed the move stated, "The mayor is not the czar, he's not king." Another charged, "The mayor is a politician, he was elected to run Cleveland. We need to elect people from education, people who know what's going on with schools" (Stephens 1996). Mayor White defended his credentials and intentions by maintaining, "I am educated, degreed, and trained to teach. I am not just some broken-down, big-mouthed politician trying to get votes.... I don't wake up in the middle of the night screaming, 'I got to have it [the system].' To me, it is strictly an accountability issue" (Jones 1996). White saw the importance of reforming the schools because "the town has no future if we don't fix the educational system" (Jones 1996). White vociferously advocated for a leadership role for the mayor. He explained:

> Every time the system runs aground, people tend to jump ship. Mayors can't jump ship. For good or bad, we are there. The buck stops at our desk (Jones 1996).

Another huge foe of mayoral control of the school system was the NAACP, calling such a move "White colonialism" (Reinhard 1997a). The organization believed that White, who is an African American, was a pawn of Cleveland's White business community

(Sloat 1999). In September 1997, the NAACP filed suit in federal district court, claiming that the appointment of White as head of the schools violated the equal-protection clause of the Fourteenth Amendment and the federal Voting Rights Act of 1965. The NAACP argued that the move disenfranchised Cleveland's predominantly African American population. Attorney James A. Ciocia, who represented the NAACP, stated, "Most of our claims relate to the community being deprived of their right to vote for a school board.... HB 269 is a law that purposely and systematically is utilized to exclude African Americans, including the African American plaintiffs, from the opportunity to participate in the educational policymaking process" (Reinhard 1997b).

Two years after the takeover, a *Plain Dealer* poll found that 68 percent of Clevelanders wanted control to return to an elected school board (Stephens and Frolik 2000). In November 2002, voters in Cleveland were given the opportunity to decide whether they wanted to continue under mayoral control of the schools and voted overwhelmingly to retain this structure. Chapter 4 discusses that the shift in approval was likely the result of a wildly popular CEO and a somewhat controversial mayor who decided not to seek reelection. The electoral provision in Cleveland was a unique part of the Cleveland mayoral control legislation. Many of the other cities where school systems have been placed under mayoral control have not and will probably never submit the policy to a public referendum.

Many lessons can be learned from the three models presented by Boston, Chicago, and Cleveland. In each of the three cases, districts achieved greater fiscal stability and increased funding, especially for renovating and building new schools. Despite the clear financial improvements and the claims of clearer lines of accountability, it remains to be seen whether student achievement has improved in any of these cities. Moreover, claims of decreased community involvement in the schools raise serious questions about participatory democracy and the role of the community in educational policy.

Detroit also followed the mayoral control trend when the Michigan legislature dissolved the elected school board and transferred power to Mayor Dennis W. Archer in 1999. Governor Jim Engler said, "Time and time again, I was told—butt out, send more money, wait until we implement our new plan, just give us a little more time, the bottom line … [is that] year after year, class after class, children are denied access to the quality education they deserve" (DeSchryver 1999). Although initial polls indicated an even split among voters regarding whether to give the mayor control (with a majority of Whites in favor and Blacks largely opposed), by the time that the legislature voted on the issue polls indicated that a majority (63 percent) favored mayoral control (Mirel 2004). Municipal unions and the largely African American Council of Baptist Pastors also backed the proposal (Bradsher 1999). Not everyone in Detroit was in favor of it; many denounced the proposed legislation as racially insensitive and contended that it fueled racial tensions throughout the city, even though the mayor was an African American. In the end, the bill passed, and Mayor Archer was given the authority to appoint six members to the board; the governor appoints the seventh, and the board appoints a CEO. However, in November 2004, Detroit voters rejected mayoral control, opting to return to an elected board (Voters 2004).

The New York State legislature recently reconfigured its educational system by granting Mayor Bloomberg control of the New York City schools. The Board of Education had been blamed for policy inertia, an inefficient and bloated bureaucracy, and the unpardonable state of schools. As one reporter said, "The NYPD doesn't need a Police Board to fight crime. The FDNY doesn't need a Fire Board to douse flames. And the schools don't need an Ed Board to teach kids to read. They need a school's boss, answerable to a mayor, who, in turn, is answerable to voters" ("Miles to Go" 2001).

The last three mayors of New York City (Ed Koch, David Dinkins, and Rudolph Giuliani) attempted to gain control of the schools, but not until 2002 did the state legislature give its approval. Complaints that the school system was deplorable and underperforming and that there was no one to hold responsible played a major role in the legislature's decision to establish mayoral control. The former seven-member school board, appointed by six different political leaders, "diffuses authority and hides the blame for the system's failings" ("Mayoral Control" 2000).

As long ago as 1999, Giuliani stated, "It's real simple. A fourth of our budget goes to education. They look to the mayor to raise money for it, and many people hold the mayor responsible for the condition of the schools. I say: then give me the authority" ("*Rudy v. Rudy*" 1999). He was quoted many times as wanting to "blow up" the Board of Education and shift the responsibility to himself ("*Rudy v. Rudy*" 1999). Among his supporters were a group of twenty successful and powerful businessmen, such as David Rockefeller and Jerry Speyer, CEO of Tishman Properties. Speyer said, "We are facing a crisis of monumental proportion, our board of education has for years struggled with improving education for the city's youth. We have failed. The best way to create change is to centralize authority and to put that authority in each city through the mayoral office" (Lipton and Goodnough 2000).

Teachers' unions are renowned for their staunch opposition to mayoral control. Thus, it was surprising that one of the advocates for mayoral control was the United Federation of Teachers; its president was quoted as saying:

> Part of what is motivating the U.F.T. to reconsider is that we're tired of this mayor or past mayors ducking responsibility for education. Each time we have a test result we have a bumpy ride. People under the most pressure, held the most accountable, are principals, teachers, and to some extent kids. The mayor ducks out of all responsibility. Every time there's some problem in the schools, the mayor says, "If I had control this wouldn't happen," knowing full well he could not get control. (Purnick 2000)

In 2000, Washington, DC, Mayor Anthony Williams narrowly won partial control of the district's 146 public schools in a referendum. The mayor is now able to appoint four of the nine members of the board. The remaining five members are elected at large. Prior to the creation of this "hybrid" form of mayoral control, an elected board had been in place. However, this largely symbolic board had been stripped of power in 1996, when the congressionally appointed Financial Control Board altered school governance in an effort to save the city financially and aid the failing schools (Henig 2004). Linda Moody, a former school board member and current chairman of the citywide coalition of parent-teacher organizations, charged that Williams "is responding to those people who have money and not to those who do not" (D. Wilgoren and Cottman 2000).

Williams is open about his ultimate goal: to bring back the middle class from the suburbs, which he believes will improve communities as well as the educational system. He is willing to harbor criticisms that such a reform would be antidemocratic: "To me, it's elitist to talk about broad principles of democracy and, meanwhile, the children aren't being educated.... Every child deserves an equal education. That's democracy. And right now, it ain't happening" (D. Wilgoren and Cottman 2000). The vote on mayoral control was ultimately split along some interesting dimensions (Henig 2004). Elites showed multiracial support for mayoral control. However, among middle-class and poorer Blacks, there was much less support for the governance change.

Baltimore represents one case that runs counter to the trend favoring mayoral control of schools (Orr 2004). Unlike cities that have recently extended the responsibilities of mayors in education, in 1997 the Maryland legislature restricted the power Baltimore's mayor formerly had over education. Prior to 1997, the mayor appointed the school board, essentially selected the superintendent, and had tremendous control over the school budget (Orr 2004, 27). For practical purposes, the Baltimore model of school governance prior to 1997 resembled many of the school systems that have recently been turned over to mayoral control. However, during Baltimore's long history of mayoral control (1899–1997), problems with the schools gained attention. "The system was in rapid deterioration. The mayor had the chance to have total control, and it didn't work out.... The mayor got bogged down in the politics and complexity of running a large school system.... It turned out to be much more complex than he bargained for," Christopher Cross, president of the Maryland State Board of Education, was quoted as saying of the situation (Heaney 1999).

Because the school system continued to struggle in terms of student performance and because the system was in need of financial assistance from the state, a deal was struck to limit the role of the mayor and create a city-state partnership on education. Today, the mayor and the governor select school board members, who have been given primary responsibility for creating budgets, appointing the CEO, and negotiating contracts. Although Baltimore falls into the category of mayoral control of the schools because of the role of the mayor in school board selection, it represents a real departure from what is currently considered mayoral control of education.

## Perspectives on Mayoral Control

Mayoral control has gained widespread support and popularity among many big-city mayors. Because of positive media coverage of Chicago's experience, many other cities and state legislatures chose to follow the mold. Many attribute the move to mayoral control to the increasing understanding that education is at the root of revitalizing cities. Fred Hess, director of the Center for Urban School Policy at Northwestern University, who has documented the takeover in Chicago, largely attributes the spread of mayoral control to the fact that "Mayor Daley became the vice president and then president of the U.S. Conference of Mayors and began to tout the powers he now had and suggested that other big city mayors ought to see this as what they should be doing if they wanted to preserve the middle class in the city. . . . To keep the middle class in the cities you have to save the schools" (Cobb 1999). Cities that have experimented with this reform approach are reporting fewer strikes, amicable labor and management relations, and healthier budgets.

Critics argue that mayoral control is not an effective way to attain quality education. Some contend that city hall is not the appropriate arena for education, and that the problems of bureaucracy and politics will soon hamper progress. As New York Assembly Speaker Sheldon Silver, a harsh critic of mayoral control, articulated, "I believe that children's education should not be part of a political football that goes around and comes around. I believe in an independent board of education that can speak out for children, can speak out independent of the political whims, that has a continuity regardless of who the mayor or city council happens to be at any particular time" (Kremer 1999).

Some oppose mayoral control because they believe it will revive the "cronyism" and corruption of the old city hall politics by which "school vending contracts and patronage goodies were simply too hard for city hall to resist" (Winn 1999). Others believe that mayoral control tramples on the principles of democracy and the system of checks and balances. Some worry that education will suffer when educational policy is added to the many other responsibilities of mayors. Still others simply question the effectiveness of mayoral control in improving the schools. As Paul Peterson from Harvard University articulates, "I'm really quite pessimistic that the mayor will be able to address the underlying fundamental problem, which is how to improve the test scores and the educational capacities of low-income minority children" (Stanfield 1997).

## Summary

As documented in this chapter, attempts to reform the educational system through mayoral takeovers have recently spread to many big cities. Although each city differs in the amount of power and responsibility granted to the mayor, they share the common hope that shifting the governance structure will solve the problems faced by urban districts. The new wave of mayors who now have control of their schools has a variety of interests in urban education. First, education is a key to a healthy city. Health may be considered in terms of the educational and occupational opportunities provided to the students in the schools or as it relates to the economic vitality of the city. Maintaining and attracting middle-class residents and business is another important consideration for mayors. If the school system is in shambles, then it will not be attractive to middle-class residents or be viewed as an asset to businesses in terms of their ability to attract blue- or white-collar workers. This is why business interests have played a significant role in the move to mayoral control of the schools in several cities.

In most cities that have adopted mayoral control, the mayor has inherited the school budget, something that is usually one of the largest municipal expenditures. Although this may appear as an incentive for mayoral control, it is also an electoral liability in the sense that if mayors are unable to turn the school system around and if they are held accountable for the lack of improvement, then they may not get reelected. The need for a "quick fix" for urban education before an election may not always produce the best long-term results for education.

In most situations in which mayors have been granted control of the schools, it is Republican-dominated legislatures handing power to Democratic mayors. Centralizing educational power in the hands of mayors is attractive to many state legislatures that have repeatedly bailed out urban schools. Republican legislatures also seem willing to merge city governments with school districts in the hope that this will lead to more fiscal efficiency. Despite the challenges associated with running urban school districts, mayors have overwhelmingly accepted this stewardship with open arms. Whether they do so for fiscal reasons, political reasons, or a deep commitment to education, mayoral control of the schools is increasingly popular.

Structural reforms such as mayoral control of urban schools are increasingly popular. We need only reflect on the 1996 Welfare Reform Act to see how the federal government devolved power to states and how the states were then encouraged to turn policy responsibility to county governments. The consequences of such structural shifts must be understood. This study makes an important contribution by analyzing mayoral control of schools in an effort to explain the consequences that this governance reform has on educational systems. Before analyzing the impact of mayoral control in Chicago and Cleveland, the next two chapters present a brief history of the two cities under investigation.

# 3 Politics and Education in the "Windy City": Chicago

Since the late 1980s, Chicago has shifted from radical decentralization to radical centralization of its school system. The city is considered an innovative leader in school reform largely because of how it has reacted to the political, economic, and racial trends that have taken place in the city. There is also no mistaking that Chicago's political machine legacy has influenced educational policy. The machine used the public education system for political purposes, especially to manipulate and control the politics of ethnic minorities and later racial minorities. Although the machine's educational policies successfully managed the politics of ethnic and racial groups during much of this century, Chicago's Black community began mobilizing against the machine in the 1960s (Grimshaw 1992; Erie 1988; Pinderhughes 1987). Even if machine rule is no longer part of Chicago politics, its policies and institutional arrangements are still apparent in Chicago's school system. This political heritage sets Chicago apart from other urban areas but did not prevent the city from being a national trendsetter in urban school reform.

Chicago's most recent school reforms, the 1988 and 1995 school reform acts, have generated a great deal of attention from scholars and policymakers alike. Creating a parent/community-controlled school system, the 1988 school reform act reflected a growing national trend favoring greater parent involvement in educational policy. Many cities have since incorporated aspects of this act in reforming their own school systems. The 1995 reform act garnered significant scholarly attention because it reversed the key feature of community control of the 1988 act, consolidating control of the public school system in the hands of Chicago's mayor.

Chicago's unique political history has influenced educational reform efforts. The political status of the minority community

42

during the reform eras is also key to understanding the nature of school reform in Chicago. Administrative power in the Chicago schools has been used as a source of political control, specifically regarding the school board and superintendent. The machine, minority political power, and governing structure constitute the three key elements of Chicago's educational reform history. These factors help explain why Chicago decentralized its educational system in 1988 and why it was recentralized in 1995.

## Chicago's Political Machine: The Richard J. Daley Era

Chicago's early machine structure is one of its most distinguishing political features. A political machine is a hierarchical, stable political organization that relies primarily on material incentives to build and maintain political support (Gosnell 1968). Incentives such as patronage jobs, government contracts, and political favors are offered in exchange for electoral support. There exists considerable evidence that the centralized power exercised by the machine was an essential part of Chicago's ability to remain financially stable from the 1930s onward (Fuchs 1992). Chicago's Democratic political machine initially established a constituency comprised primarily of European immigrants. Because of the great migration of southern Blacks to Chicago and other northern cities beginning during the World War I years, machine bosses had to appeal to the city's growing number of Black residents to maintain their political control (Grimshaw 1992). Machine support from Chicago's Black community remained strong from the mid-1950s through the 1960s (Pinderhughes 1987).

The machine sought influence over education because school districts not only oversee an abundance of resources, including large budgets, jobs, and contracts, but also possess the authority to raise taxes and sell bonds (W. C. Rich 1996; Pinderhughes 1987; Peterson 1981; Herrick 1971). Thus, Chicago's public school system was the cause of considerable conflict and political struggle. Examples of machine influence in education have been recorded (Grimshaw 1992; Pinderhughes 1987; Peterson 1976). In *Race and Ethnicity in Chicago Politics* (1987), Dianne Pinderhughes emphasizes how the machine continuously focused energy on petty patronage and symbolic benefits as opposed to investing in making real substantive educational improvements. She found that the machine provided the lion's share of teaching positions to White ethnics until the 1950s, when the need for Black electoral support made it essential for the machine to shift some of these jobs to Black teachers. These patronage jobs, along with symbolic appointments of pro-machine Blacks to the school board, served the machine's political purposes and provided the bare necessities to quiet discontent in the Black community.

Although Chicago's Democratic political machine was established in the 1930s, stable machine leadership was not achieved until the election of Mayor Richard J. Daley, who served as mayor from 1955 until his death in 1976. Prior to his election and during his tenure as mayor, Daley served as the chair of the Cook County Democratic party. The power he wielded as party chair provided an important asset in his subsequent mayoral victory. Originally, the machine relied on the electoral support of poor White ethnics. However, by the 1950s, the machine was forced to deal with several wings that had developed within the party (Grimshaw 1992, 19). As Daley embarked on his electoral campaign, he encountered the post-World War II exodus of White Protestants to the suburbs (Grimshaw 1992, 19). To his political credit, he was able to align Blacks behind his campaign and solidify a new machine base. Mayor Daley created an electoral coalition of working class White ethnics and Blacks.

## Daley and School Politics

At the same time that the U.S. Supreme Court issued its unanimous ruling in *Brown v. Board of Education*, a new superintendent, Benjamin Willis (1954–66), was appointed in Chicago. Although the *Brown* decision would have significant impact in the South, northern cities like Chicago largely avoided the issue of school segregation. Although there was a growing focus on racial issues in Chicago, Superintendent Willis opposed any discussion of these issues as they related to education. This came as no surprise considering the institutional focus of Chicago school policies until this period. In addition, the appointment of Willis occurred when White ethnics constituted an important electoral base for the machine. Because education was entangled with machine patronage and preferments, the concerns of White ethnic constituents received attention by the machine-controlled school system. Concerns about the fate of Black students were largely ignored.

As residential trends continued to make Chicago one of the most segregated cities in the nation, racial controversies about segregation in the schools gained momentum. Residential segregation and the decline in the city's White population were trends observed in other northern cities and resulted in many predominantly Black schools (Crain 1968). The inadequacy of these predominantly Black schools compared to those schools serving Whites became a primary concern for civil rights groups in many cities. Between 1953 and 1963, the city experienced a rapid increase in the size of the schools, from 375,000 to over 520,000 pupils (Cohen and Taylor 2000, 283). The added pressure on Black schools was particularly evident. Compared to all-Black or integrated schools, White schools had smaller teacher-student ratios, more certified teachers, and substitute teachers available if a regular teacher was absent (Cohen and Taylor 2000, 337). Chicago's civil rights groups were furious with Superintendent Willis for ignoring the issue of segregated and inherently unequal schooling for Chicago's urban students. Specifically, they complained that Black students were being taught in prefabricated buildings dubbed "Willis wagons" to avoid placing them in classrooms in predominantly White communities. Among the many problems identified in Black schools, there was striking evidence of overcrowding that was absent in the underutilized White schools (Pinderhughes 1987).

A new wave of school reform took hold in the United States after *Brown* (1954) and reached a critical mass by the 1960s. The equity movement centered on equalizing opportunities in education and on decentralizing administrative decision making to the school level (Sizemore 1981). This populist philosophy focused on the importance of a participatory system and equitable school aid formulas, reflecting the civil rights movement's emphases on local issues of racial equality and the need for community involvement at the local school level. Numerous civil rights groups began demanding that attention be given to widespread de facto segregation in Chicago.

They believed that political decentralization would have a widespread impact and shift the power from citywide elites to Black and White community groups.

From the mid-1950s through the 1970s, the federal government provided a variety of initiatives to support groups concerned with inequities in educational opportunities. This period began with *Brown* (1954) and included several financial provisions intended to improve educational opportunities for disadvantaged urban youth. In addition, the 1964 Civil Rights Act contained provisions that restricted federal aid to school districts found to embrace discriminatory practices (Orfield 1978). The Elementary and Secondary Education Act of 1965 required that school systems follow civil rights law as a condition for funding. When federal compensatory funding reached its peak in 1978, federal funds provided 9–10 percent of urban school districts' budgets (Gittell 1998, 155). Although the ultimate impact of federal intervention in reducing educational discrimination is debatable, especially regarding northern cities, federal legislation gave Chicago's civil rights groups a mechanism of support.

During the early 1960s, a number of Black and liberal White community groups in Chicago merged to form the Coordinating Council of Community Organizations (CCCO). This new organization, along with the Chicago Urban League, contacted the U.S. Civil Rights Commission to report continuing segregation within the Chicago school system. A 1963 lawsuit was settled out of court with the understanding that the school board was to appoint a group of experts to investigate the schools, especially Black schools, to identify race-related problems (Peterson 1976). Despite a committee report recommending immediate integration and decentralization, Willis continued to support the status quo practice of de facto segregation and used this rationale to maintain discriminatory educational patterns. He adamantly denied that there was any segregation in the Chicago schools because children were going to schools in their own neighborhoods (Herrick 1971).

The centralized administrative school system under Superintendent Willis was resistant to making any changes beyond federally mandated investigations of the racial problems within the schools. As tensions increased because of overcrowded Black schools, Willis decided to use trailers as classroom units adjacent to some Black schools. In addition, he moved some students to abandoned downtown buildings to increase the space available to Black students (Biles 1995). He hoped that these measures would ensure that integration would not occur, and that the complaints about the overcrowded Black schools would be quieted. Willis's actions represent another example of Chicago's tradition of avoiding substantive racial issues. Willis embraced the notion of "neighborhood schools" and defended his anti-integration actions based on his commitment to preserving this ideal.

White parents who opposed integrating their neighborhood schools accepted Willis's visions. Mayor Richard J. Daley attempted to avoid the integration issue, focusing primarily on the goal of preserving his electoral coalition. Mayor Daley's support of Willis and his commitment to the neighborhood school sent the message that he was not interested in integration. This position catered to Whites, the majority of the mayor's electoral coalition (Biles 1995).

Machine influence penetrated the school board. Mayor Daley's power and patronage practices even enticed Black members to oppose desegregation (Peterson 1976). By the middle to late 1960s, students in Black and racially mixed high schools demanded more Black administrators, Black studies, and greater community participation. These students staged walkouts, boycotts, and sit-ins and participated in acts of vandalism. Realizing Blacks were now an important part of his electoral coalition, Mayor Daley temporarily removed Superintendent Willis in 1965 (Grimshaw 1992). Ultimately, both the mayor and the school board members (both machine and integration supporters) were concerned with racial stability in the city at a time of great unrest in cities throughout the United States. It was evident that some changes needed to be made to end the civil disorder. However, it was feared that instituting an integration plan would contribute to more White flight, an unacceptable outcome for the mayor or his school board.

At the time that Black community protests were peaking in Chicago, increasing demands by the Chicago Teachers Union emerged because of the bargaining rights they acquired during the 1960s (Vander Weele 1994). Philip Meranto documented the strength exerted by teachers' unions in many metropolitan areas during the 1960s and how their demands for inclusion in educational policy-making were inevitable because of the tremendous strength they had come to wield (1970). In response to the growing demands placed on the machine-dominated school board and superintendent, the school administration finally saw that some decentralization was necessary.

In 1965, because of the inequalities in the Chicago schools, community groups from Chicago went to Washington, DC, seeking enforcement of the 1964 Civil Rights Act fund withholding provision. They alleged that the school board was maintaining a segregated and unequal system of public education (Cohen and Taylor 2000, 334). Adam Cohen and Elizabeth Taylor chronicle this period in their book *American Pharaoh*. They explain that this was a monumental case for the U.S. Office of Education because they had only handled cases in the South where de jure racial discrimination plagued the schools (334). For activists in Chicago, it came as a victory when the Office of Education temporarily withheld funds to the Chicago public schools until they complied with the stipulations of the act. At that time, Chicago was slated to lose $32 million of federal funding (335). Unfortunately, this attempt to amend some of Chicago's educational inequalities was largely unsuccessful because of President Johnson's order to release funds immediately after local Chicago politicians, particularly Mayor Daley, expressed their outrage (Cohen and Taylor 2000; Peterson 1976). The Daley machine was the largest Democratic organization in the country and tampering with this powerful group was obviously a political concern for the Johnson administration.

In 1966, Mayor Daley replaced Superintendent Willis with James Redmond, a superintendent who expressed an interest in changing Chicago's segregated school system. Nevertheless, problems for the Chicago public school administration mounted and reached a peak between 1967 and 1968. Superintendent Redmond initially recommended massive changes in the system such as mandatory two-way busing, magnet schools, financial incentives for teachers working in predominantly Black schools, and educational parks. Educational parks were the campuslike settings intended to replace the neighborhood schools and offering all students equal educational opportunities regardless of race or socioeconomic background. The school board was unwilling to approve such changes in light of White opposition and the machine's unwillingness to endorse such drastic measures. At the same time, Black activism continued to mount, especially during the 1967–68 school year, because of the stagnant nature of educational equality in Chicago schools.

As concern about segregated schools spiraled unabated in 1968, Mayor Daley devised a plan that would increase both community decision-making power within the schools and minority representation in Chicago's school administration. Even though the 1968 plan included provisions like a community role in the selection of principals and elimination of the city's candidacy exams for principals, these changes were primarily symbolic considering that the community role remained limited under the mayor's plan. Plus, the administrative staff was slow in implementing the plan's objectives. Consequently, this plan did not integrate the schools (Peterson 1976).

The symbolic nature of the 1968 changes merits discussion. Previously, strong support had been expressed for neighborhood schools by individuals like Superintendent Willis and Mayor Daley. Their position on this issue was a strategy primarily intended to prevent the integration of White schools. In contrast, civil rights activists and integrationists had proposed numerous plans intended to end segregation and equalize the educational field for Blacks. These plans included a host of ideas, such as two-way busing, city-suburban consolidation, and educational parks (Meranto 1970).[1] However, as the civil rights movement was winding down at the national level and resistance to integration grew among powerful Chicago interests like the mayor, the school board, business groups, and the White component of Daley's Democratic machine, integrationists altered their goal. The new focus became community control of neighborhood schools or decentralization of decision making in these majority Black schools. This was seen as the only realistic alternative left for reformers.

Mayor Daley devised a novel strategy for dealing with the teachers union because of its strength and demands for more decision-making power. As labor strikes were under way in 1968, the mayor began intervening and negotiated settlements in the union's favor by using financial gimmicks. To fund the settlements, the mayor borrowed from future years' tax receipts. Daley "managed to keep the schools open throughout the 1970s by settling teachers' strikes with promises of money the system did not have, convincing legislators to make minor changes in state aid, and asking bankers to ignore the unusual accounting and financial procedures used to keep the district's bond ratings high" (Shipps 1997, 88).

Because the mayor had influence in the Democratic-controlled state legislature, he was able to ensure the state allocated acceptable amounts of money to the school system and ignored any financial blundering that occurred (Shipps 1997). Financial blundering resulted in Chicago's 1979 financial collapse when bondholders realized that their money was used to repay previous loans, and that routine educational operations were funded by accounts earmarked for long-term loans (Vander Weele 1994). Financial mismanagement would haunt the school system for years and ultimately contributed to the ongoing budget deficit that Mayor Richard R. Daley would inherit when he was given control of the district in 1995.

By the late 1970s, the emphasis among school reformers was no longer on integration and racial equality. In addition, Chicago school authorities had agreed that progress toward desegregation had been sufficient to justify suspending the state regulations that required involuntary reassignment of students if voluntary efforts failed (Orfield 1979). In the 1971 Supreme Court case *Swann v. Charlotte-Mecklenburg Board of Education*, the court decided that desegregation required actual transportation of children, Black and White, to new schools to desegregate schools. Although this decision pushed some federal judges in the North to order busing programs in urban areas, the trend toward facilitating integration was short lived as the Supreme Court issued a series of rulings that opposed mandatory busing and integration initiatives.

The most influential of these early reversals of *Brown* was *Milliken v. Bradley* (1974), in which the court blocked interdistrict and city-suburban desegregation plans to integrate racially isolated city schools (Orfield and Eaton 1996, xxii). The justification for this case was that unless segregated residential patterns resulted directly from state or suburban actions, mandatory metropolitan integration initiatives were not necessary. This decision severely limited integration attempts in northern cities like Chicago. In addition, funding for the Emergency School Aid Act of 1972, the only federal program designed to fund integration efforts, was eliminated by the Reagan administration in 1981.

During the 1960s, Mayor Daley faced growing frustration within his Black electoral coalition regarding the blatant racial discrimination practiced against them. The selective benefits Daley distributed in Black wards of the city enabled him to maintain Black political support while dodging the issue of racial discrimination. This strategy provided only limited success, primarily because the civil rights movement began mobilizing Blacks during the 1960s. While the civil rights movement was earnestly focused on the political rights of Blacks, it still highlighted the substantive concern of public education for Black children. As residential trends in Chicago continued to segregate Blacks from Whites, the inadequacy of the city's Black schools became even more apparent. Civil rights groups in Chicago as well as those at the national level began documenting and protesting this racial gap in public education. With the goal of preventing further White flight to the suburbs, Daley continued his strategy of providing just enough teaching jobs to the Black community without actually addressing the serious issues of discrimination and inequality in public education. Because the selective benefits offered to Blacks never addressed the substantive concerns of the community, the machine was left with this as a serious problem after Daley's death in 1976. Following Daley's death, the machine politicians who had hoped to depend on Black electoral support found themselves unable to quiet Black discontent (Grimshaw 1992; Pinderhughes 1987).

## Weakening of the Machine: Bilandic and Byrne

The two Democratic mayors who succeeded Daley, Michael Bilandic (1976–79) and Jane Byrne (1979–83), were unable to exercise the tight political control over the Black community that Daley had so successfully mastered. Bilandic was widely viewed as a weak machine boss and ineffective mayor given his inability to clear the streets after the blizzard of 1979 paralyzed the city. This proved to be a tremendously costly political misstep. Bilandic's neglect of mass transit for the Black community during that blizzard motivated

Black opposition to him (Pinderhughes 1987). In contrast to Bilandic, Byrne made electoral promises to Black Chicagoans during her mayoral campaign, although she did not remain faithful to these promises once in office (Kleppner 1985).

In addition, Bilandic and Byrne demonstrated their disregard for the Black community in educational policy during their tenures in office. Fewer Black school board members were appointed during the Bilandic-Bryne years, despite the fact that Blacks composed the overwhelming majority of the student body. Neither mayor addressed the problem of race relations in the city or the other substantive concerns of Blacks, including police brutality. Thus, policy responsiveness to Blacks by the city government remained about the same in the post-Daley era as during the Daley era (Kleppner 1985). Frustration in the Black community over the clear disregard of their interests eventually mobilized Blacks and resulted in the 1983 election of Chicago's first Black mayor, Harold Washington.

As the issue of equity in schooling lost momentum at both the national level and in Chicago, the idea of school-based management took hold in the 1980s. School- or site-based management can be characterized as "a program or philosophy adopted by schools or school districts to improve education by increasing the autonomy of the school staff to make school site decisions" (White in Caldwell 1990, 304). Numerous scholars have shown that, as the focus on integrating urban schools declined, an emphasis on local control of neighborhood schools emerged (Orfield and Eaton 1996; Sizemore 1981; Peterson 1976; Meranto 1970). The supposed purpose of this change in objectives was to ensure that poor and minority urban students would have access to similar educational opportunities as those of White students in wealthy suburbs. Orfield and Eaton (1996) argue that this shift in focus mirrors the separate but equal aspect of *Plessy v. Ferguson*.

Underlying this new wave of reform in Chicago during the late 1970s, the school system's financial crisis in 1979 generated strong concerns about the economic stability of the Chicago public schools. As the 1979 fiscal crisis peaked, the school district declared bankruptcy, the Chicago Teachers Union went on strike, and Mayor Jane Byrne failed to negotiate union settlements using the traditional machine strategies employed previously by Mayor Richard J. Daley. The Board of Education, the mayor, the governor, legislative leaders, and bankers developed a bail-out scheme to keep the schools open (Kleppner 1985).

One aspect of this plan was the creation of the School Finance Authority (SFA), which was given responsibility for the oversight and approval of the school budget. The SFA was to remain intact until there were six consecutive balanced budgets (Wong and Sunderman 1994). A five-person oversight committee, the SFA was comprised of businessmen and attorneys who were appointed for fixed terms by the mayor and the governor (Shipps 1997). The plan also provided additional funds, required budget cuts, and allowed the mayor to replace any or all of the Board of Education members (Kleppner 1985). Although the financial crisis was temporarily settled, it would reemerge in 1993. In the interim, reforms of the 1980s, which emphasized decentralization and school site management, were getting under way in Chicago.

## Demise of the Machine: Emergence of Harold Washington

Rising discontent combined with a new sense of political efficacy among Blacks and a growing Black population were important factors in Washington's election in 1983. Blacks were still, however, a numerical minority in the city (Table 3.1), representing 39.5 percent of Chicago's population in 1980 and 37.5 percent of the voting age population.

Harold Washington's political experience as a member of the Illinois legislature and the U.S. House of Representatives undoubtedly bolstered his leadership skills. Furthermore, Washington's strong Black electoral coalition reflected Nelson and Meranto's (1977) assertion that group cohesion and political consciousness are also essential for Black electoral success. The centrality of his Black constituency to his electoral success was evident in Washington's electoral rhetoric and reflected the strategy of many Black mayoral candidates of appealing to racial issues.

Washington's election was not, however, an easy victory. Although he had solid backing from the Black community and support from the

Table 3.1. Racial Composition of Chicago's Voting-Age Population, 1940–80

| Year | Number (in 000s) | | | Percentage of Total | | |
|------|-------|-------|----------|-------|-------|----------|
|      | White | Black | Hispanic | White | Black | Hispanic |
| 1940 | 2,205 | 191   | —        | 86.6  | 7.9   | —        |
| 1950 | 2,236 | 345   | —        | 79.7  | 13.3  | —        |
| 1960 | 1,850 | 471   | —        | 71.1  | 20.2  | —        |
| 1970 | 1,513 | 576   | —        | 63.1  | 27.1  | —        |
| 1980 | 946   | 758   | 252      | 48.3  | 38.7  | 12.8     |

*Source*: Data as reported in Kleppner (1985, 67).

smaller Hispanic community, Washington attracted little support from the White community. This was especially true during the Democratic primary, in which he challenged Mayor Byrne and Richard M. Daley. Much to Washington's advantage, the White vote was ultimately divided between his opponents and resulted in his primary victory.

The 1983 mayoral general election was more racially charged than the primary. The Republican candidate and former state legislator, Bernard Epton, blatantly appealed to the racial fears of Whites (Kleppner 1985). In contrast to the "Vote Right, Vote White" sentiment among Epton supporters, Washington's campaign highlighted an antimachine message and unity. Washington made appeals based on social issues that addressed the desires of the Black and Hispanic communities, such as affirmative action, bilingual education, better housing, and improvment of the Chicago schools. He also campaigned on the theme "Our Time Has Come." Even though the racially charged strategy embraced by Epton was not ultimately successful, it appealed to many White voters, which kept the race close. Washington captured nearly the entire Black vote and 20 percent of the White vote and won with just 51.6 percent of the total vote (Pinderhughes 1987, 250). As Lublin and Tate found, a surge in voter turnout and the narrow margin of victory have characterized the election of many cities' first Black mayors (1995). The social movement-like mobilization of Blacks behind Washington's candidacy would later be instrumental in uniting the Black community around policy issues, including school reform. Washington's 1983 victory and 1987 reelection were facilitated by his ability to address the substantive issues of his Black and Hispanic supporters and racially liberal Whites.

Washington's electoral coalition was not enough to provide him with an effective governing coalition during his first term in office (Pinderhughes 1997). Because remnants of the Democratic machine remained in Chicago politics, Washington encountered numerous challenges, so much so that his relationship with the city council was characterized by the media as the "council wars" (Kleppner 1985). Council members representing heavily White wards still harbored resentment about Washington's Democratic primary victory and successfully blocked the mayor from numerous initiatives related to city finances, employment, and educational policy.

Nevertheless, Washington's initial victory pushed former minority machine leaders out of power or forced them to ally with his administration. Overall, Washington's 1983 election increased the number of Blacks holding countywide and statewide positions and created a sense of political efficacy among Blacks in Chicago (Pinderhughes 1997). By the time of his successful 1987 reelection victory, Washington had solidified the support of the city council and was leading public policy formation in the city. This transformation in Washington's governing power is critical to understanding the politics of education reform that was taking place.

In relation to education, Washington spoke of becoming Chicago's "education mayor" and solicited suggestions from the community regarding the shape of school reform. In addition, in 1986 Washington created an "Education Summit" composed of fifty business, community, and school leaders to advance reform proposals and build relationships between disparate interest groups (Former grassroots activist interview 7 July 1998). Washington's educational vision made a lasting impact on school reform and was largely responsible for the creation of the 1988 school reform act. Without Washington's vision, leadership, and legacy, mobilization around the 1988 school reform that decentralized control of the schools would not have occurred. On Washington's unexpected death on 25 November 1987 implementation of the reform became complicated as the progressives who had fought for the reform became increasingly marginalized as the machine reasserted itself.

Washington's supporters united behind his educational policy vision despite indications that the electoral coalition he had created was fractured.

## Machine Resurgence? Mayor Richard M. Daley (1989–Present)

Following Mayor Washington's death, the city council selected alderman Eugene Sawyer as acting mayor. Sawyer was a compromise choice because although he was the longest-serving Black city council member, he was also seen by White remnants of the political machine as someone who would cooperate with them (Grimshaw 1992). In contrast, many of Chicago's Blacks were outraged by the choice of Sawyer. They had preferred Washington's council floor leader, Tim Evans. Evans had not been selected because of White city council opposition and the support of some Black machine-minded aldermen (A. G. Hess 1995). Some members of the Black electorate were frustrated with Sawyer's machine compliance and thought a vote for Evans would protect Black substantive interests. The frustration among many in the Black community led some to denounce Sawyer as "Uncle Tom Sawyer."

The 1989 mayoral special election thus began with a serious rift in the Black community over Sawyer and Evans. This division helped Richard M. Daley, son of the former mayor, to defeat acting Mayor Sawyer in the primary and later Tim Evans in the general election. Sawyer and Evans, both Black candidates, ran against each another and divided the electorate. The racial divide that emerged in the 1983 mayoral primary, with two White candidates—Daley and Byrne—dividing White support, had been reversed. Mayor Daley benefited from this division. By appealing to Hispanic voters to join his predominantly White electoral base, Daley secured his victory. Mayor Daley was successfully reelected in 1991, 1995, 1999, and 2003. To date, a Black candidate has not emerged to fill the shoes of Mayor Washington. However, several Black candidates have challenged Daley. Congressman Bobby Rush, a Black Democratic member of Congress, challenged Daley in the February 1999 mayoral election. Rush was unable to consolidate and mobilize the Black electorate as effectively as Harold Washington had in 1983.

Several scholars have examined Chicago's postmachine political system to demonstrate that, although the city does not have an all-powerful machine as it did under Richard J. Daley (1955–76), machine politics remains an important feature of the political system (Krebs 1998, 1999, 2005; Miranda and Tunyavong 1994). Koehler and Wrightson (1987) found that although Chicago's machine dominance declined after 1976, the distribution of park facilities remained related to ward-level support of the political machine. Their findings contradict the notion that service delivery in the postmachine era is purely professional and nonpolitical. Similarly, Miranda and Tunyavong (1994) examined the distribution of community development bloc grants and capital improvement plan funds between 1976 and 1990 and found that electoral support for the mayor and ward-based politics still makes a difference in the allocation of benefits. Furthermore, the research of Timothy Krebs (1998, 1999) indicates that, although Chicago's Democratic Party organization has weakened at the county level, it remains influential in the ward-based city council elections. Krebs has also identified a distinction between political machines as organizations and the practice of machine politics. He explains:

> In the first case (political machines as organizations), a hierarchically organized party organization controls office and maintains power by granting favors in return for support; in other words, through the application of machine politics. In the second case, trading favors for political support is a key part of the system, and exists in the absence of a centralized party organization. In both cases, political insiders are valued more than outsiders. The distinguishing characteristic relates to the stability of the coalition; political machines create more stability than a system of machine politics. (2005, 49)

This distinction is useful in understanding contemporary politics in Chicago machine politics as it exists in the city today.

Even with research indicating that the political machine still has influence in city politics, the level of machine power Richard M. Daley wields remains a contestable matter because the urban, state, and federal political landscape has greatly changed since the days of his father's administration. Demographics have changed in Chicago, creating a constituency quite different from the White ethnic electoral base during the machine's heyday. Candidates today must design campaigns that appeal to Blacks and Hispanic voters and their interests if they wish to create a successful electoral coalition. The concentration of minority residents in the city contrasts with the growing number of suburban and downstate residents, who are electing a disproportionate share of Republicans to Illinois state offices. Consequently, Republican governors and the growing Republican downstate majority in the state legislature have refused to provide favorable policies for Chicago. This signifies a vast change from the era of Democratic majorities in the state.

Throughout the United States, big-city mayors have felt the pinch of declining tax bases and reductions in federal aid, causing increased reliance on private economic elites for stability. This financial strain has heightened problems in urban education because the city's tax base primarily determines school funding. All big-city mayors, including minority mayors, face the challenge of maintaining the economic base of their cities during challenging times. Not only are corporations enticed to leave cities in search of tax breaks offered in surrounding suburbs and foreign countries, but middle and upper-class taxpayers have continuously left the city for the suburbs. Because declining tax bases and limits on federal aid to cities challenge all big-city mayors, Mayor Daley has been forced to deal with problems in the school system without the protection of the favorable layering of federal-state-county Democratic-controlled governments that served as the foundation of machine dominance (Fuchs 1992).

Mayor Daley's continued control of the city council has helped him secure his educational policy goals. More than retaining relatively uncontested power to appoint school board members, Daley took over the whole enterprise of public education with his 1995 reform legislation. In addition, the Illinois State Legislature granted him control over the school system with very little oversight. The reasons the state handed over the public school system to Daley and the reasons why Daley accepted this responsibility are debated. Many assumed this was a scheme developed by Illinois Republicans, who had not only grown frustrated with financially bailing out the Chicago schools but also wanted the Democratic mayor to fail miserably.

Still, the public education system remains a great prize, especially for machine-minded leaders. Education has always been a tremendous resource for mayors because of the public school budget. In addition, Chicago's public school history has rich examples of mayors using the schools as a source of patronage. Although Mayor Daley is unable to exercise that type of power today, primarily because of civil service requirements, the schools remain an important source of power. The flexibility the legislation granted the mayor in terms of school finances is considerable. The mayor can appoint key supporters and business allies to administrative posts in the school system. Furthermore, the trend favoring privatization of services, which is used to incorporate the business community, has been applied to school services, a policy shift that enlarges Daley's potential for power through the schools.

Clearly, winning control of the school system has added to Daley's political strength. Incorporating the business community is an important part of mayoral leadership because of the economic role corporate investment plays in municipal stability. Inclusion in the educational policy process is important to the business community because it requires an educated workforce and general economic stability. The centralization of power we now see in Chicago is reminiscent of the machine domination exercised by Richard J. Daley. Mayor Richard M. Daley is receiving praise for his educational innovations from leaders across the country, including former President Clinton and other big-city mayors. Daley's successful bid for control of the school system has set a trend among big-city mayors because it opens the door to a larger universe of resources that may advantage mayors electorally and politically.

## School Politics in Chicago

Although some contend that school boards "have relatively minor policy roles," this assertion is not accurate in Chicago (Danielson and Hochschild 1998). Stakeholders in Chicago have either fought for control of the school board or attempted to gain substantive or descriptive representation on the board, demonstrating that the board does have some value. The competition for control of the school board stems from the board's influence over school district budgetary decisions, employment guidelines, curricula decisions, and policies that directly affect the lives of students. In Chicago, the position of the school board has continuously been a major source of political power. In fact, Chicago has a history of attempts to remedy educational problems through altering administrative structures by changing the size of the board or terms of appointment, adjusting the racial balance among board members, and firing superintendents. These tactics have been used to increase representation of certain groups and temporarily quiet their demands. Furthermore, the focus on the school board in the most recent pieces of school reform legislation substantiates the assertion that school boards do matter in educational policy.

Two general patterns are evident in Chicago's school board politics: the strong relationship between the mayor and the school board and the frustration expressed within the Black community over educational policy decisions that result in exclusion or neglect. The Chicago mayor has always had control over nominations for school board members. One reason for appointment of the board is favored is that elections were thought to limit membership on the board to those individuals able to run successful electoral campaigns (Policy analyst interview 18 June 1998). Placing appointment responsibility in the mayor as the only elected official accountable to the entire city has always been seen as the preferable alternative. Until the 1995 reform act, all school board nominees required city council confirmation to ensure that corruption and patronage could be negated in board selection. Given the political heritage in Chicago, the idea of city council confirmation was largely irrelevant for most of the century because of machine dominance on the council. The other theoretical safeguard against corruption was the requirement of a nominating commission for board appointments. This advisory body was, except for the brief period from 1988 to 1995, selected by the mayor (Herrick 1971). For this reason, the nominating commission has not been an anticorruption mechanism.

Black membership on the school board, as in other municipal institutions, was limited for most of the century. Michael Homel's (1984) work indicates that between 1910 and 1940 Blacks sought to increase their numbers on the board. In 1939, the first Black board member, Midian O. Bousfield, was appointed. However, substantive improvements for Black students were blocked by the White and machine-controlled board majority. Pinderhughes (1987) pointed out that the appointments of the first Pole in 1894 and the first Italian in 1927 provide evidence of the racial hierarchy in school politics. Beginning in 1944, Blacks held at least one position on the school board, a level of representation that in no way reflected the growing proportion of Black students (Herrick 1971).

During the administration of Richard J. Daley (1955–76), school board members were selected largely because of their machine allegiance. In fact, board members were threatened with removal if they operated against the mayor's wishes (Vander Weele 1994). Daley's tenure coincided with a number of important changes. The first was the increase in White flight to the surrounding suburbs. This caused concern for the mayor, especially regarding his electoral coalition and the city's tax base. Not only did changes in demographics become evident, but also the civil rights and equity movements in education reform came to fruition. Although Daley did appoint Black board members, they were machine supporters who shared his concern about Whites leaving the city. This was in direct opposition to the desegregation initiatives for which Black community members were fighting during the 1960s (Kleppner 1985).

Although the position of superintendent was eliminated under the 1995 school reform legislation, it was historically important in Chicago for several reasons. First, superintendents were selected by the school board, which made them accountable to the board of education and indicated a shared educational philosophy. Not only the superintendent's systemwide oversight duties and policy initiatives were consistent with school board interests, but also the individual in this powerful position was able to shape the goals of the school system. The second reason for the importance of this position was that selection for this high-profile position became increasingly political as educational inequalities eventually reached a peak. A trend eventually emerged in Chicago by which the racial background of the superintendent became important and served as a method of providing a selective benefit to the Black community. The decision to appoint Black superintendents became a strategically important political decision balanced with finding a Black candidate willing to embrace the philosophical background of the school board. From the middle 1950s through the early 1990s, Chicago's superintendents reflected the political struggle over the school system and the quest for minority incorporation in the policy process.

## Summary

Several conclusions can be drawn from Chicago's school board politics. One of the most apparent features is the control the city's mayor has almost consistently had over educational policy. Machine politicians took full advantage of their control over education. However, after the death of the first Mayor Daley in 1976, the reality of racial discrimination and budgetary constraints fractured the balance that had previously been established. Mobilization in the Black community over issues related to inequality and segregated education increased Blacks' descriptive and, at times, substantive representation on the board.

In addition, Black bureaucrats in the school system multiplied during the 1960s and 1970s. According to the Chicago public schools' *Racial and Ethnic Survey of Staff*, between November 1967 and October 1977 there was a 30 percent increase in the number of Black administrators in the schools (*Racial and Ethnic Survey of Staff* 2005). Although Black administrators only represented 35 percent of all administrators at the end of this period, the increase over this ten-year period was substantial. However, this did not result in the equal educational opportunities or the desegregation that community groups advocated fiercely during the 1960s and 1970s. It was not until 1985 that machine influence on Black board members truly declined or that a Black superintendent substantively worked to improve opportunities for Black students. This was, as Wilbur C. Rich (1996) explained, happening at a time when financial conditions provided a real challenge for Black administrators because of the declining tax base in the urban areas where Blacks were gaining political control. In addition, as the excellence movement emerged in the 1980s, school systems under Black administrative structures did not measure up well.

The Chicago schools, once called the "worst in the nation," are a paradigm of centralized policy control today. The city's history of machine dominance has influenced school politics and the position of the minority community in decision making. With the exception of the period following the 1988 school reform, which decentralized control of the schools and led to unprecedented community incorporation in educational policy, machine-influenced mayors have been able to dominate school policy and manage the demands of minority groups. Although minority support made Harold Washington Chicago's first Black mayor in 1983 and reelected him in 1987, minority incorporation in politics proved illusory after his unexpected death (Barker, Jones, and Tate 1999). When Mayor Richard M. Daley was elected in 1989, he presided over a city with a decentralization reform under way. This gave the mayor limited power over education in the city. However, by 1995 he was granted control of the Chicago schools and has since managed to win reelection four times. Like earlier machine politicians, Daley's electoral coalition includes only a small number of Blacks. It appears that controlling minority demands through traditional machine strategies still works in Chicago today.

# 4 Politics and Education in the "Comeback City": Cleveland

Cleveland is the fortieth-largest school system in the country ("Characteristics" 2002, 12). In comparison to Chicago, the third-largest school district in the nation, a casual observer might assume that Cleveland is inconsequential in terms of school reform because of its comparatively small size. Recently, however, Cleveland has made its mark on school reform by creating a mayoral structure of school governance as well as a controversial voucher program. In addition to Cleveland's contribution to the school reform scene, the city's political and economic history provides an instructive backdrop to educational changes in the city. Racial politics also play a significant role in the evolution of policy development in the city.

This chapter traces the history of the Cleveland public schools to chronicle the conditions prior to the 1995 mayoral takeover of the schools. Cleveland is significant for those interested in educational reform. Whereas Chicago residents were not given an opportunity to vote on mayoral control of the schools, Cleveland voters were given this opportunity four years after the mayor was granted control. As evident in Table 4.1, the overwhelming majority of Cleveland voters favored mayoral control of the schools as opposed to control by an elected school board. Even though only 30 percent of eligible voters cast ballots, just over 70 percent of those who voted supported the retention of an appointed board of education (Okoben and Townsend 2001).

## A Brief Political and Economic History

A midsize Midwestern city, Cleveland experienced peak growth during the industrial revolution but later teetered on the brink of bankruptcy in the 1970s. To date, the city has endured many

64

Table 4.1. Vote on Mayoral Control of the Cleveland
Schools, November 5, 2002

| Vote | Number of Votes Cast | Percentage of Vote |
|------|---------------------|--------------------|
| Yes | 64,690 | 72.19 |
| No | 24,919 | 27.81 |
| Total | 89,609 | 100 |

*Source*: Cuyahoga County Board of Elections.

challenging times, leading to the current recovery. Today, Cleveland is known as the home of the Rock and Roll Hall of Fame. In addition, it supports two professional sports teams, the Cleveland Indians and the Cleveland Browns; each has a new stadium. The city is also host to several major colleges, universities, and medical facilities. Not very long ago, Cleveland was best known to outsiders as the city with the river that caught fire or the first major U.S. city to default (1979) since the Great Depression.

In many ways, Cleveland has epitomized a typical midsize northern postindustrial city. During the 1930s, Cleveland was the sixth-largest city in the country (Miller and Wheeler 1997, 131). As the Black population continued to grow steadily in the following decades, largely because of southern migration, White flight from the city to surrounding suburbs intensified. By the 1960s, the city was fiscally strained. Like many other cities, it was during this period of fiscal strain that Blacks began gaining significant electoral strength. In 1967, Clevelanders were among the first to elect a Black mayor of a major city. Mayor Carl Stokes remained in office for two terms. When he stepped down, he was replaced by Cleveland's populist White mayor, Dennis Kucinich, in 1977. Mayors Stokes, Kucinich, and Voinivich (1979–89) struggled because of the terrible economic conditions that enveloped the city. Although each mayor had a different approach to improving the city, none was able to overcome the fact that their hands were tied due to a declining tax base, the loss of manufacturing jobs to the south or overseas, a growing poverty population, and an ailing school system.

Mayors Stokes, Kucinich, and Voinivich spoke of improving the city's public school system. Perhaps these proclaimed aspirations were merely symbolic rhetorical gestures. After all, regardless of the sincerity of the desires of these mayors to improve Cleveland's schools, funding an educational system via declining property tax revenues made improvements almost impossible. When seeking office in 1967, Carl Stokes campaigned on the issue of improving education and won the backing of the growing (majority) African American population. During the Stokes era, strides were made toward incorporating Blacks in the city governance and school administrative structure. Despite these steps forward, the city was financially strapped because of declining manufacturing jobs and a very difficult transition into the service-dominated economy. These factors contributed to the downward spiral of the Cleveland schools in the decades to follow. The Cleveland schools, much like the city, teetered on the brink of financial disaster for several decades following its last growth period in the early 1960s.

In 1989, Democrat Michael White was elected mayor of Cleveland. He was the second African American to hold this post, yet his electoral base was different from that of Carl Stokes. White's electoral base was largely composed of Whites. He also had the support of the business community. White, a former city councilman and Ohio state senator, narrowly defeated one of the most powerful Black politicians in the city's history, former city council president George Forbes. Forbes was backed by the majority of Black Clevelanders. He received 53 percent of the vote compared to White's 56 percent. White entered office as a self-described pragmatic idealist and had a reputation as a maverick Democrat whose governing style focused on the elimination of waste and the creation of a business climate that would attract jobs and stimulate the local economy. As a product of the Cleveland public schools, White was committed to upgrading Cleveland's overall image, especially the reputation of its public schools.

During his first year in office, White ran an ad in *Fortune* magazine reading "Cleveland—Open for Business," signifying Cleveland's desire to overcome its national image as "the mistake on the lake." This new business-friendly image brought national attention to the city and to the young reform mayor (Cohen 1997). Aside from trying to change the image of Cleveland (e.g., "the new American City") and attempting to lure businesses back, White made headlines by his support of the construction of new sports facilities and the Rock and Roll Hall of Fame (Miller and Wheeler 1997, 193). Mayor White brought the same pragmatic and upbeat attitude to his commitment to improve Cleveland's public schools. Although the Mayor's promise was initially met with plaudits, reforming the public schools proved to be a more enervating and difficult task than the downtown development component of his agenda.

White followed the lead of other mayors by garnering elite support within the business community and state legislature. He also aggressively experimented with a grassroots mobilization strategy built around large education summits attended by a cross section of stakeholders in education. Given the personal investment of the White administration in public school politics and the high expectations he may have stoked, Cleveland presents an interesting case in the sustainability of mayor-led reform across administrations. The verdict is still out on whether White's successor, Jane Campbell (elected in 2001), can plot a new strategy without undoing much of the White legacy. The bottom line is that, regardless of their ideology, race, or gender, Cleveland's mayors have not found a way to eliminate the economic challenges that haunt the city. The local economy is a major impediment to resolving the city's troubled school system. As a consequence, the economic situation has opened the door for radical programs intended to deal with public education.

## Cleveland's Public Schools: Turmoil, Crisis, and Inequality

As in other northern industrial cities, White students once dominated Cleveland's public school district. Black students were segregated in neighborhood public schools within predominantly Black sections of Cleveland, such as Glenville, the childhood neighborhood of Mayor White. In a *New York Times* article, Cleveland was ranked sixth among American cities for the highest concentration of segregated neighborhoods. Since 1990, the city has experienced a nine-point increase in segregated neighborhoods (Schmitt 2001). White flight to the suburbs (Galster 1990), combined with the lure of private and parochial schools, drew most of the White students from the city's public schools (Orfield and Yun 1999). In 1950, Whites made up nearly 85 percent of the city's population; by 2000,

Table 4.2. Cleveland Racial and Ethnic Breakdown (%), 1980–2000

|                 | 1980 | 1990 | 2000 |
|-----------------|------|------|------|
| Black           | 43.8 | 46.6 | 51.0 |
| White           | 53.9 | 49.5 | 41.5 |
| Hispanic        | 3.1  | 4.6  | 7.3  |
| Asian           | 0.59 | 1.0  | 1.3  |
| American Indian | 0.22 | 0.3  | 0.3  |
| Other           | NA   | 2.6  | 3.6  |
| Multiracial     | NA   | NA   | 2.2  |

*Source*: U.S. Census Bureau and County and City Data Book.
NA, data not recorded.

the White population had dropped to 41.5 percent. At the same time that the White population was in decline, the Black population was on the rise. Today, just over half of city residents are Black (see Table 4.2).

Today, Cleveland enrolls over 76,000 students in its public school system. Seventy-one percent of students are Black, which is 20 percent higher than the Black population of the city as a whole. Hispanics or Latinos make up about 8 percent of the public school population, which largely reflects their population in the city. Fewer than one in five students is White and non-Hispanic (see Table 4.3). This figure is well below the proportion in the pre-busing days and substantially below the proportion of Whites in the city's population

Table 4.3. Cleveland Public Schools Racial and Ethnic Breakdown (%), 1980–2000

|                 | 1980 | 1990 | 2000 |
|-----------------|------|------|------|
| Black           | 67.4 | 71.1 | 71.0 |
| White           | 28.0 | 21.0 | 19.2 |
| Hispanic        | 3.7  | 6.3  | 8.1  |
| Asian           | 0.6  | 1.3  | 0.8  |
| American Indian | 0.3  | 0.2  | 0.4  |
| Multiethnic     | NA   | NA   | 0.6  |

*Source*: Office on Monitoring and Community Relations of the Cleveland Public Schools for 1980 and 1990 figures and Cleveland Municipal School Board for 2000 figures.
NA, data not recorded.

as a whole. The current budget of the public school system is approximately $600 million. Its student/teacher ratio is 25 to 1.

Looking back on the decades from the 1970s, several noteworthy reforms and mandated changes emerged in Cleveland leading to the 1998 decision to grant the mayor control of the schools. Some of these milestones include a court-ordered desegregation plan; attempts at decentralizing the schools; state control of the Cleveland schools; publicly funded vouchers; and the mayor's summits on education. These and several minor reforms were unable to improve education sufficiently. Because the schools were unable to rebound, Mayor White took control of the city's schools in 1998.

In contrast to Chicago, where lawsuits were unsuccessful as a means to desegregate the schools, the Cleveland case tells a different story. In Cleveland, 1976 marked a monumental desegregation ruling issued by U.S. District Judge J. Frank Battisti. Finding the Cleveland and State boards of education responsible for the racial segregation in the Cleveland schools, a desegregation plan was put into place that relied on mandatory crosstown busing (Miller and Wheeler 1997, 176). Since the 1930s, Cleveland's Black community had voiced concerns and even protested segregated schools and policies on school construction that benefited Whites (177). By 1980, the district was spending $12 million annually on busing. At the same time, Black and White residents who could move to the suburbs did, and Cleveland's school enrollment dropped by more than one-third (178).

Mandatory busing remained in place until 1996, and during this period busing remained one of the most controversial issues associated with public education in Cleveland. Divisions within the Black community about busing were common. Debate centered on whether moving Black children across town to desegregate predominantly White schools was in fact the best way to improve educational opportunities for the youth of the city. In addition, crosstown busing did not address the financial problems faced by the district and led some to question whether desegregation was the solution to the problems of urban education. Although some leaders in the Black community vigorously opposed the end of the desegregation order, others were in favor of ending the order and placing more emphasis on improving all of Cleveland's public schools (Community member interview 24 August 2001; Former board member interview 30 October 2000; City council member interview 31 August 2000; Farris interview 15 August 2000).

As noted, many of the challenges the Cleveland schools faced stemmed from financial problems resulting from a declining tax base. Although busing was aimed at solving the problem of segregated schools, it did not result in broad integration or reverse other alarming trends in public education. Declining attendance patterns and graduation rates, as well as limited numbers of students going to college, continued unabated despite attempted improvements (see Chapter 7).

Mayor White's first attempt at school reform involved an invitation to all concerned citizen groups to attend a citywide forum on education. White responded to the issue of school reform with a politician's sense and sensibility. In May 1990, Mayor White launched the Cleveland Summit on Education. His strategy involved mobilizing some of his own electoral base and transferring its energy to the education arena. It entailed bringing together a large and diverse group of community activists and other school stakeholders in the hope that a more open discussion would lead to a more coherent and collective vision. For Mayor White, the citywide summits were a successful mobilizing and attention-getting mechanism. However, the summits were not open to everybody. The president of the Cleveland Teachers Union characterized the attendees:

> There were targeted invitations. [The summits included] people who had participated before and had shown a level of interest. We physically asked individual schools to send some individuals, so that every school would have at least one person who could report back to the school on what the summit had to say or what it suggested doing. . . . I believe it was kind of unique in the sense of being so broad, bringing virtually everybody in the community, even people who had nominally no connections with school districts were brought in and willingly so. The schools are plums embedded in the pudding of society. Society is not going be successful . . . unless the schools are successful. (DeColibus 23 April 2001)

On the one hand, this targeted invitation clearly sought to build citizen support and consensus for public school reform. On the other hand, targeting precluded surprises and gate crashing by unwanted outsiders. With each summit, there were more attendees and more opportunities to enhance the social capital of the city (Orr 1999). Aside from restoring public confidence in the public school reform movement, the summit became a vehicle for promoting Mayor White's desire to center the effort in city hall.

Bringing such a disparate group together to discuss public school reform was a testimony to Mayor White's ingenuity. At the first summit, participants adopted a vision statement that listed a set of ten-year goals. The summit mission of May 1990 states the goals are "to initiate an ongoing process by which the community and the schools articulate a common vision, develop shared goals and begin to identify and implement an action agenda which results in public school improvements that guarantee every student in Cleveland a quality education" (Summit on Education 1990).

At first glance, this mission statement is too broad to serve as a policy statement. Yet, the summit leaders sought to craft a statement that reflected the policy aspirations of the 700 assembled leaders, parents, and teachers. This was no easy task as each set of stake-holders arrived with their own political agendas. Some even lacked agendas because many parents came seeking answers about the failing public schools and their children's performance in them. Others were community activists using the forum to get visibility for their agendas. Still others came to the first summit just to hear what the new mayor and the superintendent had in mind for the public school system.

In 1991, the second summit drew one thousand people and produced another set of 27 policy initiatives. Although this helped define an agenda for change, it did not in itself provide the muscle needed to push reform into practice. Few, if any, of the proposals were implemented by the public schools. The lack of successful implementation of these policy initiatives stemmed primarily from limited resources and differences in terms of which initiatives should have priority (Community member b interview 23 August 2001).

Meanwhile, having apparently lost confidence in the seven incumbent members of the board, Mayor White backed a reform slate of four candidates for school board elections (White interview 25 April 2002). He reasoned that a new group of board members who shared his views would make necessary fundamental changes in public policy. The slate was known as the Four L-Slate Reform Coalition, so named because all of the candidates' names started with the letter $L$.[1] This reform coalition was victorious in the 1991 school board elections and experienced victories in 1991. The mayor was again able to elect his endorsed slate of board members in 1993. These board members were known as the Vision 21 slate. Despite having a reform-minded board, the school system continued to drift educationally and experienced fiscal and administrative problems. The Cleveland reform board was not very successful in changing the culture and the politics of the public school system. This not only was partly caused by fiscal conditions, but also was because the reform slate was merely one faction of a divisive board. The divisiveness among the board may ultimately have set the stage for mayoral control of the school system because of the centralized and hierarchical nature of that reform. Simply put, mayoral control would promise a more unified school board.

In 1993, the third summit attracted fourteen hundred participants. This summit focused on implementation of the Vision 21 plan, a comprehensive education action plan (*Vision 21* 1993). This report, designed to prepare Cleveland public schools for the twenty-first century, was Superintendent Sammie Campbell Parrish's (1992–95) effort to put her stamp on the system. Four hundred people were organized into twenty-four working teams to implement the Vision 21 plan (Summit on Education 1993). The plan predicted that, by the year 2000, the Cleveland public schools would be recognized nationally for their academic excellence. To achieve this goal, the system would require a total commitment from the local community and massive financial resources. Vision 21 did not survive Parrish's tenure, which ended in 1995.

The early summits of 1990–94 are fascinating examples of citizen mobilization. In this way, White achieved more, at least symbolically, as an education mayor than previous mayors, including Stokes, who had made improving public education a center of his campaign efforts in 1967. The summits generated several documents that not only outlined goals, but also allowed the participants to interact with a wide spectrum of stakeholders. The high profile of school reform as an issue in city politics had alerted everyone to the importance of the public schools in Cleveland's future.

However, it appears that the recruitment of summit attendees did not delve sufficiently into the ranks of ordinary Cleveland residents. Organizers had hoped that the participants would include a representative sample of parents, but most of the attendees were "targeted invitees," meaning school administrators, teachers, business people, community activists, and foundation leaders. This suggests a symbolic aspect of the summits. Because there was an informal connection between the mayor's electoral coalition and summit participation, it is likely that inviting large numbers of parents was seen as a less-important political strategy because the mayor's electoral coalition relied more heavily on other groups. Also, to the extent that the mayor was attempting to use the summits as a way to push his educational agenda and school board slates, there was less of a reason to include a broad spectrum of parents who could oppose his educational agenda.

Still, the scope of the involvement, reaching two thousand attendees at its peak, was extremely impressive. It is likely that the breadth of involvement increased over time as well. However, although the increasing numbers of attendees suggest that diversity was increasing, it may be the opposite because increasing numbers of school district employees turned out over and beyond the community stakeholders. Although White's summits effectively mobilized interest groups, residents who had children in the public schools were mobilized to a lesser extent.

By 1994, Mayor White began to assume a less-visible role in the summit. The 1996 summit, which drew two thousand attendees, marked a watershed in the structure and the function of the summit (E. M. Butler 1997, 1–4). Mayor White was away on business, yet the summit went on without him, indicating either that this organization had become institutionalized in the mayor's agenda or that it was becoming less important to him. In his absence, state-appointed Superintendent Richard Boyd presided over the summit. Site-based management (i.e., more autonomy for the building staff) was one of the primary ideas promoted at the summit. This demonstrates that the national trend in school-based management, or decentralization, did not miss Cleveland.

Although Cleveland's experiment with decentralization was neither as broad nor as complex as Chicago's 1988 decentralization plan, the city did institute a limited decentralization plan beginning in 1991, when a few local councils were created. The plan became slightly more extensive toward the later 1990s when the first eight school governance councils were created. It was anticipated that each Cleveland school would eventually have its own council. These initial councils were composed of the principal, four parents, four teachers, a staff member, a community representative, a corporate partner, and two high school students (Ryan 2001, 2). School governance councils were given several noteworthy responsibilities, including selecting principals, managing the school budget, and making curricular decisions for the schools (Ryan 2001, 3).

Another important component of the 1996 summit was the complaints by parents concerning teachers, the lack of books and computers in the schools, and the physical conditions of the school buildings (Jones 1996). This debate over the conditions of the schools came as the federal courts ended court-ordered busing in Cleveland. Busing was supposedly draining energy and resources from the schools. The new order allowed stakeholders to focus again on the operating problems of the district.

Whereas the summits generated and consolidated support for experimental school reforms, the increasing turnouts posed a potential problem for city hall. Even if the group maintained its vigor and focus, there was a risk that some members would grow restless about the slow pace of reform and subsequently challenge the assembly's sponsors for control over the agenda. Alternatively, the multiple voices might dissipate into a cacophony, with the group becoming a difficult force to control politically. Managing such turnouts required energy that could conceivably be better utilized in making much-needed administrative changes.

Perhaps because Mayor White sensed these risks, he began disengaging himself from the process. Because White did not want to lose his control over the agenda or ruin his image as an education innovator, he withdrew. It is conceivable that White realized that he could no longer safely pilot such a big boat full of so many special interests and newly engaged citizens. After all, democratically empowered citizens are difficult to control.

After White's withdrawal, the nature of the summits began to change, first evolving into a general forum for public school leadership. Because these open forums became unwieldy and the difficulties of moving from ideas to action became of greater concern, the citywide assemblies were discontinued in favor of small working committees made up of the traditional school policy stakeholders. Retaining the name of the Summit on Education, it now functions as a small nonprofit organization. As Marva Richards, the executive director of the Cleveland Summit on Education put it, "We serve the role of pulling people together for the conversation" (Richards interview 3 May 2001).

There are no plans to convene another citywide summit in the near future. The Cleveland Summit on Education, however, continues to be supported by business and local philanthropic organizations (Dempsey interview 19 August 2000).[2] Although the summits attracted attendees, they did little to address the serious fiscal problems of the public school system—something that was necessary for the schools to function well in the future.

## The Mix of Summits and the Fiscal Crises

It is noteworthy that the summits did not focus on the fiscal problems of the schools despite the seriousness of the problem. However, this omission seems related to Mayor White's original goal for the summits as a path toward a shared vision of school reform among educational stakeholders. Although the mayor was undoubtedly aware of the district's finances, his primary objective for the summits was the creation of a reform plan for the schools. The summits also gave him an opportunity to gain publicity in the area of school reform, a policy area important to voters, in a way that avoided the crisis that had continuously plagued the schools.

Mayor White's other school agenda included building public confidence in the fiscal integrity of the system, a frailty that had plagued the system prior to his tenure. A decade before Mayor White's election, the state had taken the district into receivership for three years, but fiscal troubles kept haunting the district. In 1992, Superintendent Frank Huml resigned, partly because the board refused to place a 9.8 mills operating levy on the ballot.

Dr. Sammie Campbell Parrish became superintendent, making her the third school head since Mayor White took office. Parrish was also unsuccessful in placing a 12 mills operating levy on the ballot and an 8 mills levy on the ballot two years later, a levy the mayor had supported.

In 1992, the state approved a $139 million loan to keep the district from returning to receivership. Despite the best intentions of fiscal managers, "red ink" continued to flow. A $51 million deficit forced the district to make an $18 million dollar budget reduction. The cuts ranged from teachers to school supplies.

The deteriorating conditions and the proposed desegregation settlement prompted the board to place a 12.9 mills operating levy on the ballot in May 1994. Voters rejected the levies. A second $16 million levy was voted down in November 1994. During the 1994–95 school year, the district overspent its $500 million dollar budget and was $125 million in debt. Implementation of the Vision 21 plan got a mixed reception from the district's evaluation committee, and Parrish lost the confidence of the mayor. In February 1995, she resigned.

The Parrish resignation, the failed levy efforts, and new debt added more uncertainty to the ongoing fiscal firestorm of the district. In March 1995, Judge Robert P. Krupansky of the U.S. Sixth Circuit Court of Appeals ordered the state to take over the schools. Judge Krupansky called the Cleveland public schools "a rudderless ship mired in mismanagement, indecision and fiscal irresponsibility" (Miller and Wheeler 1997, 196).

Obviously, the reform boards, supported by the mayor, had done little to extinguish the fiscal firestorm. The high turnover in superintendents (ten times between 1980 and 1992) also undermined efforts to restore public confidence in the district. Although Mayor White's school board candidates won in the 1991 and 1993 elections, the 1995 election would be different. Seventeen candidates entered the race. Following the court-ordered state takeover, Board President Lawrence Lumpkin and members Adrian Maldonado and Tony Cuda decided not to run for reelection (Stephens 1995b). Their departures were a sign that, with state receivership, membership on the board would be meaningless. White's strategy of changing school policy through a reform board had failed.

## The Search for an Alternative Solution

The school reform discourse changed in 1995 as many school activists began to observe Chicago's mayoral takeover of the school
system. Some Cleveland community leaders, such as the Rev. James
Lumsden of Westside-Eastside Congregations Acting Now, suggested that Mayor White takeover the schools (Stephens 1995a).
Support for a takeover within Cleveland's African American and
church-based communities was not typical in the other cities considering mayoral control (Henig and Rich 2004). The summits had
served to focus community activists, including religious leaders, on
the problem of the city's public education system. Moreover, in the
eyes of the public, the summits had shown the mayor's commitment
to education. As such, Mayor White's prior involvement in a cooperative, mobilization-oriented strategy laid the groundwork for
an image of mayoral control that was nonthreatening. The idea of
mayoral control was one of the topics discussed most during the
1996 summit.

After six years in office, the mayor had become more amenable
to an appointed board. The mayor's elected reform board had not
succeeded in controlling educational finances or improving student
performance. Mayor White became convinced that elected reform
boards did not work. More direct city hall involvement was needed.

In his 1996 State of the City address, Mayor White called for a
new law that would allow him to appoint the school board. He used a
medical analogy: The Cleveland school system was a sick patient. He
suggested that if nothing was done, the city's tombstone might read:
"Here lies Cleveland, a city that betrayed its children, a city that killed
its future" (Draper 1996). Interestingly, the Republican-dominated
state legislature was quite willing to hand over control of the schools
to the Democratic Black mayor. Two Republican state legislators
(Senator William G. Batchelder and Representative Michael Wise),
representing districts outside Cleveland, introduced the "Chicago-
styled" legislation. The bill was introduced without consulting
Cleveland's education leaders. Steven Minter, executive director of
the Cleveland Foundation and longtime stakeholder in school politics, asserted, "No one talked to us [about the bill]" (Minter interview 1 May 2001). The two legislators appeared to act alone.

Although the idea of a mayoral takeover had been discussed in the 1996 summit, the mayor nonetheless felt that the bill was premature. He asked the legislature to delay passage until he could appoint a commission to study the idea. Meanwhile, the mayor and Superintendent Boyd signed the "Memorandum of Understanding" to create a Cleveland-School Community Covenant. The covenant also restructured the Summit Convener Group into a Summit Strategy Council chaired by the mayor and the superintendent. The Summit Strategy Council was further divided into a group of 125 member work teams, or stakeholders, that met every month to discuss school policy. The entire process had a defined timetable with expected completion dates ("Memorandum of Understanding" 1996).

For the purpose of this study, the covenant's section H was most important, establishing a Governance Task Force. The mayor appointed Steven Minter, executive director of the Cleveland Foundation, and David Bergholz, executive director of the Gund Foundation, as co-chairs of the Advisory Committee on School Governance. After three months of research and debate, the committee produced a widely circulated report that recommended a mayor-appointed school board. Legislative hearings were held in Cleveland and Columbus on the proposed changes to the school governance structure.

In September 1997, the Ohio State Legislature passed House Bill 269, granting the mayor control of the schools. The new legislation also included a 2002 referendum on whether to retain the appointed board. The public discourse that followed the enactment of the new law created some confusion about the timing of the referendum and the mayor's day-to-day role in the schools.

In a letter to the *Plain Dealer*, the mayor tried to correct two misconceptions about the governance proposal. He asserted that the law did not provide for a referendum prior to the implementation of the new administrative changes. In addition, the mayor was not granted the authority to manage the schools directly. White asserted, "That is the job of the CEO. . . . If the new governance system is approved, the responsibility that the mayor will inherit is sobering, but I will not shrink from it. I have the fortitude, patience and unyielding confidence in our children to see it through" (White 1997).

The plight of the schools became the central issue in Helen Smith's primary challenge to Mayor White's 1997 reelection. After the *Plain Dealer* wrote an editorial supporting the takeover, George Forbes, former city council president, wrote an editorial supporting the National Association for the Advancement of Colored People (NAACP) suit against the takeover. During the campaign, Ms. Smith also wrote an editorial attacking the mayoral takeover plan. She asserted: "My goal is to have the school governance issue on the ballot for the May 1998 primary election" (Helen Smith 1997). Smith made the runoff, but White defeated her with 59 percent of the vote.

The pending 1998 mayoral takeover was met with several lawsuits. Stanley Toliver, former president of the school board, filed a suit in Cuyahoga County Common Pleas Court on behalf of the resident parents, claiming the takeover violated the city charter. Toliver explained:

> There's no question that it was unconstitutional. . . . You have to remember that this was a Republican led legislation that put the CPS under the jurisdiction of the mayor. Without the votes of the people. . . . What's so sneaky about it is that this is the same mayor, along with other people, who persuaded the voters to pass one of the biggest tax levies for the schools and then turned around and denied those same people the right to elect their own school board. There's no question that the mayor wanted control because of the financial incentives. (Toliver interview 30 September 2000)

In addition to the suit filed in Common Pleas Court by Toliver, the Cleveland Teachers Unions, the Service Employees International Union Local 47, and the local NAACP filed a federal suit. They lost the case in federal court because the judge ruled that the takeover law was constitutional.

In 1998, Mayor White appointed the Rev. Hilton Smith (1998–2003) chair of the newly created nine-member school board. The mayor then appointed Barbara Byrd-Bennett, a former New York City school administrator, as the new chief executive officer (CEO) of the Cleveland school system. She came highly recommended to the mayor and the board. She even received an endorsement by the vice president of New York State United Teachers, a federation of more than nine hundred local unions. Nevertheless, a local reporter also

warned CEO Byrd-Bennett about the politics of Cleveland. He asserted, "You're here to make White look good. You may be running
the schools, [but] don't forget he is running the show" (Afi-Odelia
1998). By all accounts, the new CEO and Mayor White had a good
working relationship. In interviews with board members and others
in the city, the consensus was that CEO Byrd-Bennett was making
positive changes in the administrative structure of the schools.[3]
Some even suggested that the new CEO, not the board, was "running the system." One former school board member noted:

> I think that there is more stability in the Cleveland schools since the
> mayoral takeover. He [Mayor White] brought in Dr. Bennett, a
> professional educator, and since then he keeps his hands off the day-
> to-day operations of the schools; it's a good marriage. Dr. Bennett is
> very much her own person and she will not be dictated to in terms
> of carrying out her responsibilities. (Farris interview 15 August 2000)

In addition to the fact that the mayor and the CEO appear to have
created a good working relationship, the school board is virtually
unanimous on all decisions, from high-level decisions on budgetary
matters to middle-level decisions involving day-to-day management
issues (Community Oversight Committee 2000). The former chair
of the appointed board goes as far as to say that there are "no politics
on the board. It is just like any other board ... [except] no one is
running for office" (Hilton Smith interview 9 May 2001). Not-
withstanding the former chair's assurances of nonpartisanship and
the lack of political ambitions by his fellow members, what they
decide *is* political.

## Public Opinion

Since Mayor White's popularly supported takeover, polls show a
slight increase in confidence in the school system. A survey of Clevelanders by the Triad Research Group identified an increase in the
percentage of people who perceive the schools as excellent or good,
from 11 percent in 1996 to 25 percent in 1999 ("Clevelanders
Expect" 1999). However, only a minority of citizens rate the schools
positively. The rest of the survey also suggests that parents wanted
higher standards, and that they felt welcome at the schools.

Confidence was also expressed in the citizens' willingness to vote for bonds to support the public schools. In the 2001 bond campaign, the public wanted assurances that money would be spent wisely. This concern explains Mayor White's decision to establish the twenty-three-member Bond Accountability Commission before the May 8, 2001, vote. This commission oversees the spending and holds regular public meetings. Simply put, the district needed more public trust before it could raise more money. The success of the 2001 bond issue and levy suggests that school officials may be achieving that goal. The election yielded a $335 million bond issue and a $46 million maintenance levy, with a $500 million state match for school facilities. With a strong turnout in predominantly Black eastside wards, 60 percent of voters approved the bond issue.

In November 2002, voters decided to maintain mayoral control of the schools, even though concerns about this governance structure had been expressed in surveys. According to a 2000 *Plain Dealer* poll, 80 percent of Clevelanders wanted to end Mayor White's control of the schools (van Lier 2001; Stephens and Frolik 2000). A poll taken in November 2001, but released in 2002, showed 41 percent of Clevelanders endorsed a mayor-appointed board. Leading up to the vote, Mayor Campbell stated her preference to retain the present mayor-appointed system. CEO Byrd-Bennett indicated that she would not work for an elected board. A November 2001 poll showed a 64 percent approval rating for Byrd-Bennett (Okoben 2002a). She took the lead in the fight to maintain the appointed board leading up to the 2002 vote (Okoben 2002b).

## Fiscal Strain

Most of the district's fiscal problems can be traced to the use of property taxes as the primary source of revenue. A declining tax base has left school budgets with severe shortfalls.[4] The revenue disparities between suburban and urban (and rural) districts have been challenged in the courts.[5] In a 4–3 decision, the Ohio Supreme Court ruled in *DeRolph v. State* (1997) that the state's system of funding schools was constitutional, but that the state must spend more to rectify disparities between rich and poor districts. The court did not specify a deadline for rectifying the disparities, but it did indicate that it would become involved with education funding if any of the districts that filed the original suit requested such action. Until a more equitable funding formula is negotiated, the Cleveland schools will remain largely dependent on a limited tax base.

The Cleveland school district has been on a fiscal roller coaster for decades. Although fiscal stability will not always translate into an exceptional school district, it can play a significant role in moving a district in that direction. In 1981, Cleveland's school district was placed under financial receivership for three years. The state of Ohio then established the Cleveland Education Fund to help stabilize the district financially. However, the city could not stay out of debt, so in 1991, and again in 1992, the state made short-term loans to the city to prevent another receivership. The loans were for $44 million and $75 million, respectively. In 1994, Cleveland voters expressed their dissatisfaction with the school district by voting against a school levy. By 1996, the district was in fiscal hot water again as it faced a $152 million deficit. In the eyes of state officials, the district was a cauldron of fiscal mismanagement. The state auditor declared a fiscal emergency and placed the district under a Financial Planning and Supervisory Commission. In 1997, voters supported a $13.5 million operating levy that would generate $67 million annually. This was the first operating levy approved in 26 years. Since the levy's passage and the mayor's takeover of the schools, the district has reached financial stability, with a cumulative surplus of approximately $158 million. Despite this fiscal recovery, there are numerous areas in which improvements in the schools still remain necessary. This is why the recently approved bond issue and its maintenance levy were so important.

The 2001 bond issue victory also highlights a more perplexing problem facing the schools: the changing political demographics of Cleveland. Black voters on the east side overwhelmingly supported the levy, but voters on the predominantly White west side were less supportive. This was consistent with previous levy votes. Nevertheless, CEO Byrd-Bennett explained the need for the bond issue in westside communities and framed the issue as a vote for all of Cleveland's children. As a result, the westside opposition was less strident than in previous times. This does not mean, however, that race is disappearing as a significant factor in the city's school politics.

## Race as a Factor in School Reform

Race continues to be a factor in school reform because of the high percentage of Black children in the Cleveland public schools. School reform has become a litmus test for racial progress. Who gets what, when, and how is a very salient school policy issue for the African American community. For many low-income inner-city parents, effective schools are seen as escape portals for their children. They want change and will accept a change in the governance structure of the schools if it means improved public education. For African American teachers and school administrators, the entire public school reform process is often regarded as an assault on professional autonomy. Like most professionals, they are leery of lay encroachment.

School demographics are changing faster than the overall population. Today, African Americans represent 51 percent of the city's population of 478,403. African American voters have needed White voters' support to pass school levies or bond issues. Although the White population continues to decline, it is still a factor in school-specific initiatives.

Class and ideological cleavages within Cleveland's Black community have translated into different perspectives among Black voters and Black leaders. Former Mayor White was not universally admired in the Black community. Among a small segment of Black Clevelanders, he was even known as "White Mike." This moniker was the result of the concessions he made to the predominantly White business community. It can also be traced to his first race against African American George Forbes. In that election, Forbes received 90 percent of his support from Blacks. White received only 30 percent of the Black community's vote, and 90 percent of his support came from Whites. Clearly, there remains some fallout from that race. Throughout his tenure in office, there were power brokers in the Black community who routinely challenged White on issues such as the end of the desegregation order, the legality of the transition to mayoral control of the schools, and the levy initiatives. These critics included Councilwoman Fanny Lewis, attorney Stanley Toliver, and George Forbes, now with the NAACP.

With the election of Jane Campbell, a White woman, as mayor, new personalities animate school politics. So far, she has continued

Mayor White's reform initiatives. Retaining CEO Byrd-Bennett was a master stoke in terms of Campbell's transition to office. It is not clear what Campbell plans to do about the schools. The fact that the teachers union endorsed her so quickly suggests that they believe they have little to fear. However, the leadership in the Black community has apparently taken a wait-and-see attitude toward the new mayor.

## School Politics in Cleveland

In terms of the institutional realities, the Cleveland school system is still struggling to overcome its history and precarious fiscal situation. This situation is not self-correcting and will require the state of Ohio to legislate a new and more equitable system of funding for the schools. If the state legislators thought that giving the mayor control over the board would allow them to disengage fiscally from the system, they were wrong.

School politics in Cleveland also highlight the importance of images to the success of mobilizing the public. Because former Mayor White and his appointed CEO, Barbara Bryd-Bennett, were at the apex of this mayor-centered approach to school reform, all eyes were on the two personalities. That the former mayor eschewed micromanaging the school system helped Byrd-Bennett's efforts to revitalize and modernize the administrative structure of the district. This constitutes a dramatic shift from White's strategy of getting very involved before the takeover, then keeping "an appropriate mayoral distance," to then letting the experts run the system after the takeover.

In Cleveland's 2001 mayoral race, public school reform and the future structure of the school board were key issues. Campbell and her opponent, Raymond Pierce, strongly supported extending mayoral control beyond 2002. Both also stated publicly that they would retain CEO Bryd-Bennett. Before the 2001 mayoral election, a poll found that Black respondents were evenly divided on the issue of an appointed board (Okoben and Townsend 2001). This poll showed an increase in support for the appointed board (the 2000 polls showed that 80 percent opposed the idea). Proponents of an elected board faced an uphill battle without the support of the new mayor. The same campaign team that led the bond issue, the Committee for Cleveland's Children, worked diligently in the 2002 referendum to retain the mayor-appointed board.

The dissident Black leadership's argument that an appointed board was undemocratic and disenfranchised the Black community did not resonate with the voters. Having a popular Black woman as CEO probably complicated the campaign for an elected board because voters' reservations about mayoral control were probably lessened as there would still be a Black female CEO if mayoral control was maintained. This guaranteed a level of minority representation at the top of the school hierarchy. The departure of Michael White may have taken some of the emotions out of the debate about who determines the makeup of the school board. Mayor Campbell is not part of the leadership rivalry in the Black community. As of this writing, she has not inherited much of the angst and hostility previously directed toward White.

The question of the efficacy of citywide public assemblies or summits as a vehicle for citizen mobilization and school reform remains open. It is unclear whether an annual meeting of citizens can be useful to public school reformers. Almost thirty years ago, Professor James Riedel warned citizen participation advocates that "officially sponsored citizen participation tends to be co-optation rather than representation" (Riedel 1972, 212). The summit members were never outsiders because the mayor had organized the group. With the institutionalization of the Cleveland Summit on Education as an in-house advocacy group, the public became spectators in the mayor's ongoing reform efforts. What is striking about the summits is that there has been little outcry over the decision to discontinue them. Yet, the more important question is whether the Cleveland school district's future policy options will result in fundamental improvements in the academic performance of Cleveland schools. After all, this was the original purpose of the school reform effort.

## Summary

Compared to Chicago, Cleveland has been more cautious with new school reform initiatives. Whereas Chicago tried massive decentralization and then a striking shift to mayoral control, Cleveland did not adopt a decentralization reform, and only after mayoral control was under way in Chicago did Cleveland adopt a more moderate form of mayoral control. In Cleveland, the mayor's power over school policy is moderated by several checks on mayoral power, such as the vote to maintain mayoral control in 2002 and the inclusion of the community in school board member selection. The reason for these checks may stem from the fact that Blacks are a clear majority in the electorate and the school system, something that likely contributed to the parameters of mayoral control in Cleveland. Yet, even though Cleveland has adopted less-radical school reforms, fiscal strain continues to hamper the city. The school system will not be able to avoid financial problems regardless of any fiscal stability mayoral control of the schools has facilitated.

# III Measuring Success in Education Reform

# 5 Responsiveness and Community Incorporation

The scene is Ocean-Hill Brownsville, New York during the 1968–69 school year. With funding from the Ford Foundation, the New York public schools began experimenting with administrative decentralization of the schools. A leading factor in this initiative was the failed effort to integrate the public schools (Gordon 2001, 95). Confusion resulted because Black and Puerto Rican parents in Ocean-Hill Brownsville interpreted the largely ambiguous new roles they were given through decentralization as constituting community control of the schools. Parents and community members, long locked out of educational decision making, used their new influence over educational policy to hire more minority teachers and minority administrators and insisted that classroom pedagogy include instruction on Black history.

Nineteen teachers, all White and primarily Jewish Americans, were reassigned because of their hostility toward the new system. The teachers were angered by their exclusion from the decision-making process. The situation erupted and became a historic clash of the community versus teachers when the teachers, with the backing of the union, went on strike. Although the schools remained open, the tensions outside the schools resulted in the constant presence of picketing teachers and the police. Ultimately, the teachers' union was successful in convincing the New York School Board to suspend the decentralization experiment. The reassigned teachers were escorted back to the schools with the backing of the mayor (Gordon 2001).

One might initially interpret the Ocean-Hill Brownsville situation as a failed attempt by minorities to assert authority over the educational destiny of their children. However, a deeper analysis is more instructive. Even though minority parents did not achieve their direct objectives, they did mobilize and make their voices heard. The Ocean-Hill Brownsville episode illustrates a monumental shift in power from a centralized school administrative structure into the hands of a newly mobilized, previously apolitical, ignored, and impoverished community. It tells us that evaluations of educational success can and should include contextual evaluations of educational change. Without the contextual background, mobilization of previously silent groups can be overlooked.

This chapter examines school reform in Chicago and Cleveland to determine how educational reform had an impact on minority communities, not in terms of educational skills assessments, graduation rates, attendance records, or student teacher ratios, but in the ways in which it changed the level of political influence wielded by these communities in the educational policy arena. How responsive has the educational system been to minority concerns and demands pre- and postreform? Did levels of political efficacy exhibited by the community improve? Is the minority community truly incorporated in educational decision making? The concept of responsiveness in this study is influenced by Berry, Portney, and Thomson's contention that revitalizing urban democracy requires citizen participation to ensure governmental responsiveness to the preferences of citizens (1993). The involvement of the minority community in educational policymaking is therefore viewed in this study as an important aspect of democracy in urban America.

I conducted interviews in Chicago and Cleveland with elites and non-elites, including minority parents and community members active in school reform. In Chicago, I conducted interviews between 1998 and 1999. These interviews took place ten years after Chicago's momentous decentralization reform and three years after mayoral control was instituted. In Cleveland, my interviews occurred between 2000 and 2002, roughly three years after the creation of mayoral control. Through these interviews, I examine the level of responsiveness of the school system to the interests of the community served by the schools.

As noted in previous chapters, Chicago experimented with a major decentralization initiative in 1988 following widespread mobilization in the minority community for control over the schools. Although Cleveland did experiment with decentralization in the early 1990s, it was never implemented in a comprehensive way. In Cleveland, the contrast to mayoral control was school boards elected at large. In both cities, the governance structure prior to mayoral control was more democratic in the traditional participatory sense. My evaluation of the degree of participatory democracy under each system is influenced by Archon Fung's contention that this type of democracy requires that individuals "have substantial and equal opportunities to participate directly in decisions that affect them" (2004, 4). The following section examines the impact of educational reform on the political representation of the community.

## Citizen Satisfaction with School Governance in Chicago: Pre-Mayoral Control

Chicago's 1988 school reform legislation decentralized the administrative structure of the school system by placing an unprecedented amount of power in the hands of parent and community members. This reform was truly aimed at getting community people into positions of power to enhance diversity. A component of the 1988 law was the creation of the School Board Nominating Commission (SBNC) and local school councils (LSCs). The LSCs are councils of elected parents and community representatives, teachers, and principals in each of Chicago's 541 public schools; the councils were created to make financial and administrative decisions.[1] The majority of LSC members are elected parent and community representatives. Twenty-eight members served on the SBNC; twenty-three of these were directly elected representatives from regional LSCs, and five of these individuals were appointed by the mayor.

Prior to the 1988 reform, mayors usually appointed members of the city's political and social elite to serve on the board-nominating commission. Chicago's minority residents were often overlooked as potential nominees. In addition, despite the fact that mayors created these commissions, a loophole gave mayors the option of selecting school board members who were not nominated by the commission. Creation of the SBNC, which provided the mayor with the list of nominees from which he could choose, signified the first time that community members were formally included in school board member selection.

In addition to descriptive representation of their community, SBNC members were committed to increasing racial, ethnic, regional, occupational, and economic diversity on the board of education (Former grassroots activist interview 7 July 1998).[2] Past school boards had minimal racial and ethnic diversity. The SBNC strategy of recruiting a racially, occupationally, and economically diverse board was a radical departure from previous searches. The SBNC advertised in newspapers and distributed flyers throughout the community urging interested individuals to come forward for consideration. The past chair of the SBNC explained:

> The SBNC was unique and important for a number of reasons. First, the mayor could not get around this democratic selection process, he was required to choose one of the three people we sent for each of the fifteen board positions. Many of us were grassroots activists who had played a role in the 1988 legislation and were willing to give a great deal of our time to finding the right people for the school board. Our selection process was very open and because we had fifteen slots to fill, we could be sure that there was diversity on the board according to race, economics, location in the city, the type of school they were representing, whether they were representing parents or business, and whether they had concerns that reflected a broad interest. You must also understand the commitment that we all had. We were not paid as LSC members, as sub-district council members or SBNC members. We had to nominate 45 people for the mayor and we usually had over 300 applications and did approximately 230 interviews. This took a lot of time and it was a challenge to get 28 strangers together to make some really tough choices. (Former grassroots activist interview 24 October 1998)

There were significant changes in the racial composition of the school board between 1986 and 1990 postreform boards, as Table 5.1 illustrates. Not only did minority representation increase on the 1990 board by 16 percent overall, but also there was an increase in economic and occupational diversity.[3] Traditionally, board members were important business or municipal actors. Under the new system, members were middle-class parents, ministers, community activists, homemakers, and professors.

Table 5.1. Racial Representation on Chicago's School Board

| Race | 1980 and 1986 Boards: 11 Members | | 1989 Interim Board: 6 Members | | 1990 Board: 15 Members | | 1995 to July 1999 Board of Trustees and Management Team | | August 1999–2002 Board of Trustees and Management Team | |
|---|---|---|---|---|---|---|---|---|---|---|
| | No. | % | No. | % | No. | % | No. | % | No. | % |
| White | 4 | 36 | 2 | 33 | 3 | 20 | 4 | 40 | 4 | 33 |
| Black | 5 | 45.5 | 3 | 50 | 8 | 53 | 4 | 40 | 5 | 42 |
| Latino | 2 | 18.5 | 1 | 17 | 3 | 20 | 1 | 10 | 2 | 17 |
| Asian | 0 | 0 | 0 | 0 | 1 | 7 | 1 | 10 | 1 | 8 |
| Total | 11 | 100 | 6 | 100 | 15 | 100 | 10 | 100 | 12 | 100 |

*Source*: The racial background of school board members provided by the Office of Communications for the Chicago public schools.

*Note*: Boards were selected to highlight the changes in racial representation after the 1988 and 1995 legislation took effect. Boards in 1980 and 1986 were selected to highlight racial representation on the board prior to the 1988 reform; both boards had exactly the same racial balance. The 1989 interim board was in place for eighteen months and was appointed by the mayor.

Interviews with parents and community members reveal a high level of satisfaction with school board selection under the SBNC process. The new diversity that was reflected on the school board appeared to provide people with a sense of direct representation. One SBNC member explained:

> The nominating commission gave the community the chance, for the first time, to have some input into how the board was selected, and consequently how the budget was run. This gave us the system-wide input that the LSCs provided at the individual school level. (Community member b interview 24 October 1998)

When asked whether they could remember any school board members selected during the time of the SBNC, many interviewees were readily able to do so. In a few interviews, respondents recalled having personal ties to board members after the 1988 law was passed. Some respondents indicated that board members had been neighbors or had children in school with their child or children. The fact that respondents reflected positively on the school board selection process after the SBNC was established is critical. There was a clear feeling among these respondents that there was finally a mechanism intended to include the desires of the minority community. This was important to all parent and community respondents.

Although there was a high degree of satisfaction with the SBNC because more community residents were involved in the educational policy process as a result of the new reform, criticisms still emerged. One of the main problems identified by SBNC members was that they were not given the resources, office space, or legislative guidelines under which to operate. Several community groups claimed that their representation on the SBNC was inadequate. The SBNC chair claimed that the dissatisfaction expressed among many groups was an indication of the democratic nature of the SBNC selection process:

> The first couple of years everybody was complaining because they saw people from all over appointed to the board. For example, the reform groups were upset because there weren't enough reform people on the board. We also received complaints from the mayor, from the unions. Because we got complaints from everyone, but also knew that many of these same people appreciated many of our choices, we felt the process was very democratic. (Former grassroots activist a interview 24 October 1998)

Despite these criticisms, the interviews revealed a high level of satisfaction with the school boards chosen through the SBNC process. The interviews also revealed a high level of contact between school board and community members regarding problems or concerns with the school system. One former Chicago public school parent and current school volunteer said:

> I used to go down to the Board of Education meetings, either once or twice a month after that '88 law. I'd go and they'd have meetings and if you had a problem with the schools you could go talk to them. You only had something like two minutes to make a case, but if enough of us got together we could usually persuade a board member to combine the time and let one person speak longer. (Community member a interview 29 October 1998)

Parents and community representatives typically said that they were aware that they could attend and have their voices heard at board meetings. Although they believed the board listened, there was a sense that board business often took too long. For example, the same parent who claimed he routinely attended board meetings said, "They sure took their time getting around to doing things" (Parent a interview 29 October 1998).

The accusation that the fifteen-member board micromanaged the schools was an issue that occasionally emerged with parent and community respondents but was voiced even more fervently by the current school administration. One current administrator, a former Chicago public schools lobbyist, said that with the post-1988 school board there were too many committee meetings, and that board members could often be found milling around the board office (Administrator interview 13 October 1998).

This perception of "inefficiency" appears to have been associated with the amount of time board members spent addressing community concerns. Ironically, this inefficiency is precisely what parent and community members seemed to value, even as they criticized the board for making slow progress.

The slow rate of response among school board members to community concerns complicates a clear assessment of responsiveness. Although board members appeared more accessible and interested in the concerns of community members after the 1988 legislation was enacted, their inability to act quickly became a problem. Depending on how responsiveness is defined, evaluations of this variable can be analyzed differently. If responsiveness is a product of listening, holding regular public meetings, making themselves available at a public office, and eventually enacting policies that met the needs of the community, then the post-1988 school board members were very responsive to minority concerns. On the other hand, if responsiveness is the rapid enactment of policies that rectify community grievances, then the board was insufficiently responsive.

Review of post-1988 school board minutes provided additional insight into the complicated issue of responsiveness. The large number of issues that the post-1988 school boards addressed, the frequency of their meetings, and their elaborate committee system that offered access to the community through open meetings are themes that also surfaced repeatedly in my interviews. As one board employee explained:

> Those boards would deal with every little problem that came their
> way. If one of the cafeteria workers in a particular school was causing
> problems, they'd deal with it. If they needed to get supplies for a
> different school, they'd deal with it. It was definitely micromanaging,
> but that was how the board was set up. (Administrator interview
> 26 June 1998)

The procedures followed by the board of education, with their
elaborate committee system, reporting procedures, and openness to
public input, clearly slowed board business. Budget deficits were also
another critical problem plaguing the Chicago public school system.
One current Chicago public school administrator and pre-1988
school board member explained:

> The school board that I was a member of, similar to the board after the
> 1988 legislation, had one extremely important restriction—money.
> We used to see huge surpluses in something like the playground fund,
> but we couldn't touch it because it was earmarked for the play-
> grounds. Never mind that the schools' roofs were caving-in and that
> schools were crumbling, we couldn't touch it or borrow money be-
> cause of the deficit and the School Finance Authority's oversight.
> Those new board members listened, but they got tied-up in red tape
> and restrictions. With that committee system there was just no way
> around it. (Administrator interview 23 October 1998)

In effect, the slow response time was sometimes the result of the
chronic budget crisis. Consequently, any request made by the community that involved funding was extremely difficult to honor.

Overall, it appears that the school board created under the 1988
legislation was more responsive to minority concerns compared to
the previous system, which seemed closed to minorities. This finding
reflects favorably on the level of participatory democracy under this
school reform. This is not to say that the structure established after
1988 was flawless. Whereas there was community satisfaction in
terms of responsiveness, there was also the sense that boards were
underfunded and inefficient. However, minority residents felt better
represented in the school policymaking process as a consequence of
the 1988 reform because of their perception that their input was
incorporated in the system. Minorities were also descriptively better

represented on the board as a consequence of the 1988 legislation, which likely enhanced their levels of political efficacy, specifically in the area of educational policymaking. In principle, the SBNC reflected the pluralist ideal in which multiple groups compete on an equal footing for resources and power.

In addition to the radical decentralization of administrative control, the other essential part of the 1988 legislation was the move toward school site-based management. The creation of elected LSCs essentially opened the doors for parents and community members to make educational decisions at their local schools. These elected officials chose to serve their schools despite lack of compensation for their service. Because LSCs are elected by voting-age individuals in the school's neighborhood, the creation of LSCs granted the community a great deal of influence.[4] As discussed in Chapter 3, this was largely possible because of the temporary alliance between the Black community and the business community, who lobbied the legislature for decentralization and an organization that would allow the community to have direct involvement in their neighborhood schools.[5]

The LSCs were granted tremendous discretion in curriculum and financial decisions for their school, in addition to the ability to hire and fire principals. Bypassing the school board, LSCs were directly allocated state "Chapter One" funds based on their low-income student enrollment. LSCs were also given the right of final approval of their school's expenditure plan. The broad and expansive power granted to LSCs made them essential parts of the school administration as they made most of the decisions for their schools. The school board retained the power to oversee the school system, but it was largely restricted by the fact that the School Finance Authority (SFA) actually managed the budget. In effect, while the school board was able to monitor the school system and mandate standards and systemwide requirements, the LSCs operating across the school district were the locus of educational policy. The balance of power between the LSC and the board favored the LSC in many respects because the vast majority of members on the SBNC were also LSC members (Community member a interview 24 October 1998). The control wielded by LSCs was monumental and especially apparent when compared to the efforts made in the Ocean-Hill Brownsville experiment. The community in Chicago succeeded in going a step further than the Ocean-Hill Brownsville community in terms of community control.

Dan Lewis and Katherine Nakagawa reported considerable satisfaction among Chicago's public school parents during the first phase of school reform (1995, 100). Although these authors did not attribute parental satisfaction to the creation of LSCs, their findings regarding parental satisfaction during the post-1988 reform period are reaffirmed in this study. The energy that respondents continuously identified regarding the first LSC elections indicated that these councils reflected the highest degree of political incorporation ever experienced at the school level.

One motivation for the reform was to get more parents involved in the education of their children. Based on my interviews, it appears that parents became more involved after the reform took effect. Many individuals said that their LSC members encouraged them to volunteer, to attend LSC meetings, and to consider running for election themselves. Seeing friends and neighbors, many of whom did not have prestigious occupational backgrounds or extensive educational backgrounds, making educational policy brought people together based on their common interest in improving educational opportunities for children. One community representative commented:

> When a spot opened on the LSC, people knew me because I was always coming to LSC meetings and volunteering whenever they needed help. You see, my children went to this school and I know not all these children don't have a parent like the kind I am. So, they said to me, "Mrs. [Name], won't you think about running?" So I did. . . . I call a lot of these parents and talk to them about activities in the school and concerns that they need to know about. I called them about the leaking sky lights and the crumbling swimming pool. I also contacted a lot of people when we heard the school was being reconstituted. They need to know what is happening in their child's school and what they can do to help. (Community member interview 30 October 1998)

The creation of LSCs offered a direct way to enter the political system for many of Chicago's minority residents, who ran for office for the first time. A tremendous shift in the number of minority elected officials occurred after the first LSC elections. By 1994, LSCs were composed of eighteen hundred Black (42 percent) and seven hundred Latino (16 percent) members (Shipps, Kahne, and Smylie 1998, 18). Table 5.2 provides voter turnout figures for the first LSC elections held between 1989 and 1998. Table 5.3 documents the number of candidates running in these elections.

Although voter turnout and the number of contenders in an election are not direct measures of responsiveness, these statistics indicate the minority community's faith in the system. Both the voter turnout figures and the numbers of candidates during the first LSC elections were high and indicate a significant level of interest in these elections compared to the decline in both areas that can be seen in subsequent elections. Tables 5.2 and 5.3 present LSC voter turnout figures and the number of people running for LSC positions from 1989 to 1998. In both tables, the decline in participation is evident over time. The 1998 LSC elections yielded the fewest candidates. Moreover, when compared to previous LSC elections, the low voter turnout reflected an almost 50 percent reduction in participation from the first LSC election in 1989. According to one board employee in the Office of Schools and Community Relations,

Table 5.2. Local School Council Voter Turnout Figures in Chicago

| Year | Total |
|------|-------|
| 1989 | 311,946 |
| 1991 | 173,767 |
| 1993 | 135,933 |
| 1996 | 175,845 |
| 1998 | 144,632 |

*Source*: Data provided by the Office of Schools and Community Relations for the Chicago public schools.

*Note*: According to the Office of Schools and Community Relations, the number of eligible voters is not available because of the complications associated with eligibility. Voters need not be registered voters to participate. They must only provide evidence that their children attend the school or that they live in the community. In addition, each resident who is eighteen years or older can vote in two schools (high school and elementary). Parents with children in multiple city schools can also vote in each school's local school council election. Finally, some students attend schools that are outside their local school's boundaries.

Table 5.3. Local School Council Candidates in Chicago

| Year | Community | Parent | Teacher | Student | Total |
|------|-----------|--------|---------|---------|-------|
| 1989 | 4,818 | 9,329 | 2,429 | 520 | 17,096 |
| 1991 | 1,858 | 4,739 | 1,545 | 248 | 8,390 |
| 1993 | 1,495 | 4,254 | 1,612 | 178 | 7,539 |
| 1996 | 1,683 | 4,501 | 1,623 | 211 | 8,018 |
| 1998 | 1,504 | 4,074 | 1,480 | 172 | 7,266 |

*Source*: Data as reported by the Office of Schools and Community Relations for the Chicago public schools.

voter turnout for LSC elections was near 30 percent during the first round of LSC elections (Administrator interview 7 July 1998). Given the low level of voter turnout for elections in the United States and the estimated 10 percent turnout for elections in cities where school board elections are held, this level of participation is considerable (Gittell 1998, 155). The community empowerment realized in the first round of LSC elections significantly declined by the next round.

When interviewees were asked about the level of LSC responsiveness to their concerns during the 1988–95 school reform period and whether they felt that participation as voters or candidates was important, respondents shared extremely positive evaluations. They also indicated that they recalled the excitement surrounding the first LSC elections. Respondents believed that the LSC was able to allocate money for programs that specifically met the needs of students at their local school. One frequently mentioned attribute of the LSC was that members would ask parents what types of programs they would like to see developed for their children. Because LSC members were seen as "common folk," they seemed approachable to many of the parents interviewed (Parent a interview 29 October 1998).

In probing respondents regarding why they felt their LSC was responsive, many answers emerged in the following categories. Some claimed that they felt comfortable talking with their representatives; others stated that LSCs tried to provide money for programs in which parents believed. Still others said that LSC members shared the goal of improving the educational environment in the particular school; that during LSC meetings parents felt welcome; and that parents felt that their presence in the schools was valued and appreciated for the first time. These comments can be seen as strong indications of a high level of responsiveness among LSC members after the initial LSCs were created after the 1988 law took effect.

However, the decline in voter turnout and the reduction in candidates seeking LSC positions does not correspond to a higher level of responsiveness. Although it could be an indication that participation declined because LSCs had become inconsequential political bodies, the responses received from parents do not support such a conclusion. When parents and community members were asked directly if they continued voting in LSC elections or considered running after the initial 1989 election, some respondents said they really did not participate very often after 1989. One parent explained that she believed the LSC at her school did a good job, and that she trusted that good people would continue to hold positions on the council (Parent b interview 29 October 1998). Another parent indicated that, although she consistently voted in the first three LSC elections, her defeat in 1989 destroyed her interest in running again (Parent a interview 29 October 1998). The most common response was that the LSC did a good job, and people felt that they really did not need to vote.

As for running for an LSC position, individuals who had served and individuals who had not said that the time commitment was challenging, especially when holding a full-time job and raising a family. In analyzing the decline in participation, one activist made an analogy between serving on the LSC and being a member of a condominium board. In both cases, you serve because you have a stake in policies, but it is a thankless duty that takes time and provides no compensation (Community member interview 25 June 98). The fact that LSC positions offered no compensation, in contrast to many other elected positions, may partially explain this large reduction in the number of LSC candidates over time. The dwindling number of candidates reduces competition and in turn may explain the declining rates of voter participation in LSC elections.

LSCs have had their share of critics. Opponents of the 1988 legislation, including many Chicago school administrators, claimed that parents and the average community member were insufficiently educated to make important policy decisions. A related criticism was the potential for too much parental interference in classroom instruction.

The initial legislation neither mandated nor provided training for LSC members in budgetary or curricular policy. One former grass-roots activist and current Chicago public schools administrator commented:

> Think about what happened in 1988. We [Black community activists] finally had some say in the schools. But the legislation came back revenue neutral. So you had all these really interested parents who felt the energy and they were elected to LSCs. Many of them had no experience with budgets or curriculum or hiring a principal because they'd never been invited in the past to do these things. Without the money for training and because the system was in bad shape in terms of money, it seemed as if they wanted us to fail. That way the blame could be placed on these unqualified, undereducated activists. (Former grassroots activist a interview 24 October 98)

As a result, some of the programs enacted by LSCs were scrutinized and criticized by observers. Despite the fact that the legislation did not initially mandate training, a number of grassroots community organizations conducted training sessions for interested LSC members. Philanthropic foundations in Chicago largely financed these training programs. The foundation community's support was essential even if they were not influential in the creation of the 1988 legislation (McKersie 1993). The role of Chicago's foundations in this training comes as no surprise given their role in funding, implementing, and evaluating school reform initiatives over the previous 20 years (Rolling 2004, 24; McKersie and Markward 1999).

Training elected officials is more complicated then it appears at first glance. Although it would be ideal for all elected officials to receive comprehensive training, elected officials in the United States do not typically receive mandated training. If legislators required that parents and community members receive mandatory training for the unpaid office to which they are elected, then this could have been viewed as a statement that voters in LSC elections were incapable of selecting qualified candidates. In turn, this might have reduced the pool of potential candidates.

The high degree of satisfaction expressed by parents and community activists about LSCs contrasts with the sentiments that emerged during elite interviews. The difference between elite and non-elite evaluations of the level of responsiveness of the post-1988 administration was very striking. Many of the current Chicago public schools administrators believed that LSC members under the 1988 legislation were unqualified and should have never been granted such vast policy discretion. This was often linked to the financial problems that lingered after the 1988 legislation and the complaint that, because the board's central office was weakened, there was not an accountability mechanism for the school system. Overall, the new school board and the LSCs received high praise from minority residents for being open and responsive, while established actors in the policymaking process, such as administrators, were strikingly critical of the LSCs, particularly of members they felt were unqualified.

## Citizen Satisfaction with Pre-Mayoral Control School Governance in Cleveland

Unlike Chicago, Cleveland did not experiment with a massive decentralization effort. Nevertheless, prior to mayoral control in Cleveland, there was community input in educational decision making. The most structured methods of community participation were evident through the elected board of education.

Cleveland has a long history with elected boards of education. Legislation passed in 1953 mandates that all large school districts in Ohio have a seven-member school board elected at large unless the state legislature agrees to different arrangements ("Bringing New Skills" 1997). During the long history of elected boards in Cleveland, voter turnout in school board elections appeared relatively strong (see Table 5.4). But, these figures are somewhat misleading because board elections were held in conjunction with citywide elections, thereby artificially inflating voter turnout. Had board elections been held independent of other elections, the turnout figures would likely be lower. Nationally, voter turnout in most school board elections typically hovers around 10 percent (Gittell 1998, 155).[6] Therefore, it is noteworthy that in Cleveland turnout never dipped below 27 percent in a nonmayoral election year.

Parent and community respondents characterized the school board during the early 1980s as responsive to their needs.[7] These

Table 5.4. Cleveland School Board
Election Voter Turnout (%)

| | |
|---|---|
| 1985 | 38[a] |
| 1987 | 28 |
| 1989 | 54[a] |
| 1991 | 27 |
| 1993 | 36[a] |
| 1995 | 33 |
| 1997 | 41[a] |

*Source*: Cuyahoga County Board of Elections.
[a]Mayoral election.

respondents reflected favorably on the early boards as "helpful" and "willing to get things done on their behalf." Many of these same respondents also admitted that even though the board was responsive, it was unable to solve the underlying problems that plagued the Cleveland schools. In addition, the respondents stated that it often took the board considerable time to get things done because of all the demands they handled and the time they spent in the community. The outreach to the community was readily apparent in minutes from board meetings during the 1980s through 1997, the period prior to mayoral control.[8] Despite its often slow pace of operation, community and parent respondents appreciated the board's inclusiveness and the willingness of board members to "reach out to the community" (Community member a interview 23 August 2001). One former board member and president of the board (1967–78) explained:

> What I did was encourage people to come to committee meetings because that's where the dialogue takes place and where the decisions take place. That way, when the committee chairperson went before the board and made a recommendation, the recommendation is already backed up because it had the involvement of the community. (Farris interview 15 August 2000)

Most of these elected officials had children in the schools and thus had a direct stake in the fate of the students. More important, as elected officials, they were directly beholden to the community for reelection. They were less likely to be highly paid professionals and more commonly individuals who ran based on a commitment to

Table 5.5. Cleveland Public Schools Racial and Ethnic
Breakdown (%), 1980–2000

|                  | 1980 | 1990 | 2000 |
|------------------|------|------|------|
| Black            | 67.4 | 71.1 | 71.0 |
| White            | 28.0 | 21.0 | 19.2 |
| Hispanic         | 3.7  | 6.3  | 8.1  |
| Asian            | 0.6  | 1.3  | 0.8  |
| American Indian  | 0.3  | 0.2  | 0.4  |
| Multiethnic      | NA   | NA   | 0.6  |

*Sources*: Office on Monitoring and Community Relations of the
Cleveland Public Schools for 1980 and 1990 figures and Cleveland
Municipal School Board for 2000 figures.
NA, data not recorded.

the education of their children (Wood interview 16 March 2002;
Community member interview 24 August 2001; Community member b interview 23 August 2001; City council member interview 31
August 2000). According to three former board members who
served in the 1980s or early 1990s, about half of the eighteen school
board members elected in the 1980s could be classified as community
activists. Although five members were classified as lawyers, several of
these individuals were also very active in representing the community
in local affairs. Of the other board members from this era, three were
classified as educators, one as a union representative, and two as
business leaders or local philanthropists. Over half of the school
board members from this period had children who attended the
Cleveland public schools.[9] Racially and ethnically, the board reflected
the community relatively well, with the exception of the Latino
community (see Tables 5.4 and 5.5). Thus, it comes as no surprise
that these early boards were seen as responsive to the community.

The costs associated with running for the board during the 1980s
were moderate, often not more than the filing fee and the time it took
to campaign (Former board member interview 30 September 2000).
However, a major shift in school board politics occurred in 1991
when Mayor Michael White decided to run a slate of candidates for
the school board. The slate was known as the Four Ls because it
consisted of four candidates whose last names began with the letter *L*.
The decision to endorse a group of candidates further politicized
board politics and increased the costs of running for office, primarily

based on the increased media expenses. As one community activist commented:

> I think the school boards in the 1980s were responsive to the interests of the community. However, I think the school board has always been a political beast, a political animal. And that part didn't have anything to do with the education of kids, it had to do with contracts and dollars. But the point when it became so publicly political was when you had the mayor running his 4 Ls slate for the school board. I think that's the time when things really started to deteriorate with the board. I personally feel that school boards should be governed by the community. The trouble begins when you have an elected body that's hand-selected. (Community member interview 24 August 2001)

Mayor White succeeded in getting his slate of candidates elected in 1991 and again in 1993. According to board members who served during this time, the cost of running for the board became prohibitive. One member of the mayor's 1993 board reported that she wouldn't have been able to run without being a part of the mayor's slate, a group that spent over $200,000 collectively to win (Wood interview 16 March 2002).[10]

In 1995, an Ohio court ordered the state of Ohio to assume control of the Cleveland schools. The judge premised his decision on the fiscal crisis of the system as well as internal dissention on the Cleveland school board. By all accounts, this was the point at which the elected school board deteriorated to complete pandemonium. The elected board that remained in place after the state takeover had absolutely no power. The factions on the board clashed constantly, and the superintendent at the time refused to deal with the board. He explained:

> The board was pretty chaotic. Not that there weren't some good people on there. In some ways they were like any other urban board. There's the racial politics, the partisan politics, there's all kinds of politics. And this group engaged in that. Lots of delving into areas that were really the prerogative of the superintendent. And board meetings were just a circus. And then they had a board election. And the real question was, why would you want to run for a board that had no authority? . . . After one particularly hideous meeting I informed the board that I would no longer attend any meetings nor would any

member of my staff. (Former superintendent interview 28 February 2002)

Although the superintendent had one set of complaints about a board of education under state control, some community members disliked state control for different reasons. As one parent noted:

> Rather than giving the board the strength it needed to make things better, like more money or teachers or better schools, they took power from the people who had elected these board members. . . . There could have been a different solution. (Parent interview 7 March 2002)

Mayor White was also unnerved that the state took control of the schools. He was not consulted prior to the takeover, which stripped his slate of board members of power (White interview 25 April 2002).

Altogether, the mayor's dominance in school board elections, followed by the state takeover of the schools, were demoralizing to both parent and community respondents. After reducing the ability for rank-and-file Clevelanders to run successfully for the school board, the state takeover sent the message that Cleveland parents and community members were only symbolically integrated in education policymaking. In contrast to parent and community respondents, elites were far more likely to view school board members as corrupt, unable to serve the children of the school system, and merely interested in climbing the political ladder. Elected board members, even some whom he had endorsed, were later characterized by former Mayor White as "seduced by power." He claims that, as a consequence, they were unable to deal with the demands of the unions, teachers, bus drivers, custodians, and so on (White interview 25 April 2002). In addition, elites were likely to see school boards prior to the election of the mayor's candidates in this same light.

The contrast between elite and non-elite assessments of elected boards is noteworthy and reminiscent of the differences in Chicago's elite versus non-elite assessments of the 1988 reform. Whereas elites assign a high value to efficiency, organization on the school board, and their own inclusion in the policy process, non-elites are more concerned with their incorporation in policy process and the ideals of participatory democracy even if the price they pay is a slower policy process. Interestingly, non-elites are overwhelmingly city residents; elites typically reside in suburbs and are therefore part of different school systems. These findings are instructive in terms of the divergent interests and how elites are typically more successful in pushing for reforms they favor. Elite-backed reforms are less likely to incorporate pluralist ideals. Next are examinations of citizens' reactions to mayoral control in Chicago and Cleveland.

## Citizen Satisfaction with Mayoral Control School Governance in Chicago

Although the 1988 legislation had decentralized control of the school system from the school board to the local community, the 1995 legislation bypassed the school board and centralized power in the hands of the mayor. The driving force behind the 1995 legislation for control of Chicago's schools was the school system's fiscal insolvency. Although the schools were able to operate under financial strain for many years, by 1993 there was a $150 billion budget deficit. Moreover, teachers' strikes were consistently causing schools to close their doors at the start of each academic year.

No longer able to accept the budget deficits that plagued the school system for decades, a statewide business coalition created a new school reform package aimed at solving the short-term fiscal problems. The legislation that resulted, the 1995 school reform legislation, dramatically reversed the previous community-centered reform effort by centralizing administrative power in Mayor Daley's office. In addition to granting the mayor the power to appoint a five-member board of trustees and a management team, the new legislation gave the board an unprecedented amount of financial flexibility.

A facsimile of the LSC system was retained under the 1995 legislation, perhaps to make the reform politically more feasible. Yet, the sources of LSC power—autonomy, decision-making ability, and financial assets—were now restricted. Because the board of trustees was established largely to create a financially stable school system, it was given complete discretion over the finances of the school system. This reversed the financial autonomy over individual school discretionary spending established for LSCs under the 1988 legislation.

Although principal selection remains the responsibility of the LSC, the board and the management team have the formal authority to replace principals they believed are not qualified. In addition, if LSCs are found to operate "inefficiently," then they can also be removed by the board and replaced with interim LSCs. The elimination of elected officials by a school administration is viewed by some as undemocratic. LSCs at two schools have been removed because of the board's conclusion that they were administratively or financially ineffective.

The 1995 legislation recalled an earlier period when Chicago's mayors exercised autonomy in school board nominations. However, the 1995 legislation granted Mayor Richard M. Daley an additional layer of authority. Throughout Chicago's history, city council confirmation of school board members had been required. The 1995 legislation no longer required city council approval. Eliminating the SBNC and the city council from board selection was a clear reversal of the democratic aspect of the previous selection process. It eliminated an important democratic check on the power of the mayor to control the city's educational policy. In addition, because the number of minority city council members had increased since 1988, eliminating the council's role in the selection of board members further reduced minority influence over educational policy.

Another unique part of this legislation was the elimination of the superintendent. Because the school board was historically responsible for selecting a superintendent, this was a monumental shift. The position of superintendent was replaced by a five-person management team, also appointed by the mayor. The management team's purpose is to work with the mayor and the board to address efficiently particular needs of the Chicago public schools. Among the most striking aspects of the school system's new administrative structure was the number of businesspeople and former employees of the mayor's office who served on the board and management team. The composition of the board and management team reflects the importance of the business community in designing this legislation. This new structure reversed the trend toward a more racially and occupationally diverse school board that had emerged after 1988.

A new Republican majority in the Illinois legislature shaped the 1995 legislative process as it pertained to school reform in Chicago.

This change in leadership largely blocked participation of those active in 1988, including Democratic legislators and minority activists. In addition, because the 1988 activists were occupied with LSC business, some suggest that they were unaware of the changes under way (Policy analyst interview 26 June 1996). The two entities consistently active in school reform were Chicago's business and Black communities. Whereas the 1988 legislation was created by a Chicago business and community coalition devoted to decentralization, the 1995 legislation was the product of a statewide business coalition focused on achieving financial stability for the school system (Shipps 1998).

Another important change in the 1995 reform was deemphasis on educational expertise. None of the board or management team members had a background in education. To parent and community respondents, this fact increased their concern about the direction of the new reform. One parent noted:

> If they know a lot about managing money or dealing with city bureaucrats, that's all well and good if we need the budget balanced and the city to listen. But, if they need to create programs for our kids, how can they do it any better than me or you? If we aren't trained in how kids learn and thrive academically, how can we know what's best. It's the same thing for the board. (Parent b interview 29 October 1998)

Many other respondents also thought that the lack of educators on the school board simply did not make sense. The appointment of someone with knowledge of educational tools, techniques, and pedagogy would have been reassuring to the community and teachers. The teachers interviewed in this study indicated that the exclusion of professional educators from the mayor's board indicated the consistent disregard for educators' input in school reform (Five-teacher interview 14 July 1998). In an interview, a Chicago radio talk show host shared an anecdote related to the educational expertise of board members:

> I had one of the board members on my show, and I didn't want to embarrass him, but he admitted he doesn't know a thing about education. These board members just don't know anything about

education. I think their orders are coming from the top and they are told, "sign here." (Community member interview 31 October 1998)

All respondents, including elite and non-elite respondents, reported that, because the finances of the school system needed improvement, including financial experts on the board was understandable. There was, however, disagreement over whether a school board dominated by business professionals and political experts could make the necessary reforms. Some middle-level Chicago public school administrators had expressed hopes that when the board of trustees expanded to seven members in August 1999 that educational experts would have been placed on the board. However, educational experts were not appointed to the board in the 1999 restructuring.

If descriptive representation is one indicator of minority incorporation in the policymaking process, then there is no question that the 1995 legislation undermined minority incorporation at the school system's highest levels. Since 1981, Chicago's superintendents have traditionally been Black, even when the Black community's first-choice candidate was not selected. In replacing the superintendent with a management team, the highest-ranking school administrative position was replaced by a team headed by a White chief executive officer (CEO), Paul Vallas, the mayor's former city budget director. Black community activists expressed a large amount of frustration when he was selected. One former grassroots activist noted:

> The mayor, by hook or by crook, stumbled across this board and team that we were really concerned about. The CEO was White and the last four superintendents had been African American. The President of the board, Gery Chico, was Latino and the last two or three were African American. Because of this, African Americans wondered, "what are you doing?" These people had fought so hard to have resources handed out more evenly, and it was just taken away. (Former grassroots activist interview 7 July 1998)

The frustration in the Black community in the wake of the 1995 legislation was evident in all community and parent interviews. With respect to descriptive representation, the new board and management team at the time this research was conducted in 1998 and 1999 had only four Black members out of a total of ten members (Table 5.1). Given that the Chicago public schools currently serve a majority-minority population, the 1995 legislation significantly decreased descriptive representation among board members. As Table 5.1 illustrates, there was a 13 percent decrease in overall minority representation (Blacks, Latinos, and Asian Americans combined) between the 1990 and the 2002 board. Although the addition of one Black and one Latino board member in the 1999 board restructuring did increase minority descriptive representation compared with the 1995 board, the new minority members on the board and management team in 2002 were occupationally and economically dissimilar from the majority of families served by the school system. All board members had prestigious business backgrounds or were formerly high-ranking municipal employees.

Another concern voiced during interviews was that few board and management team members sent their children to Chicago's public schools. Except for the board president at the time of this study, who sent his children to one of the newly established charter schools, the other board and management team members with school-aged children sent their children to private, parochial, or suburban schools (Journalist interview 3 August 1998). A journalist commented:

> Having children in the school system indicates a certain faith in the system. If board members won't send their own children to the public schools, what sort of message is that to those of us who have no choice? I mean, you at least used to know that they were sending their kids to school with yours or that they were interested in the schools for this reason. If they are making decisions for children that don't go home to them, why should they care? (Journalist interview 3 August 1998)

In addition to the changed racial and occupational demographics of the board members, the standard operating procedures of the board also changed considerably as a result of the 1995 legislation. Under the old board, meetings were held twice a month. There was also an elaborate committee system. The new board meets once a month, televises their meetings, and has eliminated the previous committee structure. The committees have been replaced with a management team that receives delegated responsibilities based on their area of specialization. The minutes of the new board reveal that meetings are run quite efficiently compared to those before mayoral control of the schools.

Community participation at board meetings continues to be encouraged under the new board structure. However, parent and community respondents indicated that there is not the same "behind the scenes" interaction with board members. Regarding the post-1988 boards, members were often in contact with community activists before meetings. After 1995, contact with community actors was characterized as more formal and exclusive.

Clearly, the new management team is making concerted efforts to reach community members through televised meetings. However, it is important to note that televised meetings do not constitute citizen participation. Although many parent and community respondents claimed that they had seen televised board meetings, few had actually attended one. Of those interviewed who claimed to have interacted with post-1988 board members or spoken at a meeting, only two of those individuals claimed to have interacted with the board of trustees or attended a board meeting (Three-parents interview 29 October 1998). One woman claimed:

> I thought the meetings would be democratic, like they were before.
> I went to two meetings and it seemed to me that people are cut
> off quicker than before. (Parent b interview 29 October 1998)

Televising board meetings has apparently not worked to reverse the opinions of community residents that the new board is less responsive than the former one created by 1988 legislation. Parents and community respondents in this study were asked whether they were familiar with school board members after passage of the 1988 or 1995 legislation. Whereas these respondents claimed to have known the names of a few school board members or to have had personal contact with them after the 1988 legislation, those respondents who identified any post-1995 board members were primarily familiar with only former CEO Paul Vallas. The interviews, however, revealed that community reaction to Mr. Vallas is positive, even among those highly critical of the mayor and his administration.

Respondents frequently stated that they believe Mr. Vallas "really cares about children." Paradoxically, some of the individuals who felt the board, mayor, and management were totally unresponsive to the minority community made this type of comment about the CEO. This seems to indicate that the CEO was able walk a fine line with the community and make a favorable impression at the same time that the community was generally displeased with the new governance structure. In addition, respondents did not have contact with board members prior to their appointment, as some claimed to have had with those serving on school boards after the 1988 legislative initiative.

Both community members and parents overwhelmingly indicated that they thought the new school board was unresponsive. Most respondents felt they were excluded from the educational policy process because board members were inaccessible and because LSCs had been stripped of a great deal of their powers. As one parent noted:

> When my daughter was held back, the LSC said they didn't have the power to help, that it was the board's decision. Then I couldn't talk to anyone at the board because they wouldn't return my calls. (Parent interview 9 November 1998)

During discussions about what a responsive school administration ought to resemble, respondents indicated that board member accessibility and LSC authority under the 1988 legislation were critically important.

Respondents consistently complained about the new policies implemented by the board of trustees. The most serious criticisms of board actions were in the areas of reconstitution of schools, reliance on standardized tests to measure achievement and determine grade promotion, creation of charter schools, and elimination of LSC power. Respondents who mentioned these policies emphasized that these were not the policies they advocated. Reconstitution, which meant that a school would essentially be closed and reopened with a new staff, was reserved for chronically low-performing schools. The policy authorized the board to strip LSCs in those schools of their governing authority. Although those LSCs would still be free to meet and generate support for the school, they would be essentially powerless.

The result of the financial and governance limits placed on LSCs has, according to many elite and non-elite respondents, made membership on the LSC an ineffectual political post. Parents and community activists claimed that although LSC members were responsive to their concerns, they now seem unable to help even if they feel committed to doing so. The sense of political empowerment that was once felt by LSC members and non-LSC parent and community members has diminished following the 1995 legislation.

Interviews with parents and community representatives indicate that since the 1995 legislation, LSCs are no longer seen as an important place to go for assistance. However, the decline in voter turnout already had begun after the first LSC election in 1989 (see Table 5.2). Nonetheless, the recentralization basically stripped the LSCs of power, and therefore it is not surprising that voter turnout and the number of LSC candidates have continued to decline. Because LSCs have been stripped of much of their power, there appear to be few compelling reasons for individuals to seek office or vote.

## Citizen Satisfaction with Mayoral Control
## School Governance in Cleveland

In 1998, with the support of the business and philanthropic communities, the Ohio legislature gave then-Mayor White control of the Cleveland schools, a decision the mayor was informally involved with crafting. The shift from state control of the schools to mayoral control marked a significant change in the governance structure of the schools. Republican state legislators who were prepared, at least figuratively, to wash their hands of the Cleveland schools led this reform effort. The mayor was given the authority to handpick a CEO and appoint a school board. The legislation granted these new leaders extensive financial flexibility with the school budget. Although the Cleveland reform was modeled after the Chicago reform, there were significant differences. First, the Cleveland reform was not preceded by a governance reform focused on decentralization and community control. Second, the Cleveland system never experienced a massive minority mobilization around a reform as was the case following the Chicago 1988 decentralization.

The most important difference between the reforms in Chicago and Cleveland was that the Cleveland reform was seen as a four-year pilot project in mayoral control. At the end of the four-year period, voters in Cleveland would have the opportunity to vote on whether to retain the new governance structure or return to the former elected board structure. Despite complaints among many community respondents that removing people's right to vote in school board elections was undemocratic, others were less concerned because of this "escape hatch" in the mayoral control model. The most public opponents of mayoral control were the National Association for the Advancement of Colored People and the Cleveland Teachers Union. Both organizations filed lawsuits in an attempt to block mayoral control.

Similar to Chicago, the post of superintendent was eliminated and replaced by a handpicked CEO. An integral component of Cleveland's new reform was the selection of Barbara Byrd-Bennett as the CEO. Mayor White clearly realized the need to find a person who could handle the politics of education in the city and deflect some of the criticism the reform was generating, primarily from the teachers union, the National Association for the Advancement of Colored People, and angry community members.

The selection of Barbara Byrd-Bennett was one of the mayor's best political decisions. A Black woman, a trained educator, and experienced administrator, Byrd-Bennett arrived in Cleveland and swept people off their feet. Byrd-Bennett is originally from New York and was the superintendent in Brooklyn before accepting the position of CEO of the Cleveland schools. Even respondents in this study who remain vehemently opposed to mayoral control of the schools agree that the current CEO has been an asset to the school system. She is able to communicate with parents, teachers, union members, and others in the school administration in a way that fosters trust and confidence. Many respondents also indicated that she was the reason that city voters overwhelmingly approved a $335 million bond issue and to retain mayoral control of the schools.

The nine-member appointed board of education is now hand-picked by the mayor, but there are several noteworthy caveats in the board selection process. First, eighteen nominees for the board were initially presented to the mayor by an eleven-member, community-based nominating panel. The state superintendent selected members of this panel. The nominating panel included three parents, three people appointed by the mayor, one person appointed by the city council president, one teacher, one principal, one representative of the business community, and one president of a local college (HB 269). In addition, the panel was instructed to strive for a board reflecting the racial, ethnic, and socioeconomic diversity in the city ("Bringing New Skills" 1997). This panel reflects Chicago's SBNC under the 1988 reform. This is notable because, in creating the Cleveland model, there was an attempt at community inclusion and participation, even if only symbolically. As one parent explained:

> The parents on the nominating panel aren't the only people included, there were a lot of other people who could tip the balance away from the parents' perspective on that panel. . . . What was more important was that every time vocal parents were identified, they were quieted by giving them jobs or what seemed like important positions. I think this nominating panel was just another way to bring parents in to make it seem like we were included. (Community member c interview 23 August 2001)

From the start, the panel solicited applications for the board by advertising in the local paper. From a list of over 200 applicants, the nominating panel narrowed the pool of applicants and gave the mayor a list of nominees. Like Mayor Daley in Chicago, Mayor White assembled a board that reflected the business community. Unlike Daley's board, Cleveland's board mirrored the city's racial and ethnic composition at least as well as previous elected boards. Tables 5.5 and 5.6 present the racial and ethnic composition of the Cleveland schools and the school board. Table 5.6 demonstrates that there was actually a 5 percent increase in Black representation on the appointed school board as compared with elected boards. In contrast to Black Clevelanders, the city's Latinos, who comprise a small but growing proportion of the Cleveland schools and general population (8.1 percent of the school population in 2000), saw a reduction in representation on the appointed school board. As evident in Table 5.5, the Black population of the schools is 71 percent, and this group remains underrepresented on the board.

Table 5.6. Cleveland Racial and Ethnic Breakdown on School
Boards, 1980–97

| | 1980–97 Elected Boards: 36 Served | | 1997–2002 Appointed Boards: 11 Served | |
|---|---|---|---|---|
| Race | No. | % | No. | % |
| White | 17 | 47 | 5 | 45 |
| Black | 18 | 50 | 6 | 55 |
| Latino | 1 | 3 | 0 | 0 |

*Source*: Board of Education of the Cleveland Municipal School District 11 May 2001 correspondence. The appointed boards include one resignation, Douglas Fear, 27 March 2001.

What is noteworthy is that, in comparison to Chicago, the shift to mayoral control did not result in a decrease in minority descriptive representation on the school board. Over time, the board has come to include more parents and individuals with a background in education. This marks a departure from Chicago's record of descriptive representation. Although some respondents insisted that the inclusion of community representatives, Blacks, residents, parents, and educators on the board is symbolic, their presence indicates a distinct difference from the Chicago case.

The school board has tended to agree almost unanimously on all decisions, from high-level decisions on budgetary matters, to middle-level decisions involving day-to-day management issues (Community Oversight Committee 2000). Reverend Smith, the former chair of the board, went so far as to say that there are "no politics on the board. It is just like any other board... [except] no one is running for office" (Hilton Smith interview 9 May 2001). The camaraderie on the board is also occurring at the same time that the district's financial accountability has improved dramatically, including a balanced budget. The 2001 bond victory has certainly been a feather in the cap for mayoral control advocates because it was approved once the new governance structure was under way. Had it been rejected, it could be inferred that voters did not have faith in the new governance structure.

As in Chicago, there were significant differences in Cleveland between elite and non-elite assessments of mayoral control. Elites in the business community and school administrators tended to favor mayoral control. Virtually all elite respondents cited the differences between the previously elected boards and the appointed boards as a significant improvement for the school system. Praise for the CEO was also forthcoming throughout interviews. Mayor White was also likely to receive accolades from elites, who viewed him as extremely concerned about the fate of Cleveland's youth. The differences between elite and non-elite respondents are striking. Whereas parents and community members reported that they are not included, elites were more likely to say that the former system that was more open to participation was riddled with flaws and inefficiency. As one current philanthropic community representative noted:

> School board meetings were ridiculous spectacles and nothing was being done for the children. Today's board doesn't allow for that type of showmanship. They remain on track and get things done. The people who complain about not having their voice heard today have simply lost sight of the accomplishments since 1998. (Philanthropic community interview 22 August 2001)

Elites were also more likely to point to the more symbolic measures to involve the community in educational policymaking as evidence of minority incorporation, such as the Cleveland Summit on Education or the representation of a community member on the board of education. The non-elites who were asked whether this signified true incorporation were united in disagreeing with the elite assessment.

On the surface, it appears that the Cleveland reform was inclusive enough to avoid some of the problems raised by parent and community respondents in Chicago. The fact that voters institutionalized this reform in 2002 appears to have given this mayoral control model even more democratic legitimacy. Although only 30 percent of eligible voters participated in the referendum, they overwhelmingly supported mayoral control of the schools. As noted in Chapter 4, the decision to maintain the current governance structure may have been the result of a very popular CEO and the fact that Mayor White had left office, thus eliminating some of the controversy he had ignited within the community.

Whereas community and parent respondents were very familiar with and gave CEO Byrd-Bennett positive reviews, they were unfamiliar with board members. The majority of respondents were able to name members of the elected boards, but with the exception of two respondents, they were unable to name appointed board members. Appointed board members were not viewed as visible in the community or responsive to the concerns of parents. One respondent even commented that many Clevelanders are unaware that there is a board of education, assuming that the mayor and the CEO "run the show" (Community member interview a 23 August 2001). Interestingly, all parent and community respondents were in agreement that the board was a symbolic body without significant power. A common critique is reflected in the following statement:

> The board is beholden to the mayor. Members are appointed by the mayor without the input of the community and without a check by the city council or any other elected body. When people have problems they don't go to the board the way they used to. Maybe they try to get in touch with Barbara [CEO], she's at least visible. The board members aren't visible to the community and they aren't really connected to us either. I'm not saying they're bad people, because they probably aren't. I'm just telling you that the board isn't where the power is at. (Community member interview 16 August 2000)

Those who previously looked to the elected boards for help explained that the current board does not allow the same level of community input as earlier boards. Like Chicago, there are complaints about the community's opportunities for input. As one respondent noted:

> We used to go to (elected) board meetings and pool our time so we'd be able to make our points. Today, they [the school board] believe in frustration and delay. If you organize and bring a group of people there, they'll go into executive session. And they'll come out of executive session and we're still there, they'll vote on a few items and go back into executive session. They'll stay back there until you leave. Try getting people to go back, it's difficult one time to get there with other obligations, much less a second or third. (Community member a interview 23 August 2001)

As was the case in Chicago, the appointed board is more efficient, without committees, and tends to agree unanimously. Even though the current board is more diverse and reflects the community better on paper, respondents in this study did not see the board as an effective tool in educational policymaking. This raises a serious question: If the school board functions as the mayor's puppet, then how can parents and community members participate in an authentic democratic process?

## Educational Policy Under Mayors

One important goal of mayoral control in Chicago and Cleveland was to facilitate administrative accountability in the school system. In placing the city's chief executive at the center of the new reform, clearly drawing on the attributes of representative democracy because the mayor is elected to represent the people, accountability to the community was thought to follow. The irony was that the administrative accountability that mayoral control was assumed to create actually minimized the level of representative democracy, especially in Chicago. In Chicago interviews, minority residents gave Mayor Daley low marks for his responsiveness to community concerns. In addition, Daley's electoral coalition has not included a large Black component but rather relies on Whites and a growing Latino presence (Pinderhughes 1997, 131). Virtually all parent and community respondents pointed out the paucity of Black appointees in the Daley administration. Among Black respondents, there was a strong sense that Mayor Daley had not made concerted efforts to help the Black community. One Chicago journalist commented on the mayor's objectives:

> I think he recognizes that in order to keep middle class people he has to have a decent school system. I think he cares about kids, but I think the first priority is certainly to keep his middle class residents happy. The mayor has created magnet schools to keep the middle class, and it remains to be seen what the impact will be on schools with poor kids because the magnet schools tend to attract middle class parents who know how to manipulate the system. (Journalist interview 3 August 1998)

Assessments of Mayor White by Black respondents in Cleveland were less scathing but still raised concerns. They viewed him as advocating pro-business policies at the expense of the minority community. As one community member explained:

> Mayor White has always been in the back pocket of the business community. Look at all the tax abatements they got for things like Jacobs Field and the Rock and Roll Hall of Fame. All of this happened while the taxpayers were struggling and the schools were a mess. (Community member a interview 23 August 2001)

This sentiment was reiterated throughout my interviews with parents and community members. In addition, respondents were united in believing that the mayor was unresponsive to their concerns regarding education and other matters. Allegations that the mayor favored pro-growth policies and that he wanted to control the schools so he could control the education purse strings were commonly expressed.

If mayors are primarily concerned with stimulating the economic growth of their cities, then the prospect for their responsiveness to concerns among the less affluent is significantly reduced (Peterson 1981). Furthermore, as Clarence Stone observed (2004), mayors are interested in quick results that can provide electoral momentum. Fixing urban school systems might not be a high-priority policy area because improving education takes time. Achieving a balance between economic growth policies and the needs of the less fortunate is a challenge for all big-city mayors. Mayoral control over public school systems brings this challenge into a vital policy arena. One community activist in Chicago expanded on the idea of mayoral responsiveness to the minority community as a secondary consideration by analyzing the improvements in school buildings after Chicago's 1995 legislation:

> One of the assets of this system could be seen in the improvements in school buildings. Although wealthier areas are clearly getting faster service and more new schools, there has been an increase in fixing problems across the city. This has a lot to do with the fact that the school system is now an official part of the city. The mayor can send his sanitation people or parks people over to improve the schools. The big question we need to consider is why didn't he do this before? There were always broken windows and playgrounds that were

dangerous, why the sudden interest? (Community member interview 7 August 1998)

Offering some additional insight on the balance between economic and educational issues, a Cleveland parent noted:

> To me, they're pimping the taxpayers instead of getting money from big business. It angers me that so many things are forgiven for business. For instance, take tax abatements and this tax implement financing for business. They'll loan these corporations millions of dollars and then they'll forgive the loans. Like Jacobs Field, they'll never pay taxes for the property. And my daughter doesn't have new textbooks and I can't even afford to paint my house. The bottom line is that the people who don't have the money are being burdened with having to pay for education. Then we don't have any influence. (Parent interview 7 March 2002)

Many current school administrators in both cities emphasize the new level of accountability in the school system because of mayoral control, identifying school building improvements, the recently balanced school budgets, or improvements in standardized test scores as indications of success. However, respondents in both cities were not in agreement that mayoral control of a school system leads to educational improvement, especially as it relates to having a responsive school board and mayor.

In contrast to the generally positive evaluations of Chicago's former CEO, Paul Vallas, a degree of skepticism about Mayor Daley's control emerged during interviews. Primary concerns among teachers were that the mayor has no educational training, and selecting a board based on political factors does not increase educational achievement (Four-teacher interview 14 July 1998). Cleveland's CEO, Barbara Byrd-Bennett, received positive evaluations across the board for her work. Mayor White, in contrast, was not viewed as responsive. In fact, it is very likely that, when voting on mayoral control, voters were actually associating mayoral control with the CEO, whom they like, and the fact that Mayor White was not seeking reelection. This raises the issue of whether mayoral control is evaluated by voters based on the personalities of the current mayor or CEO rather than the long-term potential impact of the reform with successive mayors (and CEOs).

Another important consideration is the mayor's electoral and governing coalitions and the degree to which minorities are a part of these organizations. These factors likely influence the way that a mayor makes policy decisions. Although Mayor White's electoral and governing coalition included only a minority of Blacks, he clearly saw the need to create a school board that reflected the largest racial and ethnic group in the city. The actual increase in Black descriptive representation on the appointed board may have depressed some community frustrations with mayoral control because, as Katherine Tate (2003) argues, minorities are more satisfied with policies created by representatives who reflect their racial/ethnic background. Even though Cleveland's appointed board members are not very visible, respondents in this study did not express the same level of frustration with the appointed board as Chicago respondents. It is possible that this difference stems partially from the lower level of minority descriptive representation on Chicago's appointed boards.

In terms of Mayor Daley's electoral and governing coalition, it is likely that the limited level of Black incorporation in these political structures has influenced the discontent toward mayoral control among respondents in this study. Parents and community respondents in Chicago cited their concern that the system is more political than ever before, and that the mayor has continued to ignore complaints about new policies enacted by the board. In this study, many individuals expressed frustration over Chicago's unresponsive administrative system. Similar concerns were raised by Cleveland respondents, who claimed that, despite their respect for CEO Byrd-Bennett, she is not able to deal with their concerns, and that the overall administrative structure of the schools is unresponsive.

That the minority community appeared to feel locked out of educational policymaking since mayoral control in both cities is at odds with the public praise the mayors have received for improving their school systems. (Chapter 7 includes a content analysis of national news stories on mayoral control in Chicago and Cleveland, revealing that stories on this governance structure are overwhelmingly favorable.) Despite indications of frustration among parent and community respondents, Mayor Daley has claimed credit for improvements in the Chicago public schools since he assumed control in 1995. Winning his fourth term in 2003, he has continuously referred to improvements in test scores and the fact that the school system has lost its reputation as the worst in the nation.

The media coverage does not reflect the frustration parents and teachers expressed during my interviews in both cities. In fact, one Chicago parent suggested that democratic accountability is further impaired precisely because centralization removed the principal actors from the community and thereby insulated them from community complaints. A similar observation was also raised in Cleveland interviews. One Cleveland minister who has remained opposed to mayoral control explained that previous boards did not have the same financial flexibility or money from levies to work to get the system back on track. Thus, the leverage a mayor gains from claiming to turn the system around, even if it is mainly in terms of the finances, gives that mayor a political boost (Community member c interview 23 August 2001).

In Chicago and Cleveland, the mayors and their appointed boards have successfully balanced the school systems' budgets, a challenge others were unable to conquer and something that is absolutely vital for any efficient school system. Mayor Daley has used reports of increased student performance to his political advantage despite continuous questions regarding the accuracy of performance statistics and a current federal investigation regarding whether high-stakes testing in Chicago is hurting minority students. The financial flexibility granted to mayors and their appointed boards has freed previously earmarked resources, attracted corporate investment in the schools, and possibly slowed the middle-class exodus because of the creation of new charter schools and the building of new schools. Nevertheless, we must be aware of the levels of minority incorporation under mayoral control; none of these indicators reveal the potential problems on this front.

## Summary

The differences between the structure of mayoral control and the governance structure that preceded mayoral control in each city reveal some important lessons about minority incorporation in education. First, in both cities the residents I interviewed perceived educational policy responsiveness to the community was higher before mayoral control. In Chicago, the level of responsiveness and incorporation reached an all-time peak after the 1988 community-centered reform. In contrast, Cleveland never experienced such a high level of community involvement in education. Nevertheless, community respondents in Cleveland believe that the system was more responsive when the school board was elected. In both cities, placing control of the schools in the hands of the mayor, even if the CEO is respected, did not lead to significant minority incorporation in educational decision making.

Second, although balanced school budgets, having efficient school board meetings, and reporting improvements in student performance (even if controversial) are admirable, if the community is excluded from the policy-making process, then a significant problem still exists in the governance structure of the schools. Clarence Stone advocates parental inclusion in school reform because if we expect schools to succeed, then we must work within the educational "infrastructure of support" (Waddock 1995; D. Rich 1993; Oakes 1987) that includes parents as central players (Stone 2004, 235). In addition, low levels of community incorporation make upholding the principles of participatory democracy impossible (Fung 2004).

Based on my interviews in Chicago, the community and parents believe that the board of trustees and Mayor Daley have been unresponsive to their concerns and have failed to make a convincing case for mayoral control of the schools. Post-1995 school board evaluations are much lower than those for the school boards created after the 1988 legislation. The reduction in descriptive representation of non-Whites on the school board; the absence of educational experts at the top of the administrative hierarchy; the inaccessibility of board members; and the creation of policies that many parents and community members believe are problematic paint a troubling picture of the Chicago schools and the level of minority incorporation in educational policymaking. These findings should raise concerns for other cities looking to Chicago's most recent school reform as the solution to urban education problems.

Similar to Chicago, community and parent respondents in Cleveland have not found the mayor or the school board responsive to their concerns. The findings in Cleveland are less stark concerning descriptive representation on the board, the educational background of some board members, and the inclusion of the community on the school board nominating panel. However, complaints that community inclusion is merely symbolic, that board members are not accessible, and that there is a lack of avenues for problem identification provide a troubling portrait of minority incorporation in educational policymaking.

If parents and community respondents feel that they cannot rely on the administration to respond to their concerns, then where do they go when they need assistance? One troubling finding of this research was the sense among respondents that although the governance structures in both cities prior to mayoral control were hardly perfect, mayoral control virtually eliminated the voice of the minority community. This was viewed as a significant reversal in Chicago, where people had worked so diligently for the 1988 reform. According to the minority empowerment literature, Chicago's 1988 reform can be considered a major accomplishment (Bobo and Gilliam 1990; Browning, Marshall, and Tabb 1984; Eisinger 1982). If educational policy experts are correct in asserting that parental involvement is correlated with student improvement, then the current administrative structure of the Chicago schools raises serious concerns regarding the future of student performance improvements (Hoover-Dembsey and Sandler 1997). Likewise, the low level of political efficacy among Cleveland respondents since the mayor's involvement in school board elections appears to have fostered a sense of hopelessness among respondents.

This chapter drew attention to the perception among community members in Chicago and Cleveland that, under the new system of mayoral control, the school system is unresponsive to minority concerns. Chapter 6 addresses the issue of administrative accountability by examining how school leaders described their efforts to address community concerns.

# 6 Administrative Accountability to Minority Issues

Mayoral control of the school systems in both Chicago and Cleveland grew out of fiscal chaos and the longstanding sense among many policymakers that school boards had failed to meet the needs of students and the community. Among business leaders and some politicians, there was a growing sense that placing one elected official at the head of the school district would create greater accountability. The newly centralized school system raises important questions about the level of accountability on the part of the new administration. Does a centralized governance structure alter the level of administrative accountability to community interest groups?

The urban politics literature establishes that, on a citywide scale, more centralization clearly has an impact on interest group demands. The research of Ester Fuchs (1992) and Martin Shefter (1985) found that interest groups exerted more influence over policy in cities marked by weak and fragmented leadership. If these conclusions apply to urban education, a less-centralized system could give the community more access but result in competing interests squabbling for scarce resources. Conversely, greater centralization might manage interest group demands better but limit the community influence commonly associated with decentralized governance structures.

Given the prominence of mayors under the new governance structure, it is important to examine whether the race of the mayor, their standing within the minority community, or their management style makes any difference in terms of administrative accountability to the community. Chicago and Cleveland offer some instructive findings. This chapter examines whether there was a corresponding shift in the interests to which the new school governance structures engaged and responded after the Chicago and Cleveland schools were centralized under mayoral control.

Accountability is measured by determining whom school board members and other key administrators represent in their policy decisions: the community, municipal politicians, interest groups, business organizations, or others. This chapter examines administrative accountability to the minority community under mayoral control in both cities. In addition, I compare the governance structure prior to mayoral control in terms of administrative accountability to determine whether there are differences between administrative accountability under the various governance structures. Looking at accountability through a comparative lens highlights differences in governance regimes. The concept of administrative accountability incorporates the pluralist notion of an open political system. Theoretically, an open system would include access points for the minority community to influence policymaking.

Determining to whom policymakers feel accountable when creating policy is a complicated undertaking because appointed or elected officials are unlikely to reveal that they feel an allegiance beyond those for whom they make decisions. For this reason, I use a combination of indicators to assess administrative accountability under different governance structures. I first examine school board members' accountability according to their rhetorical claims and briefly comment on my findings. Interviews with six Chicago school board members were conducted. I interviewed two who served prior to the 1988 reform, three members seated after the 1988 legislation took effect, and finally a member who served under mayoral control. A radio interview with former Chicago public schools chief executive officer (CEO), Paul Vallas, is also included. Cleveland interviews were conducted with six school board members, four of whom were elected prior to mayoral control and three who were appointed after the mayor was given control of the schools. In addition, interviews with the current CEO of the Cleveland schools and former Mayor Michael White are included. These interviews provide information about whom board members and other administrators claim they felt an allegiance, the path that brought them to their administrative positions, and their opinions regarding their accountability when making important policy decisions. Although my sample of administrators is limited, it provides instructive findings. For purposes of confidentiality, all board members are given pseudonyms.

Because of the subjectivity of evaluating individuals' accountability, I use several other indicators to strengthen my accountability measurement. In addition to asking respondents the direct question, "To whom do you feel accountable when making educational policy decisions?" I examine the ties of school board members to outside groups, their occupational backgrounds, the way they were recruited, and the criteria they used to evaluate the ideal school governance structure. These factors are significant because the ties members have to outside groups invariably influence their decisions. In addition, occupational background may also shape board members' priorities.

For instance, formal training in education prior involvement in municipal politics, leadership in religious organizations, or employment in the corporate world can differently impact what an individual brings to the school board. The method of recruitment is correspondingly important as there are likely ideological differences between members recruited by municipal politicians versus community activists. Regarding occupational background and recruitment, previous ties to organized groups may influence access for these groups with school board members. Finally, the criteria utilized by school board members to evaluate the governance structure of a school system are useful because they indicate to whom members feel an allegiance and what they feel is truly important in a school district's governance structure. All of these indicators of accountability are used to evaluate school board members' level and focus of administrative accountability under different school governance structures.

## Chicago: Administrative Accountability

Mary Smith (pseudonym) served on the board of education before mayoral control in Chicago. Smith was selected by Mayor Jayne Byrne shortly after the school system's 1979 financial crash. She served from 1980 through 1984. According to Smith, she was an "anomaly" on the board at that time for several reasons. First, as a homemaker she did not possess any formal management skills or training in education. Although there were no required credentials to serve on this eleven-member board, Ms. Smith had children in the Chicago public schools and was a member of the League of Women Voters. Her interest in school integration and educational equality caught the attention of the person organizing Mayor Byrne's school board nomination process, and she was soon selected by the mayor and confirmed by the city council. Another unique aspect of Ms. Smith's service on the board was that she was not affiliated with the citywide business coalition, Chicago United. She explained:

> Chicago United held the final card on who the mayor would consider for school board positions. Business groups had probably always been involved in the school system, but Chicago United funneled all these agencies and groups into one. I had a non-existent relationship with these business groups, so the day I heard one of them was putting my name in for the school board I figured I couldn't do any worse than the others they'd chosen because the other members were mostly suburbanites whereas I lived in the city and was very concerned about the education provided to public school students. (M. Smith interview 23 October 1998)

Smith explained that she also differed from her colleagues because many had ties to business groups or supported maintaining the practices that perpetuated segregation in the Chicago public schools, probably because many members were concerned about how integration would change the racial composition of their children's schools. Although her appointment was mediated through the business-oriented Chicago United, Smith claims that her service on the board was governed by a commitment to equal educational opportunities for Chicago's students and her sense of civic responsibility. She claims that she felt directly accountable to the students in the school system.

Although Smith underwent an informal nomination process and city council confirmation, the ability of interest groups to exert influence on board member selection was certainly present. Because she served prior to the time of large-scale Black community mobilization around educational policy, Smith primarily recognized the influence of the business community on decision making. Connections to Chicago United guided many board members' decisions and helped them to reach consensus on issues.

The second pre-1988 reform school board member I interviewed, Leona Francis (pseudonym), served from 1984 through 1988. An African American, she was appointed by Chicago's first Black mayor, Harold Washington. Francis had children in the school system and was the director of human services for Operation Push. As a supporter and friend of Mayor Washington, Francis was recommended to the mayor through colleagues at Operation Push, where she was employed at the time of her appointment to the board. According to Francis, although Chicago United was actively interested in school reform, there was not an overwhelming business influence on the school board when Mayor Washington sent his nominees to the city council. Regarding to whom she felt accountable when creating educational policy, Francis claimed:

> I felt entirely accountable to my community. You see, when the day was over I had to go home and I couldn't go home without delivering to the children of the community. I felt very passionate about this. (Francis interview 1 August 1998)

As for her allegiance to the mayor who selected her, Francis explained that she did not feel accountable to the mayor, but that she shared his vision of an equitable school system. In commenting on the best way for school board members to be selected in Chicago, Francis explained:

> Having a mayor select members on his own really depends on the mayor. Harold [Washington] was a very progressive mayor who brought an inclusiveness and made the people in Chicago feel that he was the mayor for all people. He believed and practiced coalition building and he respected us as a board and knew that we were doing our best for the children and to avoid strikes. I wasn't accountable to the mayor, but we [the board] worked well with him, there was a shared vision. Today, school board members are only accountable to Mayor Daley because he appoints them completely on his own and there is too much power in Daley's five-person board. At least when I was a member city council played a role, even if it was just a rubber stamp. There is nobody to advocate for the children today. (Francis interview 1 August 1998)

Smith and Francis remain abreast of school board issues today, and Smith is a current administrator for the board. Both agree that the School Board Nominating Commission (SBNC) process that emerged after the 1988 reform was cumbersome but created a board with a shared notion of accountability to the community at large rather than the business perspective that dominated prior to Mayor Washington's term. They also expressed similar concerns that the SBNC process inhibited school board action because members began to represent various interests in the community, including unions, parents, business, and reform groups. Francis asserts that the school board under Mayor Washington was the most efficient, balanced, and representative school board based on his appointment decisions. She claims that the 1988 reform, in trying to replicate legislatively the representativeness that Mayor Washington created, ultimately made the process too cumbersome. Nevertheless, she explained:

> Today it seems that you probably need something like that (the 1988 reform) where the community is involved in selecting board members. Otherwise, they don't behave like they are accountable to the community. (Francis interview 1 August 1998)

Although Smith and Francis were willing to elaborate on the strengths and weaknesses of the post-1988 boards, only one was willing to offer extensive comments about the current school board. Because Smith was employed by the board of trustees at the time of this interview, she was reluctant to make many comments about the 1995 legislative changes. On the other hand, Francis, who remains an ardent community activist, provided her analysis of the 1995 reform. She believes that the Black community has been relegated to an inconsequential position in education policymaking. Although she also noted her dissatisfaction with the slowness of the SBNC process, she believes that it was the best way to ensure school board accountability to the community. Moreover, she believes that mayoral control of the school system can only work well if the mayor places priority on the children of the school system. She claims that this priority seems absent in the current mayor's administration. Given the unlikelihood of having another mayor like Harold Washington, Francis believes that mayoral control is the wrong way to organize a school system because board members are accountable to one individual who might not place minority inclusion as a priority. The unfortunate result is a return to minority exclusion from a policy arena tied to future opportunities for Chicago's minority youth. Given that the current mayor seems primarily concerned about labor peace and the school budget, she remains concerned about the fate of Chicago's poor Black students.

Like the two school board members who served prior to the 1988 reform, the three board members who served after the 1988 legislation took effect conveyed a high level of commitment to the community and students during their school board service. Unlike previous board members in Chicago's history, these members were nominated through a new SBNC process. As noted in previous chapters, the SBNC intended not only to include the community in school board selection but also to diversify the board so that numerous interests would be represented. Diversity included the racial background of board members, occupational background, economic status, and geographic location in the city.

Even though the nomination process through the SBNC did become complex, time consuming, and cumbersome because of the elaborate screening process, all three of these board members believed it was a useful process because it guaranteed that members were accountable to the community. These three representatives came from very different backgrounds, although each shared a strong connection to the minority community. A priest, an educational specialist for Chicago's Urban League, and a college professor, all were recruited by community representatives on the SBNC. The three members claimed a direct connection to Chicago public schools' students either through having children in the school system or, in the case of the priest, having parishioners who were enrolled in the school system. According to these board members, their direct connections combined with their occupational diversity were assets to the board of education.

During interviews with these three former board members, all of whom were appointed in 1990 when the components of the 1988 reform were finally implemented, it was evident that the SBNC nomination process played a tremendous role in their assessment of their level of accountability.[1] Because nominees were required to go through many interviews with members of the SBNC prior to having their names sent to the mayor, all three respondents reiterated their assertion of their accountability to the community. Father James Doyle (pseudonym) explained:

> I think the process by which we were selected was a good thing. If you are talking about reform coming from the people, or the people in the community having a sense of ownership of reform, then the people who are going to serve the children and the community should reflect the community from which they come. The way we were nominated guaranteed that you'd have dedicated representatives. We were raised up from the community, so we were directly accountable to our community. (Doyle interview 10 March 1999)

Dr. Bob Clyde (pseudonym), the school board president from 1990–1995, was in agreement with Father Doyle about the entire board's accountability to the community under the SBNC process. He noted:

> Our fifteen-member board felt accountable to the community because for the first time members did not have major interests other than a commitment to the school system. If you look at the five-member board today, in addition to school based issues, they have major business interests and other professional interests. A person only has so much time in a day, so you can't possibly run to LSC [local school council] meetings, board meetings, talk to the community, and all sorts of other things when you have a significant number of additional responsibilities that consume your time. (Clyde interview 8 March 1999)

This quotation reflects a major change in school board structure today. Under the 1988 legislation, board members attended school board meetings, subcommittee meetings, and random LSC meetings. They were reportedly also available in their board office for their constituents despite the fact that they also held paying jobs. This observation about the public accessibility of Dr. Clyde's board was confirmed in interviews with several central office staffers employed during the time that these school board members served (Administrator interviews 7 July 1998; 24 October 98). It is also noteworthy that these central office staffers claimed that the "open door" policy made board business chaotic and stifled educational progress for the system. One of Dr. Clyde's fellow board members, Sandra Holmes (pseudonym), explained:

> I know we all felt accountable to the community. We disagreed on issues, but there were many of us who regularly stopped in schools we were driving by to make our presence known and to see how people felt about the job we were doing. I knew this was important for me to do in order to make good decisions for the students. (Holmes interview 11 March 1999)

Although it is possible for any elected or appointed official to make the case that they are or were directly accountable to the broader community, the sample of members who served after the 1988 legislation took effect appeared to feel a shared sense that they were giving their time to help their personal community. They considered themselves stakeholders in education because of their community ties. Each of these post-1988 board members noted that they worked virtually full time on school board responsibilities without compensation, that the nomination process was demanding, and that they were often frustrated with the financial problems of the system. More important, they all mentioned their connections with the community as a strength during their terms. Dr. Clyde commented:

> Most people in the city, and I don't mean to toot my own horn, felt some closeness to the board president at that time, and I know they would say that about other board members at that time too. I don't think the community organizers, especially in the African American community, would say that they feel that they can sit down and get an audience with current school leaders—I mean a serious and legitimate audience. They might get a perfunctory audience, but they wouldn't actually be heard and listened to now. One of the strengths of our board was that there was community inclusion. (Clyde interview 8 March 1999)

The comparisons between the previous board of education and the current board of trustees reflect the sense that these past members do not believe that the same community concern is present on today's school board.

The sample of school board members who served prior to 1988 and the sample of those who served under the 1988 legislation were in agreement that board members must feel a sense of accountability to the community. Although one former board member was reluctant to comment on the current board because of her employment in the Chicago public schools, the rest explained that accountability has changed under this new system. School board selection today eliminates the community involvement that former school board members explained was important to them and made them feel accountable to the students served by the Chicago public schools. Father Doyle elaborated on the difference between the school board on which he served and today's board:

> On the school board today there is an absence of people representing the grassroots. And because of that, there isn't the same passion. I don't mean to make a value judgment about those people, but because there isn't a passion for the school system and the community, it's just not the same as it was when we served. At that time you had a group of people who felt a passion—beyond a shadow of a doubt—to make certain that they would respond to the will of the people and make the best schools for the children. (Doyle interview 10 March 1999)

One potential problem that the 1988 legislation created was the opportunity for many organized interests to penetrate the school system. If fragmented power is a characteristic of an administration, then there may be many access points for organized groups to influence policymaking. Prior to 1988, the school system operated under severe budgetary deficiencies. In effect, the fiscal insolvency experienced by the school system after the 1988 legislation pre-dated the decentralized school initiative. Interest group competition, on the other hand, was a vibrant result of the 1988 reform. Not only did the post-1988 board members bring their connections to outside groups to the administration, but also their occupational diversity changed the nature of debates. As the chair of the SBNC noted:

> The competition was healthy. You had all sorts of people fighting to get their people on the board including reform groups, the mayor's people, the PTA, unions. Not only did this prove that selection was democratic, but a lot of voices were heard on the board all at once. (Former activist interview 24 October 1998)

Competition for school board representatives who reflect diverse groups is one indication that the policy process was open. In addition, the school board members I interviewed indicated that there was conflict on the board because of the access that organized groups had to members. Even though financial turmoil preceded the 1988 decentralization reform, the board was unable to oversee a financial recovery. This was likely related to the factionalism that stemmed from the competing interests that had access to board members.

Business and community interests supported the 1988 school reform act and certainly influenced policy decisions. Part of the reason business interests influenced the process was because the School Finance Authority (SFA), the organization that oversaw all school board expenditures, was created when local business agreed to help financially bail out the Chicago schools in exchange for oversight of the budget through the SFA (Shipps 2004, 68). The SFA remained an important presence from 1980 through 1995, when the organization was eliminated under the mayoral control legislation. All former board members mentioned the oversight of the SFA as influential but identified the community as the group to which they were accountable. Unions exercised influence with the board, but because the administration had few financial resources to meet union demands, strikes and unrest continued.

In all of the interviews, I asked respondents to whom they believed school board members were accountable under the pre- and post-mayoral control legislation. Here, too, people overwhelmingly said that school boards before mayoral control were accountable to the community, whereas they felt that the board under mayoral control is accountable only or primarily to the mayor who appointed them. Consequently, they expressed concern that board members will share a concern for those interests favored by the mayor over others. Father Doyle explained:

> I believe that when you are appointed by one person, as opposed to coming through a process involving a number of people, you lose sight that being a school board member is not about any one individual, but about a whole collection of people. I personally believe there is a difference if you feel a total allegiance to one individual. (Doyle interview 10 March 1999)

Doyle's statement also reflects what the majority of community and parental respondents expressed. Probably because today's board is less accessible to the community, there is the belief that board members are insulated and directly accountable only to the mayor who appointed them. One current board member disagreed and indicated that the board is accountable to the community because the members are always accessible at monthly board meetings (Fellow interview 23 July 1998).

Current board of trustees members understandably feel an allegiance to the mayor who appointed them. During my interview with Ben Fellow (pseudonym), one of the Black members of the board of trustees, he explained that the slogan used by the Chicago public schools today, Children First, points to whom board members feel accountable (Fellow interview 23 July 1998). He also explained that one of the assets of today's "corporate-style" board is that members are able to act as a block:

> We are all working in one direction and while we all have our own ideas, it's not me doing it because I'm representing a union or my side of town. There's a benefit to knowing that the mayor and the board are accountable. So, if we put a new policy into place, we are responsible and we work out our disagreements more easily. This is one tremendous asset of our board. (Fellow interview 23 July 1998)

Today's board members have experience in Chicago's business community or as previously high-ranking municipal politicians, including several former office staffers of the mayor. At the time of this study, board members included Mayor Daley's former chief of staff, the president of LaSalle National Bank, the vice president of government affairs at the University of Chicago hospitals, the director of finance at Salomon Smith Barney, and the medical director at the Madison Health Center, which is affiliated with Mt. Sinai Hospital (Pick 1996). Members' professional experience appears to affect the way that they evaluate their current appointive positions. Whereas previous board members placed considerable emphasis on their contact with the community and their accessibility to those whom they claimed they were accountable, today's board and management team members appear to use different criteria to evaluate themselves. Using the slogan Children First, Ben Fellow did identify his concern for Chicago's public school students. His comments regarding his sense of administrative accountability to the minority community were accompanied by statements supporting the financial stability brought to the school system by the board of trustees, a stability that has benefited the schools. The community-centered analysis used by previous board members contrasts with the more fiscally efficient, corporate management style of analysis offered by this current board member.

Although this one interview cannot definitively represent the perceptions of accountability held by current board members, Fellow's comments indicate a weaker community affiliation in comparison to interview data from school board members who served before mayoral control. When discussing his contact with individual community members, Fellow emphasized contact via monthly school board meetings, commenting:

> We do have a bit of contact with parents. We begin each meeting with public participation, so many parents come to raise issues. If I step into the hall a lot of people come up to me with concerns. They will approach me about things on the agenda or things that their LSC has been discussing. We also try to have someone visit a school a month. When we go out in public people know who you are and sometimes people have positive things to say, sometimes it's negative. But, the meetings are probably the main source of contact. The meetings are also televised on Saturday afternoons on a local cable network, so quite a few people watch on Saturday afternoons. (Fellow interview 23 July 1998)

In identifying more informal contacts with community members during board meetings, a striking contrast to the former administrative structure emerges. Whereas the pre-mayoral control school board members had contact with the community prior to their bimonthly board meetings, regularly held meetings with constituents in their board offices, and frequently visited individual schools, Fellow's description of the current board's outreach efforts pale in comparison.

Although today's school board and management team members are largely unrecognizable among community and parental respondents (see Chapter 5), former CEO Paul Vallas was one exception. During a radio interview, he conveyed views quite similar to Fellow concerning the strengths of the present board, including their management style and ability to use their political capital wisely, commenting:

Now you have a corporate board that is not involved in the day-to-day management of the system. This board is involved in approving broad policy changes, and obviously approving contracts. But, the board has a very limited role. So, you have a clear line of authority. The management team manages, and the board provides broad oversight. I think that selection of this small, focused, nonpolitical board, appointed directly by the mayor, has been important to the success of the system, as has the establishment of this corporate style management structure. (Vallas interview 15 July 1998)

The emphasis placed on corporate management structure by the current board has apparently replaced the attention focused on community involvement by the earlier board. The statement by Vallas that the new board is nonpolitical raises some interesting issues. The mayoral control legislation officially tied the school administration directly to the city's mayor. Whereas the 1988 school reform act allowed for the involvement of various interest groups and could therefore be seen as political, centralizing control in the hands of one official and limiting the involvement of newly empowered groups is equally political. The primary difference between the two models is that in the former case lower-strata groups were brought to the table and in the latter instance educational policymaking returned to an insulated elite group.

As noted, school board members are always likely to claim that their allegiances lie with public school students. Nevertheless, the manner in which they evaluate their responsibilities provides some insight into where their allegiances truly lie. Again, the information provided by school board members under mayoral control was significantly different from the data collected on current board and management team members in terms of community contact. In commenting on some of the programmatic changes initiated by the current board and management team, former CEO Vallas said:

Let's face it, we know we have to make some controversial decisions. The mayor wants people who can make decisions. The mayor's impatience is with people who refuse to make decisions. He'll support you if you make a controversial decision that he thinks is well thought out, and he'll refuse to support you if you refuse to make any decisions. (Vallas interview 15 July 1998)

Pre-mayoral control board members rarely mentioned the mayor when reflecting on their policy duties. Although the same Mayor Daley was ultimately responsible for the selection of the pre-mayoral control board and the post-mayoral control board (Daley became mayor in 1989), the community involvement that occurred between 1988 and 1995 lessened the allegiances of board members to the mayor.

The differences between pre- and post-mayoral control school board members are striking in terms of the criteria they employed to evaluate school administrative structure. The community inclusion that former board members stressed contrasts with the corporate management structure mentioned by my post-mayoral control sample. Whereas corporate management emphasizes bottom-line productivity, community inclusion stresses the need to bring people in even if it creates a cumbersome process. The corporate model, with its top-down/centralized control features, mirrors the pro-growth strategy adopted by many contemporary big-city mayors. This strategy encourages attracting mobile capital and maintaining and expanding the tax base (Swanstrom 1985).

Centralizing control of the school system in the hands of one elected official who is responsible for all educational issues was one of the primary objectives of mayoral control. Although this could work well if a mayor is committed to the pluralist notion of equal access for all groups, it can raise concerns if a mayor favors certain groups over others. Centralizing municipal policy arenas can be detrimental to minority inclusion if the mayor in control does not rely heavily on minority groups for electoral support or establishes pro-growth policies at their expense. Although Mayor Daley's electoral coalition has increasingly included more Latinos, it has never included a significant component of the Black community (Pinderhughes 1997). The limited level of Black inclusion on the board since the mayor took control comports with the composition of his electoral coalition but is at odds with the demographic composition of the student body, which is 50 percent Black.

Mayor Daley's decision to appoint school board and management team members with connections to municipal politics or business produced efficiencies that demonstrated a sharp contrast to previous boards. The board members and management team have consistently acted with speed and vigilance when implementing new policies. The financial flexibility granted to this new board has provided numerous opportunities. With the elimination of the SFA and access to previously earmarked funds, the new board has negotiated contracts with unions, privatized many school services like cafeteria and janitorial services, created charter schools, improved school buildings, identified low-performing schools, and introduced an extensive summer school curriculum for students with special academic needs.

The capacity to manage conflict and interest group demands is one very impressive characteristic of the post-mayoral control school board. Two of the important attributes the board appears to possess are a high degree of consensus among members and the ability to manage external groups. Even unions, among the most powerful educational actors, have succeeded in negotiating satisfactory contracts with the mayor. This is significant given the history of acrimony between the administration and the Chicago Teachers Union. Controlling demands placed on the school system may not necessarily indicate that the school system is responsive to the minority community, but it does produce the potential for a more organized and efficient system.

The Chicago case presents some instructive differences between pre- and post-mayoral control accountability. Board members before mayoral control, particularly those who served after the 1988 decentralization legislation, appeared more accountable to multiple interests, including, but not limited to, the minority community. These members engaged in more community outreach and were more diverse. These characteristics were primarily attributed to the structure by which they were selected, specifically the SBNC process. In contrast, the post-mayoral control board is far more efficient and financially stable. Members engage in less community outreach and are less diverse than previous boards. Although they also claim to be accountable to the people served by the schools, interviews indicate that they have stronger accountability ties to the mayor who appointed them to the board. This comes as no surprise given that there is no longer a mechanism such as the SBNC to limit the influence of the mayor in school board selection.

## Cleveland: Administrative Accountability

George Farris (pseudonym), a Cleveland resident for nearly fifty years and a former Cleveland public school parent, served as an elected member of the Cleveland school board from 1967 to 1979. During that time, he served as school board president. Following his tenure on the board, he has remained active in city politics, twice running for mayor. Farris, an African American small business owner, explained that he received 90% of the Black vote, and that he was drafted by community members to run for the board after one of the Black members of the board moved away.

> So, when I was drafted I went on for the children, that was the only reason. My decisions were always based on what was best for the kids. I felt that my constituency was who I had to answer to, not the superintendent, not other board members, not the business manager. Particularly the constituents who I had asked to vote for me. (Farris interview 15 August 2000)

Farris claims that although he subsequently ran for mayor of Cleveland after serving on the board of education, he did not use the school board position as a political stepping stone, something he acknowledges as a potential problem with an elected school board.

Although many Black politicians initially opposed mayoral control of the schools because it infringed on the democratic notion of the right to vote, Farris took a different position because of the problems in the school system. He explained:

> It would probably be more practical to have an elected board of education if the legislature and the state of Ohio would treat education like they treat other governmental bodies. School board members should be paid, just like city councilmen, county commissioners, legislators, what have you. The budget of the school district is generally as large as the budget of the city. And, in a city like Cleveland or Chicago, there are more people employed by the school system than there are in the government. But, more importantly, the responsibility of the school board members is to bring about the best education for the children. I don't think the state has the commitment under its constitution to really provide good education for children when you don't provide compensation for school board members to make it

a full-time job. Now, if you make it a full-time job, then an elected
board is the way to go. (Farris interview 15 August 2000)

Farris agrees that although this would not eliminate the possibility of
people running for the school board as a stepping stone to higher
office, making it a paid position might make serving on the board
more politically satisfying.

In stark contrast to school board members in Chicago who, like
Farris, were selected before mayoral control, he is not an opponent of
the new structure. In fact, he was one of Mayor White's key advisors
on the governance shift. Farris claims that when he served as president
of the elected school board, unions and the Catholic Church exercised a tremendous amount of influence over the school system. He
believes that this fostered a system in which "the board became too
parochial and there were too many vested interests and no accountability." Even though he describes his own service as "for the children," the fact that political groups were able to penetrate school
politics so efficiently contributed to many of the problems the school
system faced, both fiscally and academically. He worked on behalf of
the mayoral takeover of the schools specifically because he thought
there needed to be an "accountability factor" in the school system.
According to Farris:

> Somebody needed to be held accountable for the school system.
> I'd rather it be a single person than seven or nine people given what
> I'd experienced and watched on the board for so many years. If the
> mayor has a commitment to education, and any mayor should, then
> the mayor is going to appoint people with little political ambition.
> That mayor will also look for people with a concern for the commu-
> nity, and with a track record for community involvement. We have an
> excellent board today, people without political ambition and with the
> interests of the children in mind. (Farris interview 15 August 2000)

Although Farris is a proponent of the current governance structure
of the schools, he initially viewed the shift toward centralization with
apprehension. In his role as advisor to then-Mayor White, Farris
explains:

> When he [Mayor White] talked to me about taking over the schools
> I advised him that it was the worst political decision you can make.

> He said, "it might be politically wrong, but it's morally right."
> He's not going to get credit for the success of it because he won't be
> in office when the final evaluation is made. He'll only get blamed if
> there's any failure that takes place. (Farris interview 15 August 2000)

Farris claims that the selection of school board members by the
mayor in conjunction with the nominating committee is an essential
component of the success the system has experienced. In addition,
the fact that Mayor White, who was still mayor at the time of this
interview, had distanced himself from the school scene and given
CEO Barbara Byrd-Bennett complete control of the schools was another important aspect of the new governance structure. According
to Farris:

> I think there's more stability in the Cleveland schools since the
> mayor took over. He brought in Dr. Bennett. And, since he keeps
> his hands off the day-to-day operations of the schools, it's a good
> marriage. Dr. Bennett is very much her own person and she will not
> be dictated to in terms of carrying out her responsibilities. (Farris
> interview 15 August 2000)

In Farris's mind, Byrd-Bennett has proven that she is receptive to the
concerns of parents, something he believes must be a component of
any successful reform.

The second elected school board member interviewed for this
study was Sarah Wood (pseudonym), an African American Cleveland
resident who served on the board from 1993 to 1998. Wood, a
retired employee of the phone company, claims to have had limited
ties to any organized interests when she was on the board. During
her tenure, Wood had the unusual experience of serving before and
after the state assumed control of the district. Wood ran for office
three times before she was elected in 1993. She ran because her
children had both graduated from Cleveland schools and because
she felt a deep commitment to the system. Wood noted that she was
unable to obtain a position on the Cleveland board because she was
unable to raise enough money to be a force in the citywide election.
Wood was first elected to the state board of education and then
recruited by Mayor White to run once again for the Cleveland board
as a member of the Vision 21 slate. Wood explained:

After getting experience on the State Board, it was Mayor Michael White himself who approached me at his Summit on Education and asked whether I would consider running for the Cleveland board. And I had just been re-elected to the State Board and I could have served a four-year term, but he indicated to me that my problem running for the Cleveland board was that I never had enough money. And that's one of the things that bothers me, it took a lot of money. Anybody who was ever elected in the past, before this appointed board, spent tons of money. And I even spent my retirement money the first time running. . . . I believe they spent over $200,000 for our slate to win. That shows how skewed it got. (Wood interview 16 March 2002)

As with contemporary political campaigns, the majority of the campaign money was used for television, radio, and newspaper advertisements. She explained:

When I ran there were 13 people running for 3 positions. To travel to all parts of town and articulate who you are and what you felt needed to be done, it was extremely difficult. So those who had the money paid for ads because that's where people seem to learn how to vote. In my opinion, this was a problem because Clevelanders never really had a lot of candidates who examined school board issues. They just voted for who they heard of and that was usually the people with the money to win. (Wood interview 16 March 2002)

Wood's comments are interesting for a number of reasons. First, she was quite critical of the governance structure that ultimately facilitated her election. Because she ran so many times before receiving the financial backing needed to win, she viewed the system as severely flawed. She also complained that her board was extremely fractured and divided, making it very difficult to make necessary improvements in the system. Wood argues that, as a board member, she felt deeply accountable to the children of the schools, not only because her own children were products of the system. At the same time, she believes that some of her fellow members were beholden to different constituencies, including community groups and unions. These divergent allegiances made meetings ineffective. She claims that union demands were tremendous during her tenure. According to Wood, the district's finances were spiraling downward when the state finally took over. Although there were complaints that state action limited the power of elected officials, Wood claims that it was the only way to rescue a system that was failing the children.

Like Farris, Wood sees many advantages to mayoral control of the Cleveland schools. After the state took control of the schools, she began reflecting on the ideal school board structure for the district. She initially advocated a board that was elected by district. In that way, board members would have a smaller constituency and would be able to play a visible role in each of the schools in their ward, something Wood believes is essential if board members are to be accountable to the children. However, she started to believe that board elections, even if they were not at large, might still result in board members who were beholden to certain interest groups. Because this was the primary problem that she had with the boards on which she served, she changed her position on mayoral control. Unsurprisingly, when ads appeared in the newspaper asking people to apply for the appointed board of education, she applied for a position. Of the more than two hundred people who applied, Wood was selected as one of the twenty finalists for a position. Although she was not selected, she believes in hindsight that it was a wise decision because of her connections to Mayor White and the perception that members of the previously contentious board could have tarnished the reputation of the newly appointed board.

Wood believes that the current board is "tremendously efficient" compared to when she was a board member. This efficiency developed from a shared philosophy between the board and CEO to meet the needs of the community they serve. Wood feels that current board members not only are accountable to CEO Byrd-Bennett but also have a deep commitment to the children of the system, something Wood views as a necessity for an urban school board. She views CEO Barbara Byrd-Bennett as a magnificent leader primarily because she sees the children the public schools educate as her own children.

Steven Jones (pseudonym), another elected board member, served from 1982 to 1993. An African American attorney, Cleveland resident, and parent of Cleveland public school graduates, he remains very active in education politics in the city. He claims to have stood for election to the board because of his commitment to the education of Cleveland children. Consequently, he claims that he was always accountable to the community and the best interests of the children of Cleveland. Despite the fact that some spent many thousands to get elected, Jones never spent more than $12,000, something he claims as proof that people in the community went out of their way to support him even though he was unable to campaign in the same way as better-financed candidates.

Jones was one of the leaders in the Black community who fought against mayoral control because of the belief that it would disenfranchise the Black community. Although Cleveland voters would approve mayoral control in a 2002 referendum, at the time of this interview it had not yet received public endorsement. Jones's concerns reflected those of a significant segment of Cleveland's Black political leaders. In his perspective, the current board is accountable to the mayor, who sought control only after one of the largest tax levies was passed for the schools. Furthermore, he argues that because former Mayor White was not reliant on the Black community for election, he lost sight of their interests in terms of school policy. He remains deeply concerned that appointed board members will ultimately lose sight of the community's best interests, especially if subsequent mayors use education as a political tool for their own electoral gains at the expense of the poor and helpless children.

At the time of this study, Charles Lewis (pseudonym), a Black minister and executive at a major corporation, was the president of the newly appointed board of education. Lewis, a resident of a Cleveland suburb, has prior experience as an appointed official. For example, he had served on the board of the Cuyahoga County Community College. Many of his relatives are graduates of the Cleveland schools, and many members of his family are educators, factors that made this an appealing position. Lewis applied for a position on the board shortly after the announcements appeared in the papers. Although he is reluctant to comment on elected boards because he has friends who served on those boards, he noted that previous board members were accountable to the community that elected them. He claims that he is accountable to the parents, students, and taxpayers of the community.

In principle, he believes that school board elections should be a good way of getting the community involved in education. He commented:

> I don't have any problem with people saying that they want to vote, because they have the right to vote. But, when something is going wrong and it needs fixing, you have to do whatever you can to fix it. And this [mayoral control] is just one vehicle. It might work, it might not, we'll see. (C. Lewis interview 18 August 2000)

According to Lewis, Mayor White's commitment to the Cleveland schools grew out of his experiences as a product of the system. This commitment clearly gave Lewis faith that the school system under White's leadership would place the best interests of the Cleveland students on center stage. Lewis asserts that White never called the shots on educational matters, preferring to delegate complete authority to CEO Byrd-Bennett, someone he claims to respect and admire. One difference between previously elected boards and the appointed board was that, whereas other boards micromanaged, the current board is totally unified in their concern for making good policy. Lewis noted:

> Our role is to make policy, not to micromanage. I don't get involved in the day-to-day running of the schools or this board. For example, when people call me looking for jobs, I simply tell them where to go and they're on their own merit. (C. Lewis interview 18 August 2000)

Although Lewis is willing to admit that more improvements are necessary, he believes that the new board has made major strides. In his estimation, this has happened because board members have direct family affiliations with the community, which creates a sense of ownership. In addition, he commented on the peace that has developed with the unions since mayoral control. He also believes that the role of the philanthropic community is important to the improvements seen today. According to Lewis:

> Every major foundation in this city has played a significant role in where we are today. They give their time, money, and expertise–the large foundations as well as the small–and we are just outstandingly pleased with our relationship with the foundation community. (C. Lewis interview 18 August 2000)

The role of the foundations comes as no surprise given the fact that they also played a large role in the mayor's education summits.

The second appointed board member interviewed for this study was Lisa Butler (pseudonym), a lifelong Cleveland resident, attorney, and assistant dean of a local law school. She submitted her name for consideration for the board because of her commitment to the children of the Cleveland schools and out of gratitude for the education her son received as a student in the district. Butler explained:

> My son is a graduate of the Cleveland schools, he's what I call a success story. He graduated from Collinwood High School, went on to the University of Texas, and he just graduated from Columbia Law School. I knew that there were a lot of good teachers in the school system and there were a lot of students who could succeed too. So often you just hear the negative things about urban school systems and I wanted to be there to tell the positive side too. (L. Butler interview 18 August 2000)

Butler believes that the previous governance structure of the schools was "too political" and not "child centered." Although she is unwilling to comment on the allegiances of former elected board members, she was willing to discuss her general concerns with elected school boards:

> There were stories of elected board members, and not just in Cleveland, but elected board members who were beholden to the people who got them campaign money and helped them get elected. (L. Butler interview 18 August 2000)

For Butler, the ability to improve opportunities for students is the most crucial factor in evaluating the ideal governance structure of the schools. She believes that without a shared commitment to the children, it is very difficult for a board to succeed. She claims that the current board has this commitment.

She explained that she is accountable to herself and her fellow board members when making decisions. Central to all of their decisions is their focus on what is in the best interest of the Cleveland students. Butler claims to have had limited attachments to outside interest groups prior to her appointment to the board. According to

Butler, one of the most important aspects of the current board is the important role played by Cleveland's philanthropic community.

> One of the things that has been very important for us [the board] is that you have a group behind you who can help you learn about group processes. There were nine of us, most of us had never seen each other before. We were all really committed to urban education, but we were very fortunate that the Cleveland Foundation and the Gund Foundation gave us money to be educated. We brought in a number one facilitator. We needed to learn how to work together, to govern together. . . . I think in a lot of ways that the foundation support was a key to a lot of this. And they did a lot of studies before about this form of governance and they were the ones who really suggested this form of governance too. (L. Butler interview 18 August 2000)

Whereas opponents of mayoral control argue that the democratic ideal of electing board members is absent under this new governance structure, Butler insists that this is not the case because the mayor is elected, and an elected official is indeed accountable to the people. Furthermore, because the legislature created this governance shift, the people can register their concerns with their legislators if there are problems.

Roberta Keane (pseudonym) was appointed to the board as a representative of the community. Another lifelong resident of Cleveland, Keane is a Black woman who was the parent of four Cleveland graduates and one high school student at the time of this interview. Keane has been active in Cleveland school politics since the mid-1980s. She was a plaintiff in the desegregation case and was a member of the district community councils that were a federal requirement for districts receiving Title I money. She was also a participant in Mayor White's education summits.

Keane says that her constituency is the Cleveland community, even if she is not an elected official. Similarly, she agues that she and the entire board are directly accountable to the community. She explained:

> We're accountable to the community because I keep my mouth open. I get a lot of calls, but we all do. None of us distances ourselves from the community. So, I can bet you that all nine of us and the two

ex-officio members each get at least two calls a day from the community. (Keane interview 31 August 2000)

She believes that it is less important to have school board elections than to have members with direct community connections and people who will work to support the person at the head of the system, the CEO. Keane credits CEO Byrd-Bennett with many of the successes in the schools and for the consensus-building relationship among board members. She, like all of the other current board members, argues that Mayor White took a totally hands-off approach to governing the schools. Rather, he chose to delegate to the CEO, a strategy that many believe has worked well. At the time that this research was conducted, it was impossible to determine whether Jane Campbell, the current mayor of Cleveland, garners such positive sentiments among board members. The fact that there have been no public complaints and that CEO Byrd-Bennett has remained in her position are good indications that the White model of governance is also Mayor Campbell's strategy.

The group cohesion seen on today's board, as measured by the unanimity on most votes, is further complimented by the good working relationship the board has with CEO Barbara Byrd-Bennett. Byrd-Bennett is a Black woman with a background in education. Before accepting the position as CEO in Cleveland, she was a school superintendent in New York, where she managed a $438 million budget. Several aspects of her background appear responsible for the wide acclaim she has received from divergent groups in Cleveland, including immense credibility with the teachers union. She explained:

> Part of the reason for my strong relationship with the unions has to do with the idea that the person at the head of the system does need to have an education background. I've walked in their shoes. I was a teacher. I understand the frailties of the job, of classrooms, the intricacies of what it means to have lots of children and no books, and furniture, and sometimes the administrator who seems hell-bent on making your life miserable. I understand that. (Byrd-Bennett interview 25 April 2002)

Among parents, her ability to respond to their concerns and her visibility in the schools appears key to her positive evaluations. The board members, who now have the responsibility for selecting the

CEO (a detail in the legislation that placed the board in control of the CEO after thirty months of mayoral control), are all extremely pleased with her performance as the leader of the schools. Mayor White credits her with all the success of the schools since her arrival. However, beyond her background as a professional educator and beyond the fact that she is a Black woman in charge of a predominantly minority district, she insists that her management background is also a key factor in her success.

Byrd-Bennett sees many advantages to mayoral control of the schools. Before the 2002 referendum, she made it abundantly clear that should the referendum fail, she would leave the district. She commented on her level of accountability as follows:

> As the CEO you are accountable to an individual, and that in my head is the mayor. At least that's how it started in Cleveland. . . . So, for the first 30 months of my tenure I reported to the mayor. I now report to the board and the board reports to the mayor. (Byrd-Bennett interview 25 April 2002)

Similar to the other members of the appointed board, Byrd-Bennett emphasizes the influence of her students in all her decisions as CEO. In fact, Byrd-Bennett calls the children of the Cleveland schools "my children," something many respondents viewed favorably. In her discussion of elected versus appointed boards, she focused on "her children," explaining that:

> Elected boards haven't served our children well for the most part, for whatever reasons, and I don't want to lay blame. I just think that their role and responsibility and their relationship to the district, those by definition became muddled and people lost focus. (Byrd-Bennett interview 25 April 2002)

She, like many other mayoral control advocates, believes that elections only involved a small sector of the electorate and therefore do not reflect the ideal of a participatory democracy. More important to Byrd-Bennett is the fact that the mayor is accountable as an elected official.

Although the Cleveland and Chicago boards are different in that Cleveland's board was more diverse racially and occupationally from the start, the emphasis on the corporate model for school reform is a striking similarity. Byrd-Bennett commented on the strengths of this model by saying:

> The benefit to serving under this governing structure is because I do believe that education is in fact a business. It's a business particularly when you have a budget of this size and the number of people that work for me, and when you consider the implication of all this for an inner city urban school district in terms of neighborhood and economic development.... I think this kind of a business needs to be run very much like a corporate model, which is that you have a board of directors who set the direction and policy course. And it becomes the responsibility of the CEO to carry the mission out, and you need to be engaged in economic development in the city. (Byrd-Bennett interview 25 April 2002)

Interestingly, her discussion of the business aspects of her job were equally balanced with her discussion of improving educational opportunities for Cleveland students. According to Byrd-Bennett, one of her greatest accomplishments has been taking control of a school system that had given up on students of color and labeled their parents apathetic. Regarding the potential of the students and the level of concern on the part of their parents, Byrd-Bennett believes that she has been able to change the minds of business leaders, teachers, and the broader higher education community. She commented:

> So, it's like assembling a team. A team that says, "we can win." And it's a team that looks into children's eyes and doesn't see a little demon who will be a future criminal, but sees the potential of all the Barbara Byrd-Bennetts and Michael Whites if you simply provide them with the environment, time, and space they need to get it done. (Byrd-Bennett interview 25 April 2002)

Former Mayor Michael White was interviewed for this study shortly after his retirement as the head of the city and the school district. During interviews with several individuals who know White personally, there was a shared perspective that White wanted control of the schools because he felt a deep sense of commitment to Cleveland's youth. This commitment was reflected in comments he made during my interview. White explained:

> I went to the Cleveland Public Schools at a time when the subur-
> banites paid to have their children attend the Cleveland Public
> Schools. It was one of the best urban education systems in the
> country.... The one thing I wanted most in my life they denied me,
> I wanted to be mediocre. I chased it, I pursued it and they just edu-
> cated me with capital letters to the point that I couldn't be medio-
> cre. And that was a gift that the system gave me that I don't know if
> I sat here for three hours I could ever tell you what it meant to me.
> Nor could I tell you what it means to me to see other children who
> are far brighter and more capable than Mike White still struggle in a
> system that has screwed over children for three decades, children
> who could have been anybody they wanted to be, but had their
> dreams snuffed out. (White interview 25 April 2002)

White also explained that as an observer of mayoral politics in
Cleveland for thirty years, he watched as other mayors distanced
themselves from education. A part of his platform when he ran for
mayor was the promise to improve education because he believed
that Cleveland would never be a great city without a great school
system.

Mayor White's initial attempt to improve education occurred
when he endorsed slates of school board candidates. His goal was to
find a group of school board members who shared a commitment to
the education of Cleveland's kids. Although his slates won, he admits that his interactions with his candidates had consequences:

> I did exactly what I said I would do, I left them alone once they were
> elected. I wasn't there everyday, I didn't have an educational liaison.
> So, you still had the unions, the teachers, the custodians, the bus
> drivers, the people who wanted the land, the people who wanted
> folks hired. I don't think the people I put there were prepared. I don't
> think I had prepared them. I assumed that if you put the right
> person on the board, a person who would do right by the kids, that
> they'd take care of business. I learned that that doesn't mean that
> you can stand up to the garbage. And the other thing is that politics
> is a very seductive thing, and you can be seduced pretty quickly.
> So between being overrun by the bad people and being seduced
> by power, it was only partially successful. (White interview 25
> April 2002)

Ultimately, White came to the realization that elected school boards introduced too many problems to guarantee that the education of Cleveland's children would be a priority. He explained:

> I do not believe elected boards will work in large cities anymore. I'm not completely sure why. Maybe the notion of sustained citizen contribution is a played out concept in America. Maybe we're now in an era in education where the numbers are now so large that an elected situation creates the opportunity for sustained hands in the cookie jar. Or maybe the politics around education has now become so ingrained, so high-stakes. The Cleveland Municipal School District has a bigger budget than the city of Cleveland. Just as many employees. They're the largest land owners in the City of Cleveland. Maybe we're at a point where all of those resources are seen by the people who run for office not as an opportunity to be good, but as an opportunity to go wherever they want to. (White interview 25 April 2002)

White admits that the structure of the school system is less important than a shared commitment first and foremost to pursue the best educational opportunities for the city's children. Although he believes that an appointed structure is best for big cities, he believes it can be diluted if the people coming to the table—the mayor, the CEO, the board—do not possess the proper mindset. He claims that he was able to take a relatively hands-off approach to education once he selected CEO Byrd-Bennett. He explained:

> One of the things I told Barbara was, there are some days when I'm going to stand behind you, and some days I'll stand in front of you. You'll always know the days I'm going to stand in front of you because those are the days when the arrows are coming. Those are the days when it's about politics. And I never got in front of her on education issues. (White interview 25 April 2002)

From all accounts, White operated invisibly as the head of the schools, allowing the CEO to take center stage. In addition, White appointed a diverse board with the assistance of his nominating committee. The board reflects the community racially, including representatives from the community and a broad range of professional experts from business, to higher education, and the law.

One of the critical issues that White's control raises is whether his leadership style and board selections influenced public support for the referendum on mayoral control. Although the referendum occurred after White left office, Cleveland voters gained familiarity with mayoral control under White's stewardship. White's decision not to run for reelection probably deflected some of the potential opposition in the Black community, a constituency that had offered White only tepid support. Combined with the praise CEO Byrd-Bennett has received from all constituencies, this probably led to the success of the referendum.

## Summary

The differences between pre- and post-mayoral control school board accountability in Cleveland are less striking than in the Chicago case. School board elections preceded the mayoral control governance structure; those elections created a unique situation in which members were reliant not only on Clevelanders' votes, but also often on the financial support of various groups to fund their campaigns. Interviews provide evidence that pre-mayoral control board members may have been accountable to the minority community, but there were also many access points for other interested groups to influence the system through the electoral process. According to many respondents in this study, the school board prior to mayoral control was actually chaotic and often ineffective because of fiscal problems and the many groups to which board members were accountable when making decisions.

The structure of mayoral control in Cleveland has created a school board that is remarkably efficient in terms of decision making and their finances. The current board is also diverse in terms of race, ethnicity, and occupational background because of the nomination process that shapes the mayor's ultimate nominations. In addition, Michael White, the mayor at the time of this study, appears to have delegated most of his responsibility to the CEO, who remains strongly committed to the children of the schools. Rhetoric about accountability among mayoral control board members does center on making decisions that directly benefit the children of the schools. This concern appears to stem from the fact that many of the board members are graduates of the system, have relied on the Cleveland schools for the education of their own children, or have relatives who attend the schools.

This study of mayoral control of the schools in Cleveland and Chicago offers some interesting contrasts in administrative accountability. In both cities, the school governance structure prior to mayoral control was more open to pluralist demands. Under Chicago's decentralized system, community groups exerted considerable influence according to past and present school board members interviewed for this study. Administrative accountability appears to have been heavily weighted toward the concerns of the community. This is not surprising given that the move to decentralize the schools in 1988 was influenced by community activists who wanted to carry out former Mayor Washington's vision for the schools. Along with administrative accountability to the community also came pluralist competition with other entities such as unions. This resulted in a less efficient system in many respects.

Based on interviews with past and present board members, Cleveland's formerly elected school boards also reflected a considerable level of administrative accountability to the community. However, even though elected board members were directly beholden to an electoral constituency, they also relied heavily on financial backing for their campaigns; this backing frequently came from unions and business interests. This financial dependence likely broadened their sense of commitment to groups beyond their electoral base. According to past and present members, pluralist competition remained strong when boards were elected. In addition, community groups, unions, the Catholic Church, and even the mayor were able to exercise considerable influence in terms of administrative decision making. In both cities, the governance structure preceding mayoral control not only led to greater community responsiveness on the part of administrators, but also contributed to a cumbersome policy process. In both cities, past and present board members, even those who favored a more decentralized or elected governance structure, acknowledged the slow rate of progress prior to mayoral control.

School board members appointed by mayors in both cities reflect similarities with the mayor and CEO regarding their educational vision about the future of the schools. By eliminating any constraints to board member selection in Chicago, Mayor Daley has had virtual autonomy in selecting a board and CEO with his vision. His selections, however, reflect his electoral support and appear to limit the range of administrative accountability to the community served by the schools. Chicago's appointed board under mayoral control has remained dominated by corporate types and former high-level city administrators. Although current board members share a concern for improving education for Chicago children, their connections to the community pale in comparison to former boards. Among past school board members in Chicago, there was a sense that appointed board members share the perspective of Mayor Daley, a leader who is not electorally beholden to minorities, particularly Blacks. Consequently, administrative accountability to the minority constituency has remained limited.

The background of Cleveland's appointed board members is far more diverse in terms of race, occupation, and method of recruitment since the inception of mayoral control. This might have something to do with the fact that the Cleveland board is actually larger than Chicago's, providing more opportunities for board membership. In addition to a corporate presence, members have come from the community served by the schools, higher education, and the religious community. Although Cleveland's mayor has the power to appoint the board, the mayor does so with the assistance of a nominating committee. This structure might be responsible for the apparent level of diversity on the board and the fact that members of Mayor White's appointed board included board members who were more diverse than his electoral base. During interviews, Cleveland's administrators under mayoral control appear connected to the community they serve. This sentiment was reiterated among former board members who were elected by the community. Most of these members believe that the appointed board and the CEO are accountable to the community. In most instances, these former board members believe that the new system is far more effective because of the commitment to the community among current administrators and their ability to manage demands placed on the system from various groups.

Certainly, the policies of the school boards under mayoral control reflect the governing philosophy of the mayor who appointed the boards. Differences between the style of educational leadership of Chicago's Mayor Daley and Cleveland's Mayor White have been documented by Kirst (2002). Daley is more hands-on, whereas White placed more authority in his CEO. White was leaving office shortly after being granted control by the legislature. Daley has repeatedly run for reelection after he gained control of the system. This is a key difference between the two governance regimes. Whereas Cleveland's White was no longer concerned about reelection, it is likely that he experienced more freedom in decision making than Chicago's Daley, who remains beholden to his electoral coalition. Mayor White, who was often criticized for responding to the business community at the expense of the minority community, was able to leave office knowing that he had chosen a competent CEO, appointed the board with the help of a nominating panel, and ultimately appointed a diverse school board. He did all this while avoiding attention and escaping his reputation as a micromanager because he gave considerable power to the CEO. It is possible that being free from the weight of a pending reelection allowed White the political flexibility to reach out to the Black community through a more diverse and apparently accountable school governance system.

As other big cities grapple with whether to adopt a mayor-centric school governance structure, the contrasts between the Chicago and Cleveland models are instructive as they relate to administrative accountability to the minority community. The structural differences between the two mayoral governance structures and the type of leadership and electoral coalition of a mayor appear to contribute to the level of administrative accountability board members demonstrate for the minority community.

# 7 Reform and Measuring Student Improvement

In January 2002, the Bush administration announced its new education initiative, *No Child Left Behind*. A centerpiece of this initiative is an emphasis on student performance on standardized tests. The new federal policy has direct consequences for schools that do not reach state-established standards, including the drastic corrective action of allowing parents the choice of moving their children out of underperforming schools. Just as the Bush administration expects improvement in the nation's low-performing schools, so should observers of school reform in cities like Chicago and Cleveland. The quality of education ought to be the top consideration in any urban education reform as students are the number one stakeholders in educational policy.

Whereas the new national standards emphasize student performance on state tests, there are numerous other ways to evaluate student performance. In this chapter, student performance is evaluated in Chicago and Cleveland to assess the impact of mayoral control. As discussed in other chapters, mayoral control was established in Chicago in 1995 and in Cleveland in 1998. In addition to measures of student improvement, a review of national newspapers and their coverage of the post-mayoral reform period was conducted to gain an understanding of the national perception of these school districts and their new governance structures. Rather than looking at local papers, I selected national newspapers so that I could specifically comment on the impressions of mayoral control outside the respective cities. Such impressions might well affect support for a shift to mayoral control in other cities.

The findings in this chapter are instructive beyond the Chicago or Cleveland scenarios because as other cities move toward establishing mayoral control of their school systems they must try to understand how the governance structure of a school system affects student performance. This is especially important because improving student performance is commonly cited as the reason for turning schools over to mayors. Giving mayors control of their schools may improve the management of the district's finances or create a sense that one elected official is accountable for the schools, but we must also understand whether improved student performance follows. In both the Chicago and Cleveland cases, the school systems have experienced tremendous financial stability since the inception of mayoral control of the schools. Although this is certainly a high priority, urban systems must also demonstrate evidence of educational gains if we hope to see urban education improve.

## Measurements of Student Performance

In the wake of the 1983 *A Nation at Risk* report, the Excellence Movement emerged and heightened awareness of objective measures of performance, including the use of standardized tests, more stringent graduation requirements, teacher testing, and tightened state curricula standards (Gittell 1998). Among the numerous standards-based assessments of student performance, standardized test results have become one of the primary statistics used to evaluate student achievement in this country.

In this study, standardized tests are used in conjunction with other indicators of student performance to evaluate student improvements under mayoral control. I have created a multilayer assessment tool largely because of the shortcomings of the reliance on these tests as the sole measure of student performance. As David Berliner (2002) has argued, educational research can be one of the most complicated social science undertakings because of frequent changes in social, cultural, and intellectual environments. This is not to say that educational research to evaluate school reform is impossible, just that it is often more complicated to determine causal links. As an example of the complications with educational research, during the period of this study some tests were evaluated and changed or altogether aborted, making it extremely difficult to draw conclusions about student performance over time. Although some test score data are presented in this chapter, I also evaluate student attendance and graduation rates to broaden the analysis of student improvement. As with any measurement of student performance, each of the measurements included tells only a portion of the student performance story. For this reason, a multilayer assessment of student performance under mayoral control of the schools provides the most useful method of assessing this issue.

## Indicators of Student Performance

Standardized tests represent a controversial way to measure student performance. Advocates of standardized tests argue that these tests offer a potentially consistent way to assess the progress and competency of students. Moreover, they claim that comfort with standardized tests at a young age prepares children for tests they will need for higher education or occupational requirements. If students are not demonstrating competency on standardized tests, advocates argue that the necessary arrangements to reverse trends can be made. Consistency in testing also ensures that teachers are covering adequate material. Although it would be ideal to include subjective measures of student performance such as teacher evaluations or grades, creating a formula for this is extremely difficult in a large urban school district. In addition, the general public is able to understand this simple formula by which students are expected to reach a predetermined level of academic proficiency as indicated on tests.

On the other side of the test debate, scholarly research indicates that these tests are often not as objective as their proponents assume. Some view standardized tests as culturally biased and therefore discriminatory against poor and minority students. In addition, students who do not do well on multiple choice exams may be penalized when their academic career suddenly relies on them, especially when the tests are used for high-stakes purposes. The stress teachers now experience relative to the performance of their students on standardized tests may also reduce the level of creativity and depress the development of alternative pedagogical tools. Those who oppose the recent emphasis on standardized tests often cite the skill-and-drill phenomenon by which teachers spend time drilling students for upcoming tests to ensure adequate performance.

Teaching students to pass a test may actually get in the way of their education as teachers are forced to sacrifice creative learning approaches for drills. In addition, the possibility that there is a time lag before the results of a reform may be seen complicates developing a causal link between a school reform initiative and educational improvement. Research indicates that urban school reform initiatives often take five or more years to develop, and that test scores do not reflect improvement for several years (Comer 1980). Finally, there are certainly other factors that can account for increased scores on standardized tests, including better classroom instruction, a surge in the number of students who attended preschool, or the omission of students who do not tend to test well.

Despite this controversy, standardized tests are used to evaluate student performance at the local, state, and national levels. In the case of Chicago and Cleveland, I have selected standardized tests that were given both before and after mayors assumed control of the school systems. The before-and-after test results may help to evaluate the educational significance of mayoral control. I focus on reading and math tests administered in Grades 4, 6, and 9 in both cities. These grade levels and subjects were chosen because both cities test students at these levels and on these two subjects. In addition, National Assessment of Educational Progress (NAEP) data for thirteen-year-olds on reading and math sections are also incorporated because it is the one national standardized test against which achievement in both cities can be compared. NAEP data are the only nationally reliable long-term assessment of educational progress. Thirteen-year-olds were selected as the focus group for this analysis because they are roughly comparable to ninth graders in Chicago and Cleveland.

Student attendance and high school graduation rates are relatively straightforward student evaluation tools. Truancy among school-aged children is a sign that there is a problem with the system. High school graduation is an indication that students are prepared to enter the workforce or continue with their formal education. Granted that a diploma does not in itself tell us about the quality of education received, it does specify that students have reached a level of knowledge that is acceptable to the district.

## Chicago Findings

There is indisputable evidence that test scores in Chicago have improved since the mayor assumed control of the school system during the 1995–96 school year. I have included scores for two tests, the Illinois Test of Basic Skills (ITBS) and the Test of Achievement and Proficiency (TAP). The ITBS is used to measure math and reading comprehension in Grades 3 through 8. The TAP assesses high school math and reading comprehension and was given in Grades 9 and 11 until the 1997–98 academic year for the math test and 2000–01 for reading. The TAP was replaced with the Prairie State Test. I have not included results for the Prairie State Test because that test has only been used since 2001 and therefore does not provide a useful measure of student performance prior to mayoral control.

Before presenting data on test score increases in Chicago, there are a few issues that must be acknowledged. First, in 2001 the state created a formula to calculate the overall performance on all state tests at the district and at the overall state levels. Comparing Chicago's performance to overall state levels provides an interesting place to begin the test score analysis. The first noticeable difference between state and district levels is that Chicago continues to lag behind overall state test score levels. For example, during the 2001–02 academic year, Chicago earned a 37.6. The state ranking during that same year was 60.1. In 2002–03, Chicago received a 39.9; the state received 61.0. Finally, in the last year for which these scores are available, Chicago received 42.6, and the state received 62.4. Despite ranking behind state levels, Chicago's ranking is actually increasing at a faster rate than the state as a whole. For example, between 2001 and 2003, Chicago scores increased by 5, whereas the state increase was only 2.3. This speaks well for the rate of improvement in the Chicago schools. However, just as Chicago continues to lag behind the state, when looking at many of the city's surrounding suburban districts, Chicago's improvements are dwarfed because the city ranks so far behind most suburban neighbors.[1]

Figures 7.1 and 7.2 present test score results on the ITBS from the 1990–91 through the 2002–03 school years for Grades 4 and 6. Scores for these tests are only available starting in the 1990 school year as the board of trustees has only released data going back to the

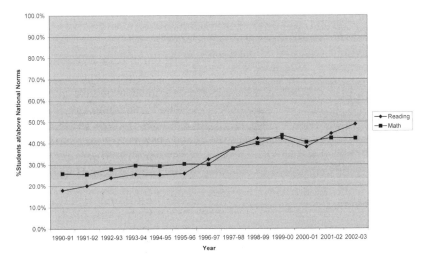

Figure 7.1. Chicago ITBS test results, Grade 4.
*Source*: Chicago Public Schools.

1990–91 school year. The ITBS results in Figures 7.1 and 7.2 reveal some clear and indisputable test score improvements since the 1995–96 school year. These figures illustrate the percentage of students at or above the national norms in reading and math. As the figures indicate, test scores in both math and reading comprehension began an upward trend the year after the initiation of mayoral control, with the exception of a modest 2.2% dip in sixth grade math the year that mayoral control began. Prior to that time, student performance in math and reading in all grades never moved beyond 35 percent achievement at or above national norms. In fact, the scores generally hovered in the 20–30 percent range. After 1995, the performance increases are notable, especially in Grade 4, for which scores rose roughly 20 percent between 1995 and 2003.

Having noted these impressive improvements, it is important to acknowledge that none of the ITBS results from Grades 4 and 6 ever reached a point at which 50 percent of the students were at or above national norms. The overall low rate of proficiency is alarming because, although there have been improvements, Chicago's elementary students remain woefully below national norms.

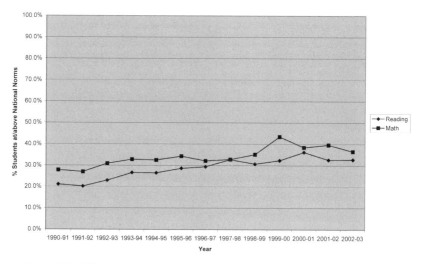

Figure 7.2. Chicago ITBS test results, Grade 6.
*Source*: Chicago Public Schools.

TAP test results, the test formerly used at the high school level, also reveal some positive gains (see Figure 7.3). Math scores in Grade 9 show consistent improvement after 1995. Like the ITBS test results for the younger cohort, there were fluctuations during the 1990–91 school year, but scores began to show a positive upward trend during the 1995–96 school year. This finding substantiates the mayor's pronouncements about increases in student performance since he assumed control. TAP results for reading comprehension paint a slightly less-promising picture. Reading scores embarked on a slow rise that resulted in a moderate decline during the final years of the test in Grade 9. However, what is most important is that there were significant improvements in all three grades and at no point do scores drop to their point prior to the mayoral takeover. This suggests that mayoral control contributed to the test score increases. Even if causality cannot be determined, the shift did not interfere with test improvements.

Evaluating these test results introduces a number of problems. First, without knowing the specific lag time before the results of a school reform are reflected in student test scores, any assessment of

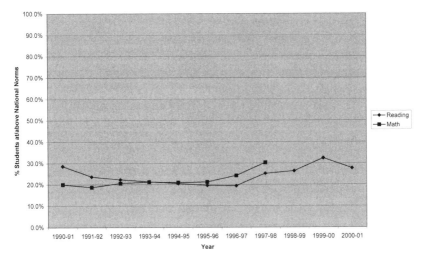

Figure 7.3. Chicago TAP test results, Grade 9.
*Source*: Chicago Public Schools.

the impact of mayoral control remains tentative. Whereas the mayor may persuasively claim that his administration is the cause of any test score increases seen after the 1995–96 school year, critics who claim that this demonstrates the effect of the 1988 community control reform may be correct. One of the dangers that frequently occurs when student test scores become the focus of political arguments about school governance is that the students behind the scores can get lost in the shuffle. If standardized tests do in fact provide an accurate assessment of student performance, it is clear that Chicago public school students are suffering considerably as test scores have remained low during both reforms, not often reaching even 50 percent at or above national norms.

A further complication noted by many who have followed Chicago's school system under mayoral control is that students retained in a grade based on their test scores are retested at the same grade level the following year, thereby inflating scores. If students are retested after an additional year of training, this could prevent an accurate assessment of student performance. Indeed, one of the most influential analysts of Chicago school reform, Tony Byrk, asserts that the policy of holding back students who receive low scores on tests inflates citywide test gains (Duffrin 1998). Linda Lenz, editor of *Catalyst: Voices of Chicago School Reform*, points out that in 1997 some 15,000 students with low scores in Grades 3, 6, 8, and 9 were forced to repeat the same grade; as a consequence, the following year the fourth, seventh, and ninth grade tests benefited from the elimination of low scores. Along the same lines, those who were retained helped the third, sixth, eighth, and ninth grade scores the following year because those who had been retained had an extra year of preparation (Lenz 1998).

Although comparing standardized tests is useful, there remain concerns about the validity of doing so based on inconsistencies in testing procedures. In the future, the effects of social promotion will become irrelevant, and test score shifts will no longer be attributed to that policy because Chicago abandoned the emphasis on social promotion after the 2003–04 academic year (Herszenhorn 2004). In addition, even if improvements on standardized tests are influenced by students being retained in a grade, the impact of this policy should only have a one-time effect on scores because once the policy is implemented, we should expect roughly the same number of students to be retested in the future, thus equalizing the impact of social promotion on test scores. Looking at test scores in the future will be interesting because the hard-line policy against social promotion was eliminated. If scores remain stable, we will know that social promotion did not affect test scores.

In addition to test scores, high school attendance is another way to evaluate student performance and an indicator that shows improvements since 1995. Student attendance is perhaps a less-obvious way to assess student performance. This indicator is included because, to receive an education, students must attend school. Therefore, I view this measurement as a precondition for student improvement. Figure 7.4 provides data on average high school student attendance between the 1989–99 and the 2002–03 academic years. Student attendance embarked on an upward trend during the 1995–96 school year when an increase of 2.9 percentage points occurred at the high school levels. Then, the next year attendance rose by 8.6 percentage points, suggesting that the new regime was working on reforms that did not reflect improvements all at once.

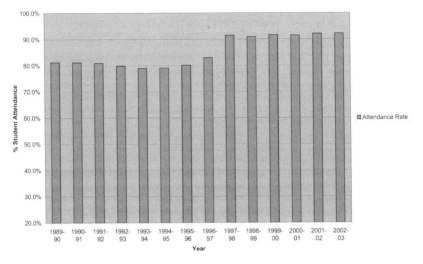

Figure 7.4. Chicago high school attendance rate.
*Source:* Chicago Public Schools and the Illinois State Board of Education.

It is noteworthy that attendance rates increased at the same time that the Chicago schools developed a comprehensive attendance improvement program in 1996. The initial program mandated that each school in Chicago develop an attendance improvement plan. Then, beginning in 2003, the district created a districtwide attendance initiative program. This initiative identifies chronically truant students, works with parents, and offers social service support to resolve the problem. The program also offers incentives to students with exceptional attendance, such as tickets to sporting events, computers, clothing, and concert tickets.[2] The attendance rate findings presented here reflect favorably on the post-1995 school reform and are something Mayor Daley may justifiably use to strengthen his new reputation as the "education mayor" (Shipps, Kahne, and Smylie 1998).

Student graduation rates can also be an important indication of the overall educational success of a school system. Although complaints about socially promoted students who graduate from high school without basic skills have raised questions about the meaning of a high school degree, the importance of a diploma remains

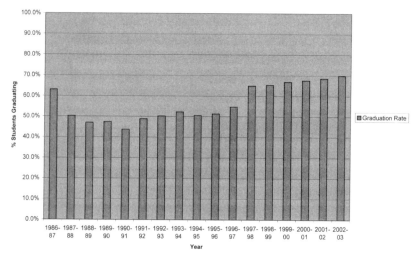

Figure 7.5. Chicago high school graduation rate.
*Source*: Illinois State Board of Education.

essential for occupational opportunities and higher education. As Figure 7.5 illustrates, graduation rates declined considerably (12.5 percent) after the 1986–87 school year, the period just preceding the 1988 school reform act.[3] The graduation rate continued to decline or hover in the low 50 percent range until the upward trend started in 1996–97, roughly the same time that test scores embarked on their ascent. The 2002–03 figure shows a steady graduation rate near 70 percent that has been in place since 1998–99. The gains since 1995 have been remarkable, increasing by 18.5 percentage points between 1995 and 2003.

Despite the limitations of these measures, several conclusions may be drawn. First, there have been significant test score improvements since mayoral control began in 1995. In fact, these improvements amount to a 50 percent improvement in math and reading scores in some grades. Similarly, there have been impressive attendance increases and an upward swing in graduation rates. These indicators, despite their limitations, do provide rather compelling evidence in support of mayoral control of the Chicago schools. In general, there was a lag of one to two years after mayoral control occurred before these trends became evident, adding to the evidence that the shift in control made a difference.

## Cleveland Findings

Whereas test scores in Chicago started an upward climb following mayoral control of the schools, the Cleveland picture is not as clear-cut. The Ohio statewide proficiency test provides the best standardized test measurement tool available over time. This exam requires a 75 percent student passage rate, or a district is placed on the state's special academic watch list. Figures 7.6 through 7.8 illustrate, respectively, the results on the fourth, sixth and ninth grade proficiency tests in math and reading from the 1995–96 through the 2002–03 academic year. As noted, mayoral control occurred in Cleveland in 1998.

Fourth grade tests are presented in Figure 7.6. Over time, gains in reading are impressive because scores almost doubled between 1998 and 2003. However, the sometimes-erratic shape of the reading data line tells us that there has not always been a steady

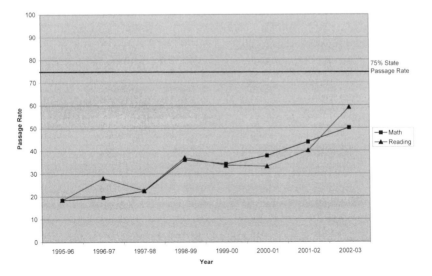

Figure 7.6. Cleveland Grade 4 proficiency test results.
*Source*: Ohio Department of Education.

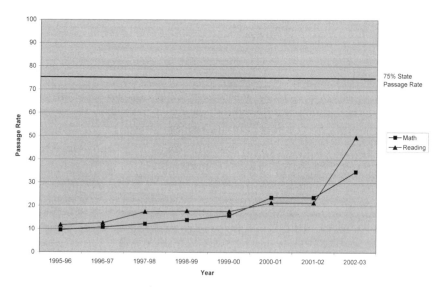

Figure 7.7. Cleveland Grade 6 proficiency test results.
*Source*: Ohio Department of Education.

increase in scores prior to or directly after mayoral control of the schools in 1998. Math scores have shown relatively steady gains over time, with some of the greatest gains during mayoral control of the schools. Despite these gains, the goal of 75 percent has not been reached at the fourth grade level during the period under investigation. As important as it is that fourth grade reading and math scores have finally reached the 50 percent passage rate, this still leaves students behind the state goal and half the class unable to pass the test in these subject areas.

Sixth grade test results also reveal gains in student performance after mayoral control. From the inception of mayoral control, moderate gains have been made, with a noteworthy jump in both subject areas between the 2001–02 and 2002–03 years. As Figure 7.7 illustrates, the overall gains, especially on the reading portion of the test, are as seen on fourth grade tests. However, as with the fourth grade results, fewer than 50 percent of sixth grade students passed the test during the period under investigation. As such, they remain woefully under the state passage rate.

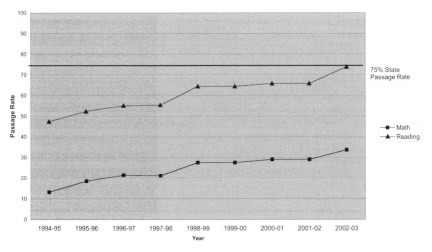

Figure 7.8. Cleveland Grade 8 proficiency test results.
*Source*: Ohio Department of Education.

Finally, Figure 7.8 presents ninth grade proficiency test scores. Improvements on this test reflect a very steady upward trend. In both subject areas, there has been consistency in the scores since mayoral control, with a notable gain of approximately 10 percent between the 2001–02 and 2002–03 academic years. It is difficult to credit mayoral control with this most recent rise in scores given that a similar jump was evident just preceding mayoral control of the schools and the first year under the new governance structure. Although it is difficult to tell whether mayoral control was the cause for the jump, it is important that the increase continued. Ninth graders finally met the state passage rate on the reading portion of the test in 2002–03. Unfortunately, math scores have remained below the 50 percent passage rate during the period under investigation.

In comparison to the other 607 public school districts in the state, the Cleveland schools continue to struggle. Since 1999, when the state began designating schools on academic watch and the lower ranking of academic emergency, Cleveland has consistently been on the list. Although there have been some changes in the percentage of the Ohio schools that receive the lowest rankings, the majority of the schools on this list have not improved enough to move off the list.

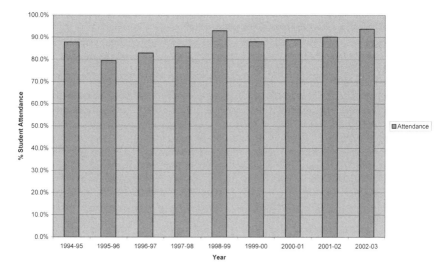

Figure 7.9. Cleveland high school attendance.
*Source:* Ohio Department of Education.

And, it comes as no surprise that most of Cleveland's suburbs exceed the state passage rate and have superior ratings.[4] Overall, despite some academic improvements, the Cleveland schools have remained among the lowest-performing districts in the state. In addition, the city performs below most of the surrounding suburban districts.

By 2002–03, attendance rates in Cleveland moved beyond 90 percent. This impressive rate has remained relatively stable since mayoral control began. The moderate attendance increase prior to mayoral control and the slight decline right after this new reform are evident in Figure 7.9. However, these dips and rises are minor, telling us that major changes in attendance have not taken place under mayoral control.

Figure 7.10 illustrates troubling graduation rates.[5] Not since the 1996–97 academic year has the graduation rate exceeded 40 percent. This is extremely alarming. If fewer than half of eligible seniors are completing high school, it indicates that serious problems remain in the school system. However, since mayoral control the graduation rate has steadily increased by 6.5 percentage points over

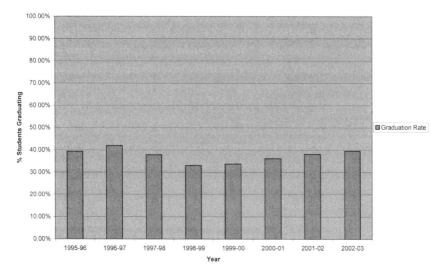

Figure 7.10. Cleveland high school graduation rate.
*Source*: Ohio Department of Education.

the low point reached in 1998–99. It is interesting that, at the same time that test scores began to climb, graduation rates also started to increase slowly. This could be an unintended byproduct of policies of the new regime. However, it is striking that graduation rates declined by 4.8% just before mayoral control and then began an upward climb. In time, it will be interesting to see whether Cleveland's graduation rate trends mirror those observed in Chicago, the city with a longer record under mayoral control.

The impact of mayoral control in Cleveland is not as clear as in Chicago because of the shortened timeframe for analysis. Nevertheless, some of the patterns in Cleveland reflect what was observed in Chicago. In particular, there is typically a two-year lag before improvements are evident. In addition, there is no disputing that there have been noteworthy test score improvements in Cleveland despite the city's disconcerting state rankings. In contrast to Chicago, attendance and graduation figures have all remained relatively stable throughout the period under investigation. Even with these positive improvements, it cannot be argued that mayoral control is completely responsible or that the system has turned itself around.

This introduces an important question for those cities considering a move to mayoral control of the schools. Given the mixed evidence on student performance, can mayoral control of big-city schools be justified on these data alone?

## National Test Score Data

Since 1969, the NAEP has collected the only nationally representative assessment of student achievement. The students tested attend public and private schools and fall into three age categories: nine, thirteen, and seventeen years. The results from these tests are only available as aggregated national data. In other words, they are not released for individual schools or school districts. Rather, the data provide an assessment of student performance in the United States according to indicators such as race, gender, and parental education. These federally sponsored tests examine student knowledge on a variety of subjects, but for the purpose of this study, only math and reading are included. Both reading and math tests are scored on a scale of 0–500. One of the remarkable findings when looking at all available long-term NAEP data is the stability of results among virtually all racial groups.

The purpose of using NAEP data in this study is to evaluate whether national trends in student achievement on reading and math tests in Cleveland and Chicago followed the basic trends as seen in the NAEP data. Direct comparisons are impossible because of the differences between the tests administered in the two cities and at the national level. However, because of the scarcity of national data on student achievement, this is the best way to compare changes. In the future, NAEP data will be more useful in assessing student achievement in specific cities because in 2002 the organization launched their Trial Urban District Assessment of Educational Progress. Representative samples of students in nine cities, including Chicago and Cleveland, are tested in reading and math annually, and district results are released. The reading test was first administered in 2002, and math tests began in 2003. Eventually, these data will allow researchers to evaluate changes in specific cities and to compare performance between cities and against national averages. Chicago results on the reading portion of the test were

released for 2002 and 2003. For eighth graders, the results fluctu-
ated by merely one point. Cleveland only started participating in
2003, so there are not enough data to draw conclusions. The results
from the Trial Urban District Assessment of Educational Progress
are not comparable to the long-term NAEP trends reported in this
study because the latter data are only available through 1999.

NAEP long-term trends results for thirteen-year-olds are compared
to ninth graders in Chicago and Cleveland because of the roughly
similar age of the students taking the test. Because the Chicago and
Cleveland schools serve a majority of minority students, I have broken
down NAEP results by race so a more accurate assessment of comparable groups can be made (see Figures 7.11 and 7.12). Because the
NAEP has long-term data available from 1978 through 1999 in math
and from 1971 through 1999 in reading, I plotted all of these data to
present a more detailed picture of change over time.

Figures 7.11 and 7.12 illustrate consistency with modest fluctuations on both reading and math sections of the NAEP among
thirteen-year-old Blacks, Whites, and Hispanics since the 1970s.
However, among minorities, there have been greater, yet still

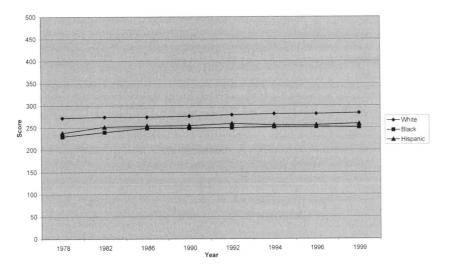

Figure 7.11. Math: long-term NAEP trends.
*Source*: National Assessment of Educational Progress.

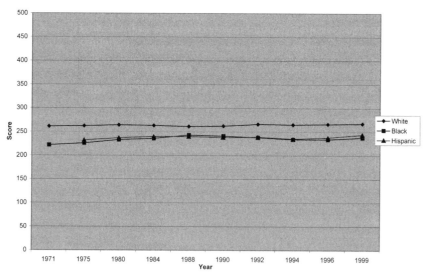

Figure 7.12. Reading: long-term NAEP trends.
*Source*: National Assessment of Educational Progress Data.

modest, gains. Because mayoral control in Chicago occurred in 1995, it is possible to make some comparisons. However, making comparisons in the Cleveland case is more difficult because mayoral control only occurred in 1998, and NAEP data are only available through 1999. Compared to the Chicago reading test results for ninth graders in Figure 7.3, NAEP data in Figure 7.11 show more consistency and fewer fluctuations. Compared to NAEP's very modest fluctuations, the upward trends in Chicago suggest that there have been impressive improvements on ninth grade reading scores in that city since mayoral control of the schools in 1995. Again, a causal link between mayoral control and student improvements is difficult because there are too many other factors to control. Nevertheless, comparisons to NAEP data reflect well on reading gains in Chicago. Math scores in Chicago are not available past the 1998 school year as the math section of the TAP test was no longer administered (see Figure 7.3), making comparisons and generalizations about the impact of mayoral control impossible.

Despite the fact that direct comparisons between Cleveland and NAEP data cannot be made because NAEP data are only available for the first two years of mayoral control in Cleveland, it is fair to say that improvements in Cleveland before mayoral control appear to have been taking place ahead of, or at a faster pace than, national trends. This could suggest that the gains we see in Cleveland after mayoral control could be attributed to different factors from those that contributed to test score gains since 1995, the date when these scores were available.

## National Media Evaluations

National news coverage of mayoral control in Chicago and Cleveland provides an important lens to assess public perceptions of mayoral control. It is likely that media attention to this reform will have an impact on the interest in replicating this reform in other cities. For this reason, and to get a sense of the accuracy of national news coverage of mayoral control in the cities under investigation, a content analysis was conducted of *The New York Times* articles since mayors in Chicago and Cleveland were granted control of their city's schools. Articles about mayoral control in each city were retrieved, as were those that evaluated student performance under mayoral control.

As expected, the number of stories on Chicago vastly out-numbered those on Cleveland. This is because of the length of time the Chicago model has been in operation; because Chicago has been seen as the model for mayoral control; and because of its size as the third largest urban school system in the country. The twenty-four articles on Chicago portrayed mayoral control of the schools in an overwhelmingly positive light. Early articles centered on the inno-vative nature of the reform, emphasizing that the purpose of this reform was to turn around failing school systems. These initial ar-ticles documented the early emphasis placed on new programs, such as the use of standardized tests to end social promotion. In his 1999 State of the Union address, former President Clinton used Chicago as a shining star of urban school improvement because of its ending of social promotion and improvements in test scores over three years (Belluck 1999). The president's comments reverberated in the news media during that time. Interestingly, Chicago's social promotion policy was recently revised after two studies released in April 2004 revealed that the nine-year emphasis on ending social promotion based on test scores is too costly and led to increases in the dropout rate (Herszenhorn 2004).

Although numerous articles discussed Chicago's social promotion policies, many of the articles since 2000 discussed student performance improvements as measured by increased attendance and graduation rates and improvements in some test scores. Interestingly, articles on test performance were quick to point out that any gains have been modest or they were on the rise prior to mayoral control (Greenberg 2002; Lewin 2002; Rothstein 2001, 2002; J. Wilgoren 2001). As noted in this chapter, we must consider the complications that arise from using test scores to measure the impact of a reform given the lag time associated with school reform initiatives. However, the data presented in this chapter on student performance have caused mayoral control advocates to claim credit for improvements in student performance caused by the timing and duration of the improvements.

In most cases, the most impressive gains occurred after mayoral control. This gives advocates of the reform added credibility even if there are other factors that could contribute to improvements. The observations in news stories about test score increases were often prefaced by statements about fiscal stability, the number of new and renovated buildings, or the streamlining of city services under mayoral control (Lewin 2002). Comments from Chief Executive Officer Arne Duncan often alluded to broad improvements in student performance as measured by attendance, graduation rates, and test scores (Herszenhorn 2004). The overarching message in the national articles on mayoral control in Chicago was that there have been improvements under this governance reform.

Although the majority of *The New York Times* articles on Cleveland focused on school vouchers, the seventeen articles on mayoral control of the Cleveland schools were also relatively positive. Articles frequently pointed out the problems in the Cleveland schools, such as the frequent turnover of superintendents prior to mayoral control and the fiscal problems of the schools. The following is representative of Cleveland articles:

> By most accounts, mayoral control has brought improvement.
> Student achievement and attendance are rising, the district is now

squarely in the black and much of the original opposition to the new system has melted away into warm admiration for Barbara Byrd-Bennett, the school district's chief executive brought in by former Mayor Michael R. White, and now serving under Mayor Jane L. Campbell. (Lewin 2002)

References to rising student achievement are rather vague, but as seen in the Cleveland test score data, there have been some dips and peaks in some of the test score increases.

In articles on both cities, there were many references to the attention mayoral control is receiving among big-city mayors. When New York's Mayor Bloomberg took control of his city's schools in 2002, a slew of articles appeared on this topic. One article pointed out:

> If experience in other cities is any guide, neither mayoral control of the schools nor putting someone with corporate experience in charge is a guarantee that children will learn more or better. In cities like Chicago, Boston, Cleveland, Detroit, Washington, and Baltimore, where there has been some form of mayoral control, superintendents have been able to solve financial and administrative problems much more quickly than academic ones. (Hartocollis 2002)

This quotation was contained in one of the most critical articles on mayoral control of the schools. In contrast, the overwhelming amount of press on this topic was positive, making reference to improvements in the schools and student achievement. Although articles do not advocate mayoral control as the solution to the problems in urban education today, it is not surprising that this governance reform is viewed as a way to improve failing schools.

## Summary

Since granting mayors control of the Chicago and Cleveland schools, evidence of student improvement is present in both cities. Progress or stability has been established in the areas of high school attendance, graduation rates, and even standardized tests. In fact, standardized test scores have in many instances revealed some spectacular gains relative to scores prior to mayoral control. Despite these improvements, neither city has experienced a massive turnaround. This is particularly evident when comparing standardized test scores between the cities and their surrounding suburbs. In addition, even with gains in both cities, comparing city scores to state averages does not paint a very positive picture of student achievement in these city school systems. At a certain level, this is understandable because both school systems have been plagued with poor student performance for so many years. Still, if one of the primary goals of mayoral control is improving student performance, this reform might not be a panacea. On virtually every student performance indicator included in this chapter, gains have been modest if we consider that, even with gains, the majority of the students are not demonstrating competency in reading or math. Instituting mayoral control of a school system has enabled mayors to rescue their schools from fiscal problems, but the evidence of student performance improvements remains mixed.

Media coverage of mayoral control of the Chicago and Cleveland schools is overwhelmingly positive. Vague references to student performance improvements are prevalent in articles in *The New York Times*. Even though these school systems have not experienced massive performance turnarounds, mayors such as Milwaukee's Tom Barrett are looking to this reform as a way to rescue city schools. The positive press the governance structure receives is likely influencing perceptions. Especially with the emphasis placed on standardized tests results under the *No Child Left Behind* policy, any student performance improvements are viewed as beneficial. The bottom line is that these urban school systems remain far behind their suburban counterparts, and until urban school students reach the same level as their suburban neighbors, further efforts to elevate urban schools will be needed.

# IV Conclusion

# 8 Resolving Tensions in Urban Education

This book has examined whether mayoral control has improved urban education. Couched within this question, I specifically investigated whether mayoral control of urban school systems leads to greater democracy through increased minority incorporation in education policymaking and whether mayoral control results in higher levels of student performance. Together, these questions raise a tension in urban education. What happens when, as I have found, student performance improvements come at a cost to democracy? Is it acceptable to see some educational improvements at the same time that participatory democracy is limited? Allowing these two values to persist in conflict with one another is unacceptable. But, resolving this tension will require us to reconceptualize the role of democracy in public education broadly. We must not only prioritize minority incorporation in educational policymaking but also look to public education to prepare students for a future in which they are civically engaged.

## Evidence of the Tension in Urban Education

### Minority Incorporation and Policy Responsiveness

Chapter 5 explored the level of school board responsiveness to parents and the minority community in Chicago and Cleveland before and after mayoral control of the schools. This was determined through interviews with community and parent respondents. In both cities, those interviewed said that the governance structure prior to mayoral control fostered more community incorporation and was more responsive to community concerns. In addition, those who were interviewed said that, prior to mayoral control, board members were more accessible to community members.

Yet, the two cities differed in some respects. Frustration with mayoral control in terms of the level of school board responsiveness to minority concerns was stronger in Chicago. In contrast, mayoral control in Cleveland resulted in greater Black representation on the school board. Mayor White and his nominating panel made a concerted effort to create a diverse and descriptively representative school board. Although Cleveland parent and community respondents also expressed dissatisfaction with board and mayoral responsiveness to their concerns, it was not as strong as in Chicago. The fact that the majority of voters upheld mayoral control in Cleveland tells us that, even with concerns about board responsiveness, there is a willingness on the part of voters to give this reform a chance. The vote upholding mayoral control could be attributed to the popularity of the Black chief executive officer, or the fact that there is a diverse nominating panel that influences school board appointments as a check on the mayor's power. The fact remains, however, that the racial, ethnic, and occupational diversity on the school board likely had some influence on the willingness of voters to support mayoral control. Descriptive representation on school governance bodies appears to be a way to satisfy community members and possibly lead to a greater sense of community incorporation in educational policymaking. Indeed, if parental inclusion in school reform is important to the success of urban education (Stone 2004; Waddock 1995; D. Rich 1993; Oakes 1987), then descriptive representation is an important consideration.

A second factor that is at least partially responsible for the higher levels of dissatisfaction among Chicago respondents has to do with the governance structure before mayoral control and the different ways that mayoral control was instituted in the two cities. Chicago's 1988 school reform, which decentralized school governance, placed an emphasis on community participation and was supported by minority activists. The 1995 mayoral control act recentralized the school system; much of the discontent within the community stemmed from these changes. With the removal of the School Board Nominating Commission, a mechanism that controlled the mayor's school board appointments, the school board increasingly reflected the views of business interests and high-ranking municipal employees who had fewer community connections. In contrast, the Cleveland school system went from a long history of school board elections to an ap-pointed board. We might expect that such centralization would also foster discontent within the community because the mayor appoints the board; however, there is a complex nomination process that en-sures community involvement. This involvement, combined with Mayor White's interest in selecting a diverse board, resulted in a board that was ultimately more diverse in terms of race, ethnicity, and oc-cupation, thus achieving the descriptive representation that was miss-ing in Chicago.

Even though Mayor White's electoral and governing coalition was not overwhelmingly Black (the largest racial minority in the city), his commitment to diversity on the school board was likely influenced by his perception that problems would emerge if the Black community was not incorporated in the governance process. White was able to distance himself from mayoral control through the appointment of a popular chief executive officer who has connected well with the community and presided over several years of union peace. It is possible that White felt obligated to strive for broader community representation because the mayoral control governance shift would be placed on the ballot after four years. Regardless of his motivations, White succeeded in neutralizing much of the com-munity opposition to mayoral control despite the fact that this study identified a low level of perceived policy responsiveness among the mayor and school board in the minds of parent and community respondents.

Mayor Daley, in contrast, was less cautions about minority dis-content when it came to mayoral control of the schools. His limited concern is not surprising given that his electoral and governing co-alition has never relied on Blacks, the largest racial minority in the city. Furthermore, Daley was not constrained in the same way as Cleveland's mayor because mayoral control gave him broader powers without the requirement that the reform be approved by voters a few years into the new governance structure. If we consider the pressure for economic growth that mayors face, then it is not surprising that Mayor Daley's board was dominated by business interests and was less diverse.

Comparisons of the findings from the two cities reveal interesting differences that may provide a framework for increasing community satisfaction with the schools as part of new educational reforms. In her book *Black Faces in the Mirror* (2003), Katherine Tate argues that descriptive representation is important for representative bodies because it is directly linked to greater satisfaction among minorities with their representative's performance. Although Tate's study examines this issue at the national level, her findings are also instructive in the case of mayoral control of schools. In the Chicago case, mayoral control resulted in a decline in descriptive representation on the school board. Regarding race and representation on school boards, Kenneth Meier and Robert England discovered that Black membership on school boards leads to more equitable educational opportunities for Black students (1984).

I found that the level of minority dissatisfaction with mayoral control in Chicago is considerable. Based on interviews from this study, it appears likely that the minority community has remained dissatisfied with mayoral control in Chicago largely because of the decline in descriptive representation on the school board and the overall decline in minority inclusion in educational policymaking.

## Minority Incorporation and Administrative Accountability

In Chapter 6, I examined whether the different governance structures in Chicago and Cleveland affected school board members' accountability to the minority community. This was determined through interviews with past and present school board members, administrators, teachers, and Cleveland's former mayor. I assessed accountability in terms of the individuals and groups that board members tended to include in school policy decisions. Prior to mayoral control of the schools, in both cities there was a significant level of board member accountability to the minority community. In Chicago, the decentralized system created in 1988 included school board members who were very receptive to community concerns. At the same time, other interest groups, such as unions and business groups, also influenced these board members. These pluralist demands made the board receptive to external groups, including parents, but likely caused slow progress on educational matters. Cleveland's elected board was beholden to the community for election, but the cost of running for office meant that candidates needed to obtain funds from moneyed interests. My findings indicate that, although the elected board was reportedly accountable to parents and community groups, the pluralist bargaining in which it engaged also slowed progress, likely contributed to disputes among board members, and resulted in a negative reputation for the Cleveland school board among many elite and non-elite respondents.

In Chicago, the appointed board's level of accountability to the minority community remains limited after reform. This is probably because of the background of most members of the current board, who often have limited connections to the community served by the schools. The board today is dominated by members with business backgrounds and appears to reflect the concerns of Mayor Daley's electoral coalition, a coalition that consists of few Blacks. Although the board is efficient and has apparently managed pluralistic demands, the decrease in administrative accountability to the community raises concerns about the future of minority incorporation in educational policymaking.

In contrast to Chicago, Cleveland's appointed board is diverse occupationally and racially. Members were recruited carefully to reflect such diversity. Board members have more community ties than the Chicago board, often because they have direct family connections to the schools. The pluralistic demands faced by elected board members are now effectively managed under the current governance structure, and the school board is able to operate in an efficient way while reportedly sharing a deep concern about the minority community. It is, however, important to note that the level of accountability reported by current board members contrasted with the perception among non-elite respondents that the board is generally unresponsive to their concerns and not visible. This inconsistency indicates that there are some unresolved issues in Cleveland that must be addressed if minority community incorporation in educational policymaking is to be realized fully.

## Student Academic Outcomes

Evaluating student improvement under mayoral control was accomplished by evaluating several measures of student performance. Standardized tests, attendance rates, and graduation figures were all examined to create a broad measure of student performance. Compared to long-term trends on the National Assessment of Educational Progress, the improvements on standardized tests in both cities reflect positively on student achievement since mayoral control of the schools. Attendance and graduation rates in Chicago have improved considerably since the inception of mayoral control of the schools. In Cleveland, attendance and graduation rates have remained stable.

Despite the test score gains we see in the two cities, student performance remains a concern because so many students continue to lag behind other districts in their states, particularly their suburban neighbors. Nevertheless, advocates of mayoral control frequently use test score improvements as evidence that mayoral control is redefining public education. Although I make no explicit claims that mayoral control is the direct or only cause for these improvements, mayoral advocates will continue to claim credit until another cause for the improvements can be identified. Local pronouncements about test score improvements have also received national attention. National news stories about mayoral control in both cities have been overwhelmingly positive, contributing to the increasing interest in mayoral control among elected officials at various levels; these officials see it as a way to rescue failing urban schools.

## Resolving Tensions in Urban Education

Here lies the tension between participatory democracy and student performance in evaluating urban school reform: What should we do if the dual goals of minority incorporation in educational policymaking and progress in terms of student achievement pull us in different directions? Although advocates of mayoral control focus on higher student test scores, I argue that this limited analysis overlooks an essential part of a successful school system: the level of minority incorporation in policymaking. Without consideration of this important issue, urban schools will never completely succeed. Minority incorporation in urban educational policymaking is important for many reasons. Locking out minorities, the very individuals who rely on the public schools for their children's futures, from the educational policy process goes against democratic ideals. Ever since the days of Horace Mann and nineteenth century common school reform, a central reform mission of America's public schools has been to cultivate democratic citizenship for the long-term health of the republic. In addition, if the minority community's voice is limited in policy debates, then those with the most fundamental understanding of what is happening in their schools run the risk of being sidelined from the process. Even in the best-case scenario, in which compassionate White policymakers who control the resources of education care about improving urban education, the exclusion of minorities means that the people with the closest understanding of the schools will have limited influence on the direction of reform. The omission of this perspective will make it difficult to resolve the problems associated with urban education. Furthermore, minority exclusion from educational policymaking could result in alienation and ultimately a decline in minority involvement in municipal politics. Given the diversity in our cities and the fact that minorities have played an important role in city politics since the 1960s, the potential fallout from mayoral control is problematic.

Proponents of mayoral control in cities like Chicago and Cleveland too readily accept the criticism that there is "too much democracy" in urban education (Chubb and Moe 1990). But this position overlooks the fact that reducing democracy in the educational policy process can result in the alienation of those who are served by the schools. When centralization advocates ignore the issues of race and class, they overlook a defining feature of urban education that contributes to unequal educational opportunities and reduces democracy. In this respect, mayoral control in Chicago and Cleveland reduced democracy by limiting minority incorporation in educational policymaking. Interviews conducted for this study indicate that minority parents and community members care deeply about the shape of educational policy. Such policy decisions are linked to the future for their children. Contrary to the notion that these parents are apathetic when it comes to the politics of school reform, this study indicates that minority parents have informed opinions and want to play a role in educational policy. The shift to mayoral control in both cities suggests that depressing minority incorporation in education poses a problem for the future success of urban education reform.

Even with the decline in minority incorporation in the two cities, evidence of test score improvements cannot be ignored. At face value, test score improvements give us hope that urban education is transitioning toward success. However, reformers' current emphasis on test scores views them narrowly, as tools for economic competition rather than as tools of democracy. Tests should also be used to measure whether our schools provide the necessary skills to prepare future generations to participate as full citizens. American public education was originally aimed at educating future citizens. Our public education system has lost this focus and the importance of ensuring that all children receive the skills to have their voices heard in the future, thereby creating a problem for the health of our democracy.

Imagine an urban school system that prioritizes providing students with the skills to participate in a democracy. Beyond understanding the basics of how the government is structured (i.e., civics), schools would teach students about the practice of democracy and how to participate effectively in the system. For example, to participate fully in the school budget process one needs basic math skills. If we look at standardized tests as a way to evaluate student preparedness for full participation in a democratic society, then they take on a different meaning. After all, low-skilled parents and students face additional challenges in the democratic process. Ensuring that they have the basic skills needed is important and can contribute to their sense of political efficacy and their ability to make sure that their voice is heard in the policy process. We could also imagine that students would learn about how governments operate in the face of fiscal strain, how coalitions are formed, the different resources that different groups possess, or how to influence the political system. Regardless of the details, the goal would be to transform tests so that they would serve the broader objective of democracy, thereby resolving the tension as seen in this study between student performance and minority incorporation in educational policy.

## Broadening Evaluations of Urban Education Reform

If we rethink the tension between democracy and student performance under mayoral control, then it is useful to extend this concept to other reform movements. Urban education remains a persistent challenge despite myriad school reforms now under way across the country. For those concerned about the fate of urban students or the future of cities, improving urban education remains an important goal. The numerous influential factors outside public schools make improving urban education a significant obstacle for mayors and school boards. Although school reforms alone cannot resolve the challenge of poverty that shapes the lives of many urban youth, accepting the educational status quo is unacceptable. Although some see alteration of funding mechanisms for public education to alleviate reliance on local property taxes as an appealing solution, there is enough resistance to this idea among suburban voters that it is not a viable option.

Given the realities of urban education today, many school systems have adopted different reforms. When we consider some of the most recent and highly publicized school reforms, such as voucher programs, charter schools, privatization, and mayoral control, it is clear that no single reform has been able to transform urban education to the point at which it is viewed as the clear choice to rescue public education. Voucher programs are particularly divisive because the idea of using public money to send needy children to private schools strikes some as contrary to the goal of using public money to create high-quality public schools for all children. Vouchers have also ignited controversy because religion-based schools frequently accept students who use vouchers for their tuition. In 2002, the U.S. Supreme Court (*Zelman v. Simmons-Harris*) upheld Cleveland's voucher program, concluding that it did not violate the constitutional doctrine of separation of church and state. Conflicting studies of student achievement among voucher students makes evaluating this reform difficult (see Witte 1996; Greene, Howell, and Peterson 1999).

Charter schools are essentially publicly funded independent schools. They are far more common than voucher programs and generate less controversy. Nevertheless, they also have achieved mixed results in terms of student performance. In 2004, a controversial study indicated that charter school students are performing no better than their non-charter school counterparts (K. Smith 2005; Feinberg 2004). Privatizing management of individual schools, or even entire school districts, has also become a trendy reform technique. Although some communities initially welcomed for-profit companies like Edison Schools to run their failing schools, these experiments have often resulted in failure and pull-outs once the job of running the schools began. Mayoral control of the schools is yet another idea in a long list of recent experiments in urban education.

Educational policymaking that considers community incorpo-ration as a fundamental part of the policy process may profoundly shape the future for urban school students, give them a sense of political efficacy, and teach them that their participation matters in our democratic society. I argue for a deeper analysis of educational reform than is possible with the current policy emphasis on test scores as the sole indicator of educational success. This study also calls for a new way to evaluate student performance indicators by linking them with measures of whether public schools are preparing students for full participation in a democratic society, a society in which their voice is heard and valued and people have the literacy and numeracy skills to think and evaluate conflicting policy pro-posals critically.

Mayoral control of urban schools is no panacea. The tension it creates between the dual values of student performance and minority incorporation raises serous concerns for us all. Although assessments of student performance should be based in part on performance data, we should reconceptualize tests as a measure of whether the schools are fulfilling their democratic responsibility of giving people the skills they need for success in our political system. Democracy ought to be a top priority of public education. For this to happen, we must reconceptualize the purpose of public education in a way that values citizen participation and the skills required for future engagement in the policy process.

# Appendix: Interview Questionnaires

## Chicago

Sections I–IV of this questionnaire were administered, with modifications when necessary, to all respondents.

### I. Background Questions

1. How long have you lived in Chicago?
2. Do you now have a child or children in the Chicago public schools? If yes, how many?
    (if yes) How long have your children or child been in attendance—during what years?
3. Are you an active member of a political party? If yes, which party?
4. Are you a registered voter?
    (if yes) Are you a regular voter, somewhat regular voter, or do you usually not vote in elections? What factors have motivated you to take this position toward the electoral process?
5. Have you ever run for public office? If yes, what office and when?
6. Have you ever held a public position, either elected or non-elected?
    (if yes) What was the position and when was it held?
7. Have you ever been actively involved in public education? Please explain.
8. Are you actively involved in community organizations?
    (if yes) What are they and how would you assess your participation in the organization's activities?

## II. Questions Concerning Pre-1988 School Reform Period

As you know, in 1988 the school governance process in Chicago was altered to emphasize parental and community control. My first questions have to do with the period before the 1988 school reform.

1. How would you assess the responsiveness of the city school administration (school board) to your needs and interests prior to 1988? For example, could you rely on the board to respond to your concerns, and did their decisions reflect your desires?
2. In your perspective, was there opportunity for meaningful input into governance procedures on the part of the community before the 1988 legislation was enacted?
3. Were there certain interests that were represented over others by the school system? Please explain.
4. How would you assess the role of big business in the school governance process prior to 1988?
5. How would you assess the role of unions in the school governance process prior to 1988?
6. Please describe the structure and procedures for school board member selection prior to 1988.
7. In your opinion, did this process allow for substantial community representation and input?
8. What type of individuals tended to be most successful in getting positions on the school board under this process?
9. Did they have connections to outside groups? Explain.
10. In your perspective, was race or ethnicity a part of this process? Please explain.
11. What issues or policies were normally incorporated in the school board agenda, and what issues or policies were generally left out? Please explain.
12. How would you assess student performance prior to the 1998 governance changes?
13. Were there any significant problems with the school system prior to 1998? Please explain.

14. Is there anything you would like to add about the period prior to the 1988 school reform?

## III. Questions Concerning Post-1988 School Reform Period

1. Please identify the fundamental changes in school governance that occurred in the wake of the 1988 reform.
2. Were political alliances an essential part of the 1988 reform initiative?
   (if yes) In what way?
3. Were you active in making the changes that resulted in the 1988 reform legislation?
   (if yes) Why or why not?
4. What was the overall impact on your own children due to the changes initiated in 1988?
5. How would you assess the responsiveness of the city school administration (school board) to your needs and interests after 1988? For example, could you rely on the board to respond to your concerns and did their decisions reflect your desires?
6. In your perspective, was there opportunity for meaningful input into governance procedures on the part of the community after the 1988 legislation was enacted?
7. Were there certain interests that were represented over others by the school system? Please explain.
8. How would you assess the role of big business in the school governance process after 1988?
9. How would you assess the role of unions in the school governance process after 1988?
10. Please describe the structure and procedures for school board member selection after 1988.
11. In your opinion, did this process allow for substantial community representation and input?
12. What type of individuals tended to be most successful in getting positions on the school board under this process?
13. Did they have connections to outside groups? Explain.
14. In your perspective, was race or ethnicity a part of this process? Please explain.

15. What issues or policies were normally incorporated in the school board agenda, and what issues or policies were generally left out? Please explain.
16. How would you assess student performance prior to the 1998 governance changes?
17. Please assess the role of the School Board Nominating Commission under the 1988 reform.
18. What impact did local school councils have on the school system in general and responsiveness to community concerns in particular?
19. What lessons were learned from the 1988 reform efforts?
20. Can you name any of the members of the school board between 1998 and 1995?
21. Is there anything you would like to add about the period before the mayor took control of the schools?

## IV. Questions Concerning the post-1995 Reform Period

As you know, in 1995 a major reform in school governance was instituted. This policy change gave the mayor authority to appoint members of the school board.

1. Please identify the fundamental changes in school governance that occurred in the wake of the 1995 reform.
2. Were political alliances an essential part of the 1995 reform initiative?
   (if yes) In what way?
3. Were you active in making the changes that resulted in the 1995 reform legislation?
   (if yes) Why or why not?
4. What was the overall impact on your own children due to the changes initiated in 1995?
5. Do you agree or disagree with the strategy of placing mayors in charge of city school systems?
6. How would you assess the responsiveness of the city school administration (school board) to your needs and interests after 1995? For example, could you rely on the board to respond to your concerns, and did their decisions reflect your desires?

7. In your perspective, was there opportunity for meaningful input into governance procedures on the part of the community after the 1995 legislation was enacted? Please explain.

8. Are certain interests represented over others by the school system today? Please explain.

9. How would you assess the role of big business in the school governance process after 1995?

10. How would you assess the role of unions in the school governance process after 1995?

11. Please describe the structure and procedures for school board member selection since 1995.

12. In your opinion, does this process allow for substantial community representation and input?

13. What type of individuals tends to be most successful in getting positions on the school board under this process?

14. Do they have connections to outside groups? Explain.

15. In your opinion, is race or ethnicity a part of this process? Please explain.

16. What issues or policies are normally incorporated into the school board agenda, and what issues or policies are generally left out? Please explain.

17. To what extent does the current board structure reflect prevailing political alliances?

18. How would you assess the mayor's performance as head of the public school system?

19. In your mind, does the mayor favor certain interests over others? Explain.

20. Comment on the performance of the chief executive officer and his interactions with the community?

21. What evidence do you see of improvement since 1995? (Can probe on community involvement in the schools, district finances, student performance indicators.)

22. Are there significant problems with the school system today? Please explain.

23. If you were to recommend the ideal governance structure for this or any other urban school district, what would you recommend?

24. Can you name any of the members of the school board after 1995?

25. Is there anything you would like to add about the current governance structure?
26. Are there other individuals you recommend to speak with who are familiar with the governance change?

## V. Past and Present School Board Members

Were asked these additional questions:

1. When did you serve on the school board?
2. Describe your educational and occupational background.
3. Describe any coalitions or factions you observed as a school board member.
4. Discuss any ties you have to groups outside of the school system.
5. Explain how you were recruited to serve on the board.
6. Why did you pursue a position on the board?
7. How would you assess the school board during your tenure in office?
8. Describe alliances on the board and between the board and outside groups.
9. To whom were you (or are you) accountable when making educational policy decisions?
10. Accountability of other boards. (Members who served prior to mayoral control of the schools were asked to comment on the accountability of members of the school board since the 1995 legislation was enacted. Members who served after mayoral control of the schools were asked to comment on the accountability of members of the school board between 1988 and 1995.)
11. Please evaluate your level of involvement with the community on educational matters during your tenure on the board.
12. Describe your major accomplishments as a member of the board.
13. Those currently on the board were asked to evaluate their relationship with the mayor and chief executive officer on educational matters.
14. What were the primary consequences on the policy process resulting from the 1988 school reform initiative?
15. What were the primary consequences on the policy process resulting from the 1995 school reform initiative?

16. What do you believe to be the ideal relationship between the school administration and the community?
17. Do you believe that mayoral control of the school board (appointment power) has an impact on democratic participation? What is the impact?

## Cleveland

Sections I and II of this questionnaire were administered, with modifications when necessary, to all respondents.

### I. Background Questions

1. How long have you lived in Cleveland?
2. Do you now have a child or children in the Cleveland public schools? If yes, how many?
    (if yes) How long have your children or child been in attendance—during what years?
3. Are you an active member of a political party? If yes, which party?
4. Are you a registered voter?
    (if yes) Are you a regular voter, somewhat regular voter, or do you usually not vote in elections? What factors have motivated you to take this position toward the electoral process?
5. Have you ever run for public office? If yes, what office and when?
6. Have you ever held a public position, either elected or non-elected?
    (if yes) What was the position and when was it held?
7. Do you consider school board elections a useful vehicle for promoting community participation in the school governance process? Explain.
8. Did you regularly participate in school board elections? Why or why not?
9. Have you ever been actively involved in public education? Please explain.
10. Are you actively involved in community organizations?
    (if yes) What are they and describe your participation in the organization's activities?

## II. Pre-1998 Questions

As you know, in 1998 the school governance process in Cleveland was altered to create mayoral control of the schools. My first questions have to do with the period prior to mayoral control of the schools.

1. How would you assess the responsiveness of the city school administration (school board) to your needs and interests prior to 1998? For example, could you rely on board members to respond to your concerns and did their decisions reflect your desires?
2. How would you characterize the school board before and after state receivership?
3. Did the state takeover of the schools have any impact of school board responsiveness to community concerns?
4. In your perspective, was there opportunity for meaningful input into governance procedures on the part of the community before the 1998 legislation was enacted? Please explain.
5. Were there certain interests that were represented over others by the school system? Please explain.
6. How would you assess the role of big business in the school governance process prior to 1998?
7. How would you assess the role of unions in the school governance process prior to 1998?
8. Please describe the structure and procedures for school board elections prior to 1998.
9. In your opinion, did this process allow for substantial community representation and input?
10. What type of individuals tended to be most successful in winning election to school board under this process? Explain.
11. Did they have connections to outside groups? Explain.
12. In your perspective, was race or ethnicity a part of this process? Please explain.
13. What issues or policies were normally incorporated in the school board agenda and what issues or policies were generally left out? Please explain.

14. How would you assess student performance prior to the 1998 governance changes?
15. Can you name any of the members of the school board prior to 1998?
16. Were there any significant problems with the school system prior to 1998? Please explain.
17. Is there anything you would like to add about the period before the mayor took control of the schools?

## II. Post-1998 Questions

As you know, in 1998 a major reform in school governance was instituted. This policy change gave the mayor authority to appoint members of the school board.

1. Please identify the fundamental changes in school governance that occurred in the wake of the 1998 reform.
2. Were political alliances an essential part of the 1995 reform initiative?
   (if yes) In what way?
3. Were you active in making the changes that resulted in the 1995 reform legislation?
   (if yes) Why or why not?
4. Do you agree or disagree with the strategy of placing mayors in charge of city school systems?
5. What was the overall impact on your own children due to the changes initiated in 1998?
6. How would you assess the responsiveness of the city school administration (school board) to your needs and interests since 1998? For example, can you rely on board members to respond to your concerns, and do their decisions reflect your desires?
7. In your perspective, are there opportunities for meaningful input into governance procedures for community since 1998 legislation was enacted? Please explain.
8. Are certain interests represented over others by the school system? Please explain.

9. How would you assess the role of big business in the school governance process after 1998?

10. How would you assess the role of unions in the school governance process after 1998?

11. Please describe the structure and procedures for school board selection after 1998.

12. In your opinion, does this process allow for substantial community representation and input?

13. What type of individuals tends to be most successful in getting positions on the school board under this process? Explain.

14. Do they have connections to outside groups? Explain.

15. In your perspective, is race or ethnicity a part of this process? Please explain.

16. What issues or policies are normally incorporated in the school board agenda, and what issues or policies are generally left out? Please explain.

17. How would you assess student performance since the 1998 governance changes?

18. How would you assess the mayor's performance as head of the public school system?

19. In your mind, does the mayor favor certain interests over others? Explain.

20. Please comment on the performance of the new chief executive officer and her interactions with the community?

21. What evidence do you see of improvement since 1998? (Can probe on community involvement in the schools, district finances, student performance indicators.)

22. Can you name any of the members of the school board since 1998?

23. Are there significant problems with the school system today? Please explain.

24. If you were to recommend the ideal governance structure for this or any other urban school district, what would you recommend?

25. Is there anything you would like to add about the current governance structure?

26. Are there other individuals you recommend to speak with who are familiar with the governance change?

III. Past and Present School Board Members

Were asked these additional questions:

1. When did you serve on the school board?
2. Describe your educational and occupational background.
3. Describe any coalitions or factions you observed as a school board member.
4. Discuss any ties you have to groups outside of the school system.
5. Explain how you were recruited to serve on the board.
6. Why did you pursue a position on the board?
7. How would you assess the school board during your tenure in office?
8. Describe alliances on the board and between the board and outside groups.
9. To whom were you (or are you) accountable when making educational policy decisions?
10. Accountability of other boards. (Members who served prior to mayoral control of the schools were asked to comment on the accountability of members of the school board since the 1998 legislation was enacted. Members who served after mayoral control of the schools were asked to comment on the accountability of members of the school board prior to 1998.)
11. Evaluate your level of involvement with the community on educational matters during your tenure on the board.
12. Describe your major accomplishments as a member of the board.
13. Those currently on the board were asked to evaluate their relationship with the mayor and chief executive officer on educational matters.
14. What were the primary consequences on the policy process resulting from the 1998 school reform initiative?
15. What do you believe to be the ideal relationship between the school administration and the community?
16. Do you believe that mayoral control of the school board (appointment power) has an impact on democratic participation? What is the impact?

## IV. Mayor and Chief Executive Officer

The mayor and chief executive officer were asked a modified set of questions based on Section III. They were also asked to describe and evaluate their position as leaders of the school system. Both were also asked to describe their interactions with the school board and with one another.

# Notes

## Chapter One

1. One need only look at the *No Child Left Behind* (2002) legislation to understand the politically important role of student performance in American education.

2. Cleveland's Mayor White did not run for reelection in 2002 and was succeeded by a White Democrat, Jane Campbell. Campbell's electoral coalition was multiracial, and she received significant support from the Black community. Campbell was defeated in the 2005 Mayoral election by Frank Jackson.

3. In Chicago, the forty-six interviews were conducted with the following groups: eleven parents, six community activists, four former grassroots activists, one journalist, two state legislators, six past and present school board members, six teachers, two principals, seven administrators, and one recent Chicago Public Schools graduate. Ten of these individuals were past or present local school council members. Thirty-six of the respondents were African American, five were Latino, and five were White. Interviews were conducted between summer 1998 and winter 1999.

4. These scholars are affiliated with the Center for Inner City Studies at Northeastern Illinois University, University of Illinois at Chicago, and Olive Harvey College.

5. My initial list of respondents was generated through consultation with experts on Cleveland politics at Ohio State University and the Maxine Goodman Levin College of Urban Affairs at Cleveland State University.

6. In Cleveland, the thirty-seven interviews were conducted with the following groups: twelve parents, four community activists, one journalist, six past and present school board members, two teachers, one former superintendent, a recent chief executive officer of the schools, two teachers' union representatives, one former mayor, one former member of Congress, four representatives from the philanthropic community, one member of city council, and one current school board administrator. These interviews were conducted between summer 2000 and spring 2002.

## Chapter Two

1. Education Week, Glossary of Terms. Available at: http://www.edweek.org/context/glossary/decentra.htm. Accessed August 1, 2002.

2. There was, however, a provision in the Cleveland legislation that gave the school board control over selecting the CEO after 30 months.

## Chapter Three

1. Two-way busing was the idea to move Black students to predominantly White schools and White students to predominantly Black schools. City-suburban consolidation was considered as a way to work with the large suburban White school population and to deal with the declining tax base that was harming the city because of White flight.

## Chapter Four

1. Leon Lawrence, Susan Leonard, Lawrence Lumpkin and James Lumden.
2. The foundations include the George Gund Foundation, Cleveland Foundation, Martha Holden Jennings Foundation, and Joyce Foundation.
3. Interviews conducted between summer 2000 and spring 2002.
4. White's attempt to lure more business with tax abatements may have had reverse effects on schools funding (see Lewin 1997).
5. *DeRolph v. State*, 78 Ohio St. 3d 193 (1997).

## Chapter Five

1. There were 541 schools at the time that the 1988 reform legislation took effect.
2. This was also noted by the majority of respondents in this study.
3. The 16 percent increase includes Black, Latino, and Asian American representation.
4. For more detail on the 1988 reform and the creation of LSCs, see Bryk et al. 1998; Bryk, Kerbow, and Rollow 1997; A. G. Hess 1991, 1995; Epps 1994.
5. This short-lived alliance between community groups and business associations is documented by Shipps' research and substantiated by interviews for this study (Shipps 1998).
6. The city, county, and state do not have records of the number of people who participated in school board elections. These are the only data available through the Cuyahoga Board of Elections.
7. The school system was under state control briefly from 1979 to 1981, and respondents were asked to evaluate the boards in place after state receivership when the board had more power.
8. School board minutes during the pre- and post-mayoral control periods were reviewed for this study. Although I was able to review these minutes at the Board of Education's office, there were some problems that made it difficult to

do a thorough analysis of the pre-mayoral control minutes. Many times, the minutes from a meeting were missing, vague, or inconsistently recorded. Minutes from the post-mayoral control period are readily available.

9. Three former board members were contacted to recall the background of board members from the 1980s. I have approximated some of the details as there was some uncertainty about the exact occupational background or family background for two members of the board from this era.

10. Unfortunately, the campaign finance records from school board elections are no longer available. By law, the Cuyahoga County Board of Elections and the candidate are only required to keep records for six years. The last school board election took place in 1993; therefore, all records are destroyed. The only information available on school board elections is the outstanding balance from them. There are only five candidates with outstanding balances, but this information is not helpful in terms of analyzing the cost of races.

## Chapter Six

1. Again, immediately after the 1988 school reform act passed, an interim school board was seated until the new school board was established. It was not until 1990 that the school board designed in the 1988 legislation was seated.

## Chapter Seven

1. Data are available at fttp://ftpirptcard.isbe.net'ReportCard2004/150162990_E.pdf.

2. Information is available at www.attendance.cps.k12.il.us (accessed 13 June 2005).

3. The board reported a change in the way graduation rates are calculated. This change occurred during the 1994–95 academic year. Because they included graduation rates calculated under the old and new formulas for two consecutive school years (1994–95 and 1995–96), I estimated the difference and adjusted the graduation rate under the old formula for the 1996–97 and 1997–98 academic years. The new formula differs as it includes students who graduate late.

4. In 1999, the list had 24 percent of the state's school districts. In 2000, the list shrunk to 8 percent and remained at this level for the next year. In 2002, the lowest rankings were received by 11 percent. And, in the last year for which the scores are available, 6 percent of the districts were on academic watch or academic emergency (www.ode.state.oh.us/faq; accessed 6 June 2005).

5. Graduation rates as reported by the state are used because the Cleveland schools changed their method of calculating graduation rates during the period under investigation. State figures provided the most consistent figures.

# References

Administrator interview. 1998. Interview by author, Chicago, Ill., 26 June.
———. 71998. Interview by author, Chicago, Ill., 7 July.
———. 131998. Interview by author, Chicago, Ill., 13 October.
———. 1998. Interview by author, Chicago, Ill., 23 October.
Afi-Odelia, E. Scruggs. 1998. "What Works in NY May Not Work Here." *The Plain Dealer*, 25 November, p. 1B.
Barker, Lucius J., Mack H. Jones, and Katherine Tate. 1999. *African Americans and the American Political System*, 4th Ed. Upper Saddle River, N.J.: Prentice Hall.
Belluck, Pam. 1999. "State of the Union: Education Programs." *The New York Times*, 20 January, p. A20.
Berliner, David. 2002. "Educational Research: The Hardest Science of All. *Educational Researcher* 31:18–20.
Berry, Jeffrey M., Kent E. Portney, and Ken Thompson. 1993. *The Rebirth of Urban Democracy*. Washington, D.C.: Brookings Institution.
Biles, Roger. 1995. *Richard J. Daley*. DeKalb, Ill: Northern Illinois University Press.
Bobo, Lawrence D., and Franklin D. Gilliam Jr. 1990. "Race, Sociopolitical Participation and Black Empowerment." *American Political Science Review* 84:379–93.
Bradsher, Keith. 1999. "Control of Detroit Schools Is Transferred to Mayor and Governor." *The New York Times*, 26 March, p. A17.
"Bringing New Skills to the Task of Governing the Cleveland Public Schools." 1997. The Cleveland Public Schools.
Browning, Rufus P., Dale Rogers Marshall, and David H. Tabb. 1984. *Protest Is Not Enough*. Berkeley: University of California Press.
———. 1997. *Racial Politics in American Cities*, 2nd Ed. New York: Longman.
Bryk, Anthony, David Kerbow, and Sharon Rollow. 1997. "Chicago School Reform." In *New Schools for a New Century*, pp. 164–200. Edited by Diane Ravitch and Joseph Viteritti. New Haven, Conn.: Yale University Press.
Bryk, Anthony, Penny Sebring, David Kerbow, Sharron Rollow, and John Easton. 1998. *Chartering Chicago School Reform*. Boulder, Colo.: Westview Press.
Butler, Esther Monclova. 1997. "The Changing Role of the Cleveland Public School Board (1965–1995): Should Urban Governance Be Restructured?" Ph.D. diss., Cleveland State University.

Butler, Lisa (pseudonym), interview. 2000. Interview by author, Cleveland, Ohio, 18 August.

Button, James W. 1989. *Blacks and Social Change*. Princeton, N.J.: Princeton University Press.

Byrd-Bennett, Barbara, interview. 2002. Interview by author, Cleveland, Ohio, 25 April.

Caldwell, Brian J. 1990. "Educational Reform Through School-Site Management: An International Perspective on Restructuring in Education." In *Advances in Research and Theories of School Management and Educational Policy* 1:303–333.

"Characteristics of the 100 Largest Public Elementary and Secondary School Districts in the United States: 2000–01." 2002. Washington, D.C.: U.S. Department of Education.

"Chicago Public Schools Race and Ethnic Survey." 1998. National Center for Education Statistics.

Chubb, John E., and Terry M. Moe. 1990. *Politics, Markets, and America's Schools*. Washington, D.C.: Brookings Institution.

City Council member interview. 2000. Interview by author, Cleveland, Ohio, 31 August.

"Clevelanders Expect Better Schools." 1999. Cleveland, Ohio: Cleveland Summit on Education and Cleveland Initiative for Education, p. 6.

Clyde, Bob (pseudonym), interview. 1999. Interview by author, Chicago, Ill., 3 March.

Cobb, Kim. 1999. "Takeover Plan Raises Racial Tensions; Move for Mayor to Lead Detroit's Schools Spurs Voting Rights Fears." *The Houston Chronicle*, 7 March, p. A14.

Cohen, Adam. 1997. "City Boosters." *Time*, pp. 22–25.

Cohen, Adam, and Elizabeth Taylor. 2000. *American Pharaoh: Mayor Richard J. Daley, His Battle for Chicago and the Nation*. Boston: Little, Brown, and Company.

Comer, J. 1980. *School Power: Implications for an Intervention Project*. New York: Free Press.

Community member a interview. 1998. Interview by author, Chicago, Ill., 24 October.

———. 1998. Interview by author, Chicago, Ill., 29 October.

———. 2001. Interview by author, Cleveland, Ohio, 23 August.

Community member b interview. 1998. Interview by author, Chicago, Ill., 24 October.

———. 2001. Interview by author, Cleveland, Ohio, 23 August.

Community member c interview. 2001. Interview by author, Cleveland, Ohio, 23 August.

Community member interview. 1998. Interview by author, Chicago, Ill., 25 June.

————. 1998. Interview by author, Chicago, Ill., 7 August.

————. 1998. Interview by author, Chicago, Ill., 30 October.

————. 1998. Interview by author, Chicago, Ill., 31 October.

————. 2000. Interview by author, Cleveland, Ohio, 16 August.

————. 2001. Interview by author, Cleveland, Ohio, 24 August.

Community Oversight Committee. 2000. Report 2: 1999–2000. Cleveland, Ohio: Cleveland Municipal School District.

Crain, Robert L. The Politics of School Desegration. Chicago: Aldine Publishing Company.

Dahl, Robert. 1961. *Who Governs?* New Haven, Conn.: Yale University Press.

Danielson, Michael N., and Jennifer Hochschild. 1998. "Changing Urban Education: Lessons, Cautions, Prospects." In *Changing Urban Education*, pp. 23–44. Edited by Clarence N. Stone. Lawrence: University of Kansas Press.

Dempsey, Louise, interview. 2000. Interview by S. Chambers, Cleveland-Marshall College of Law, Cleveland, Ohio, 19 August.

DeColibus, Richard, interview. 2001. Interview by Wilbur Rich, Cleveland, Ohio, 23 April.

DeSchryver, Dave. 1999. "Mayors: Take Charge!" The Center for Education Reform. Available at www.edreform.com/oped/990306DAD.htm. Accessed 13 August 2000.

Draper, Lawrence. 1996. "Mayor White Outlines His Plan to Save City Schools," *West Side Sun News*, 8 February, p. 3A.

Drury, Darrel, and Douglas Levin. 1994. "The Changing Locus of Control in American Public Education." Report prepared for the U.S. Department of Education, Office of Educational Research and Improvement by Pelavin Associates. February.

Duffrin, Elizabeth. 1998. "Lessons from San Francisco." *Catalyst*, June, p. 11.

Doyle, James, Fr. (pseudonym), interview. 1999. Interview by author, Chicago, Ill., 10 March.

"The Education President." 2001. *The Economist*, 27 January, pp. 25–26.

Eisinger, Peter K. 1982. "Black Empowerment in Municipal Jobs: The Impact of Black Political Power." *American Political Science Review* 76: 380–92.

Epps, Edgar G. 1994. "Radical School Reform in Chicago: How Is It Working?" In *Radical Educational Reforms*, pp. 95–116. Edited by Chester E. Finn Jr. and Herbert J. Walberg. Berkeley, Calif.: McCutchan.

Erie, Steven P. 1988. *Rainbow's End*. Berkeley: University of California Press.

Farris, George (pseudonym), interview. 2000. Interview by author, Cleveland, Ohio, 15 August.

Feinberg, Cara. 2004. "Do Charter Schools Outpace Public Schools or Lag Behind? It Depends on Which Researcher You Ask." *The Boston Globe*, December 5, p. D5.

Fellow, Ben (pseudonym), interview. 1998. Interview by author, Chicago, Ill., 23 July.

Five-teacher interview. 1998. Interview by author, Chicago, Ill., 14 July.

Flint, Anthony. 1999a. "Mayors Applaud Take-Charge Approach to Education." *The Boston Globe,* 1 May, p. B3.

———. 1999b. "Shared Lesson Plans: Chicago, Hub Schools Agendas Similar, Results Aren't." *The Boston Globe,* 3 May, p. B1.

Four-teacher interview. 1998. Interview by author, Chicago, Ill., 14 July.

Former activist interview. 1998. Interview by author, Chicago, Ill., 24 October.

Former board member interview. 2000. Interview by author, Cleveland, Ohio, 30 November.

Former grassroots activist interview. 1998. Interview by author, Chicago, Ill., 7 July.

———. 1998. Interview by author, Chicago, Ill., 24 Ocotber.

———. 1998. Interview by author, Chicago, Ill., 7 July.

Former superintendent interview. 2002. Phone interview by author, 28 February.

Francis, Leona (pseudonym), interview. 1998. Interview by author, Chicago, Ill., 1 August.

Fuchs, Ester R. 1992. *Mayors and Money.* Chicago: University of Chicago Press.

Fung, Archung. 2004. *Empowered Participation.* Princeton, N.J.: Princeton University Press.

Galster, George. 1990. "White Flight from Racially Integrated Neighborhood in 1970s: The Cleveland Experience." *Urban Studies* 27:385–99.

Gittell, Marilyn J. 1998. *School Equity.* New Haven, Conn.: Yale University Press.

Gordon, Jane Anna. 2001. *Why They Couldn't Wait.* New York: Routledge-Falmer.

Gosnell, Harold F. 1968. *Machine Politics.* Chicago: University of Chicago Press.

Greenberg, Arthur. 2002. "One Man Can't Fix New York's Schools." *The New York Times,* 1 August, p. A25.

Greene, Jay P., William G. Howell, and Paul E. Peterson. 1999. "An Evaluation of the Cleveland Scholarship Program." Cambridge, Mass.: Harvard University, Program on Education Policy and Governance.

Grimshaw, William J. 1992. *Bitter Fruit.* Chicago: University of Chicago Press.

Hartocollis, Anemonia. 2002. "The New Schools Chancellor." *The New York Times,* 30 July, p. B4.

Heaney, James. 1999. "Mayors in Charge." *The Buffalo News,* 24 January, p. A1.

Henig, J. R., R.C. Hula, M. Orr, and D. S. Pedescleaux. 1999. *The Color of School Reform.* Princeton, N.J.: Princeton University Press.

Henig, Jeffrey R. 2004. "Washington, D.C.: Race, Issue Definition, and School Board Restructuring." In *Mayors in the Middle*, pp. 191–220. Edited by Jeffrey R. Henig and Wilbur C. Rich. Princeton, N.J.: Princeton University Press.

Henig, Jeffrey R., and Wilbur C. Rich, eds. 2004. *Mayors in the Middle*. Princeton, N.J.: Princeton University Press.

Herrick, Mary J. 1971. *The Chicago Schools*. Beverly Hills, Calif.: Sage.

Herszenhorn, David M. 2004. "Studies in Chicago Fault Policy of Holding Back Third Graders." *The New York Times*, 7 April, p. B1.

Hess, Alfred G., Jr. 1991. *School Restructering, Chicago Style*. Thousand Oaks, Calif.: Corwin.

———. 1995. *Restructuring Urban Schools*. New York: Teachers College Press.

Hess, Frederick M. 1998. *Spinning Wheels: The Politics of Urban School Reform*. Washington, D.C.: Brookings Institution.

Hoover-Dembsey, Kathleen V., and Howard M. Sandler. 1997. "Why Do Parents Become Involved in Their Children's Education?" *Review of Educational Research* 67:3–42.

Holmes, Sandra (pseudonym), interview. 1999. Interview by author, Chicago, Ill., 11 March.

Homel, Michael W. 1984. *Down from Equality*. Urbana: University of Illinois Press.

Hunter, Floyd. 1953. *Community Power Structure*. Chapel Hill: University of North Carolina Press.

Jones, Patrice. 1996. "Give White Control of Schools, Panel Says." *Plain Dealer*, 11 December, p. 1A.

Journalist interview. 1998. Interview by author, Chicago, Ill., 3 August.

Karnig, Albert K., and Susan Welch. 1980. *Black Representation and Urban Policy*. Chicago: University of Chicago Press.

Katznelson, Ira, and Margaret Weir. 1985. *Schooling for All*. New York: Basic Books.

Keane, Roberta (pseudonym), interview. 2000. Interview by author, Cleveland, Ohio, 31 August.

King, Elizabeth. 1998. "Impact Evaluation of Education Projects Involving Decentralization and Privatization." Washington, D.C.: World Bank Policy Research Department. Available at http:www.worldbank.org/html/dec/Publications/Abstracts. Accessed 12 September 2001.

Kirst, Michael. 2002. "Mayoral Influence, New Regimes, and Public School Governance." Consortium for Policy Research in Education, University of Pennsylvania Graduate School of Education, Philadelphia.

Kirst, Michael, and K. Buckley. 2000. "'New Improved' Mayors Take Over City Schools." *Phi Delta Kappan* 81:538–46.

Kleppner, Paul. 1985. Chicago Divided: The Making of a Black Mayor. DeKalb: Northern Illinois University Press.

Koehler, David H., and Margaret T. Wrightson. 1987. "Inequality in the Delivery of Urban Services: A Reconsideration of the Chicago Parks." *The Journal of Politics* 49:80–99.

Kozol, Jonathon. 1991. *Savage Inequalities*. New York: Crown.

Krebs, Timothy B. 1998. "The Determinants of Candidates' Vote Share and the Advantages of Incumbency in City Council Elections." *American Journal of Political Science* 42:921–35.

———. 1999. "The Political and Demographic Predictors of Candidate Emergence in City Council Elections." *Urban Affairs Review* 35:279–300.

———. 2005. "Money and Machine Politics: An Analysis of Corporate and Labor Contributions in Chicago City Council Elections." *Urban Affairs Review* 41:47–64.

Kremer, Timothy G. 1999. "Politicizing City School Boards Won't Raise Quality of School Boards." *The Buffalo News*, 2 June, p. 2B.

Lenz, Linda. 1998. "Glaring Omission on Test Scores." *Catalyst*, June, p. 2.

Levin, Henry. 1968. *Community Control of Schools*. Washington, D.C.: Brookings Institution.

Lewin, Tamar. 1997. "Tax Breaks Squeeze Schools in Cleveland." *New York Times*, 21 May, p. B8.

———. 2002. "For Mayoral Control of Schools, Chicago Has a Working Blueprint." *The New York Times*, 15 June, p. B1.

Lewis, Charles (pseudonym), interview. 2000. Interview by author, Cleveland, Ohio, 18 August.

Lewis, Dan A., and Katherine Nakagawa. 1995. *Race and Educational Reform in the American Metropolis*. Albany: State University of New York Press.

Lipton, Eric, and Abby Goodnough. 2000. "Giuliani Leads New Effort to Take Control of the Schools." *The New York Times*, 7 December, p. B3.

Lublin, David Ian, and Katherine Tate. 1995. "Racial Group Competition in Urban Elections." In *Classifying by Race*, pp. 245–261. Edited by Paul E. Peterson. Princeton, N.J.: Princeton University Press.

"Mayoral Control of the Schools." 2000. *The New York Times*, 18 December, p. A26.

"Mayor Power." 1999. *The Economist*, 19 June.

McKersie, William S. 1993. "Philanthropy's Paradox: Chicago School Reform." *Educational Evaluation and Policy Analysis* 15:110.

McKersie, William S., and Anthony Markward. 1999. "Lessons for the Future of Philanthropy: Local Foundations and Urban School Reform." In *Philanthropy and the Nonprofit Sector in a Changing America*, pp. 385–412. Edited by Charles Clotfelter and Thomas Ehrlich. Bloomington: Indiana University Press.

Meier, Kenneth J., and Robert E. England. 1984. "Black Representation and Educational Policy: Are They Related?" *American Political Science Review* 78:392–403.

Meier, Kenneth J., and Joseph Stewart Jr. 1991. *The Politics of Hispanic Education*. Albany: State University of New York Press.

"Memorandum of Understanding between Cleveland Schools Superintendent Richard Boyd and Cleveland Mayor Michael R. White." 1996. Cleveland, Ohio: Cleveland Municipal School District, 11 March, pp. 1–8.

Meranto, Philip J. 1970. *School Politics in the Metropolis*. Columbus, Ohio: C.E. Merrill.

"Miles to Go on School Reform." 2001. *Daily News*, 6 June, p. 32.

Miller, Carol Poh, and Robert A. Wheeler. 1997. *Cleveland: A Concise History, 1796–1996*. Cleveland, Ohio: Case Western Reserve University.

Minter, Stephen, interview. 2001. Interview by Wilbur Rich, Cleveland, Ohio, 1 May.

Miranda, Rowan A., and Ittipone Tunyavong. 1994. "Patterned Inequality?: Reexamining the Role of Distributive Politics in Urban Service Delivery." *Urban Affairs Quarterly* 29:509–34.

Mirel, Jeffrey. 1999. *The Rise and Fall of an Urban School System: Detroit, 1907–81*. Ann Arbor: University of Michigan Press.

———. 2004. "There Is Still a Long Road to Travel, and Success Is Far from Assured." In *Mayors in the Middle*, pp. 120–158. Edited by Jeffrey R. Henig and Wilbur C. Rich. Princeton, N.J.: Princeton University Press.

National Commission on Excellence in Education. 1983. *A Nation At Risk: The Imperative for Educational Reform*. Washington, D.C.: U.S. Government Printing Office.

Nelson, William E. 2002. *Black Atlantic Politics*. Albany: State University of New York Press.

Nelson, William E., and Philip J. Meranto. 1977. *Electing Black Mayors: Political Action in the Black Community*. Columbus: Ohio State University Press.

*No Child Left Behind*. 2002. Public Law 107-110, 115 Stat. 1425. 8 January.

Oakes, Jeannie. 1987. *Improving Inner-City Schools*. Santa Monica, Calif.: Rand.

Okoben, Janet. 2002a. "Cleveland Divided on School Control, 41% Back Mayor Running, Poll Finds." *The Plain Dealer*, 17 May, p. 1A.

———. 2002b. "Mayoral Control of Schools OK'd." *The Plain Dealer*, 6 November, p. 1A.

Okoben, Janet, and Angela Townsend. 2001. "Mayor's School Control Unpopular." *The Plain Dealer*, 27 September, p.1A.

Orfield, Gary. 1978. *Must We Bus?* Washington, D.C.: Brookings Institution.

———. 1979. "Voluntary Desegregation in Chicago." A Report to Joseph Cronin. ERIC Document 171832.

Orfield, Gary, and Susan E. Eaton, eds. 1996. *Dismantling Desegregation*. New York: New Press.

Orfield, Gary, and John T. Yun. 1999. "Resegregation in American Schools." Cambridge, Mass.: The Civil Rights Project, Harvard University.

Orr, Marion. 1999. *Black Social Capital: The Politics of School Reform in Baltimore*. Lawrence: University Press of Kansas.

————. 2004. "Baltimore: The Limits of Mayoral Control." In *Mayors in the Middle*, pp. 27–58. Edited by Jeffrey R. Henig and Wilbur C. Rich. Princeton, N.J.: Princeton University Press.

Parent a interview. 1998. Interview by author, Chicago, Ill., 29 October.

Parent b interview. 1998. Interview by author, Chicago, Ill., 29 October.

————. 1999. Interview by author, Chicago, Ill., 30 January.

Parent interview. 1998. Interview by author, Chicago, Ill., 9 November.

————. 2002. Interview by author, Chicago, Ill., 7 May.

Peterson, Paul E. 1976. *School Politics Chicago Style*. Chicago: University of Chicago Press.

————. 1981. *City Limits*. Chicago: University of Chicago Press.

Philanthropic community interview. 2001. Interview by author, Cleveland, Ohio, 22 August.

Pick, Grant. 1996. "Corporate Style Board Backs the CEO." *Catalyst*, December, pp. 11–12.

Pinderhughes, Dianne M. 1987. *Race and Ethnicity in Chicago Politics*. Urbana: University of Illinois Press.

————. 1997. "An Examination of Chicago Politics for Evidence of Political Incorporation and Representation." In *Racial Politics In American Cities*, 2nd Ed, pp. 117–136. Edited by Rufus P. Browning, Dale Rogers Marshall, and David H. Tabb. New York: Longman.

Policy analyst interview. 1998. Interview by author, Chicago, Ill., 18 June.

————. 1996. Interview by author, Chicago, Ill., 26 June.

Portz, John. 1996. "Problem Definitions and Policy Agendas: Shaping the Education Agenda in Boston." *Policy Studies Journal* 24:371–86.

————. 2004. "Boston: Agenda Setting and School Reform in a Mayor-centric System." In *Mayors in the Middle*, pp. 96–119. Edited by Jeffrey R. Henig and Wilbur C. Rich. Princeton, N.J.: Princeton University Press.

Portz, John, Lana Stein, and Robin Jones. 1999. *City Schools and City Politics: Institutions and Leadership in Pittsburgh, Boston, and St. Louis*. Lawrence: University Press of Kansas.

Presser, Arlynn. 1991. "Revolution Needed." *National Review* 43:20.

Purnick, Joyce. 2000. "Teachers' Leader Yielding on Mayor's School Role." *The New York Times*, 4 June, p. A1.

*Racial and Ethnic Survey of Staff*. 2005. Chicago: Office of Accountability, Research, and Evaluation of the Chicago Public Schools. Provided by phone on 1 June.

Reinhard, Beth. 1997a. "Bill to Give Cleveland Mayor School Control Advances." *Education Week*, 21 May, p. 12.

————. 1997b. "Lawsuits Oppose Mayor's Role in Cleveland Schools." *Education Week*, 17 September, p. 3.

Rich, Dorothy. 1993. "Building a Bridge to Reach Minority Parents." In *Families and Schools in a Pluralistic Society*, pp. 235–244. Edited by Nancy Chavkin. Albany: State University of New York Press.

Rich, Wilbur C. 1996. *Black Mayors and School Politics*. New York: Garland.

Richards, Marva, interview. 2001. Interview by Wilbur Rich, Cleveland, Ohio, 3 May.

Riedel, James. 1972. "Citizen Participation: Myth and Realities." *Public Administration Review* May/June, 212.

Rolling, Ken. 2004. "Reflections on the Chicago Annenberg Challenge." In *School Reform in Chicago: Lessons in Policy and Practice*, pp. 23–28. Edited by Alexander Russo. Cambridge, Mass.: Harvard Education Press.

Rothstein, Richard. 2001. "Decrees on Fixing Schools May Fail the Reality Test." *The New York Times*, 3 October, p. A19.

———. 2002. "Mr. Mayor, Schools Chief. Mr. Fix-it Is Another Tale." *The New York Times*, 17 April, p. B9.

"*Rudy v. Rudy*." 1999. *The Economist*, 8 May, pp. 22–23.

Ryan, Patrick J. 2001. "Can't Let Go: Just a Few Years Back, School-Based Management Was the Rage in Cleveland. Except that the Central Office Wasn't All That Interested in Relinquishing Control." *Education Next* 1:36–41.

Schmitt, Eric. 2001. "Segregation Growing Among U.S. Children" *The New York Times*, 6 May, p. 28.

Shapiro, Rose. 1986. "It's Time to Re-evaluate New York City School Decentralization." *The New York Times*, 5 May, p. A18.

Shefter, Martin. 1985. *Political Crisis Fiscal Crisis*. New York: Basic Books.

Shipps, Dorothy. 1997. "The Invisible Hand: Big Business and Chicago School Reform." *Teachers College Record* 99:73–116.

———. 1998. "Corporate Influence on Chicago School Reform." In *Changing Urban Education*, pp. 161–183. Edited by Clarence N. Stone. Lawrence: University Press of Kansas.

———. 2004. "Chicago: The National 'Model' Reexamined." In *Mayors in the Middle*, pp. 59–95. Edited by Jeffrey R. Henig and Wilbur C. Rich. Princeton, N.J.: Princeton University Press.

Shipps, Dorothy, Joe Kahne, and Mark Smylie. 1998. "Legitimacy and Professionalism in Chicago's Layered School Reform." Paper presented at the annual meeting of the American Educational Research Association, San Diego, CA, April 13–17.

Sizemore, Barbara. 1981. *The Ruptured Diamond*. Washington, D.C.: University Press of America.

Sloat, Bill. 1999. "Court Sounds Some Doubts about NAACP's School Suit." *The Plain Dealer*, 9 June, p. B5.

Smith, Helen. 1997. "Who Will Run the Schools?" *The Plain Dealer*, 21 October, p. 11B.

Smith, Hilton, interview. 2001. Interview by Wilbur Rich, 9 May.

Smith, Kevin. 2005. "Data Don't Matter? Academic Research and School Choice." *Perspectives on Politics* 3:285–99.

Smith, Mary (pseudonym), interview. 1998. Interview by author, Chicago, Ill., 23 October.

Spielman, Fran. 1996. "Mayor's Clout Even Bigger for New Term." *Chicago Sun Times,* 25 February, p. 6.

Stanfield, Rochelle L. 1997. "Bossing City Schools." *National Journal,* 8 February, p. 273.

Stephens, Scott. 1995a. "More Mayors Taking Control of Schools" *The Plain Dealer,* 29 October, p.1B.

———. 1995b. "Seventeen Seek Cleveland School Board Seats." *The Plain Dealer,* 25 August, p. 1B.

———. 1996. "People at Meeting Criticize Plan to Give Mayor Control of Schools." *The Plain Dealer,* 18 December, p. 4B.

Stephens, Scott, and Joe Frolik. 2000. "Few Want Schools in White's Hands." *The Plain Dealer,* 29 May, p. 1A.

Stone, Clarence N. 1996. "The Politics of Urban School Reform: Civic Capacity, Social Capital, and the Intergroup Context." Paper presented at the annual meeting of the American Political Science Association, San Francisco, August 29–September 1.

———. 1998. "Introduction: Urban Education in Political Context." In *Changing Urban Education,* pp. 1–22. Edited by Clarence N. Stone. Lawrence: University of Kansas Press.

———. 2004. "Mayors and the Challenge of Modernization." In *Mayors in the Middle,* pp. 232–248. Edited by Jeffrey R. Henig and Wilbur C. Rich. Princeton, N.J.: Princeton University Press.

Summit on Education. 1990. "1990 Report to the Community." Cleveland, Ohio: Cleveland Summit.

———. 1993. "1993 Report to the Community." Cleveland, Ohio: Cleveland Summit.

Swanstrom, Todd. 1985. *The Crisis of Growth Politics.* Philadelphia: Temple University Press.

Tate, Katherine. 2003. *Black Faces in the Mirror.* Princeton, N.J.: Princeton University Press.

Three-parent interview. 1998. Interview by author, Chicago, Ill., 29 October.

Toliver, Stanley. 2000. Interview by author, Cleveland, Ohio, 30 September.

Tyack, David. 1974. *The One Best System.* Cambridge, Mass.: Harvard University Press.

Tyack, David, and Larry Cuban. 1995. *Tinkering toward Utopia: A Century of Public School Reform.* Cambridge, Mass.: Harvard University Press.

Vallas, Paul. 1998. Radio interview, Odyssey. WBEZ, Chicago, Ill., July 15.

Vander Weele, Maribeth. 1994. *Reclaiming Our Schools.* Chicago: Loyola University Press.

Van Lier, Piet. 2001. "District to Ask for Levy" *Catalyst,* January/February, p. 4.

*Vision 21: An Action Plan for the 21st Century.* 1993. Cleveland, Ohio: Cleveland Public Schools.

Vitullo-Martin, Julia. 1996. "Chicago Hope: Can You Turn a City's Schools around by Turning Them over to the Mayor?" *The New Democrat,* September/October, p. 43.

"Voters Turn Down Proposal for Mayoral Control of Detroit Schools." Associated Press State and Local Wire. November 3, 2004. Accessed through Lexis-Nexis, http://web.lexis-nexis.com/universe/document?_m=ab90f8 782ba2b222205a643c1990b6a.

Waddock, Sandra A. 1995. *Not by Schools Alone.* Westport, Conn.: Praeger.

White, Michael. 1997. "Appointed CEO Will Focus on Children, Improvements." *The Plain Dealer,* 21 October, p. 11B.

White, Michael, interview. 2002. Interview by author, Cleveland, Ohio, April 25.

Wilgoren, Jodi. 2001. "Chief Executive of Chicago Schools Resigns." *The New York Times,* 7 June, p. A26.

Wilgoren, Debbi, and Michael H. Cottman. 2000. "Williams Seeks Control of School System." *The Washington Post,* 2 January, p. C1.

Winn, Stephen. 1999. "Bad Mix: Mayor and Schools." *The Kansas City Star,* 13 March, p. B7.

Wirt, Frederick, and Michael Kirst. 1972. *The Political Web of American Schools.* Boston: Little, Brown and Company.

———. 2001. *The Political Dynamics of American Education.* Richmond, Calif.: McCutchan.

Witte, John F. 1996. "Who Benefits from the Milwaukee Choice Program?" In *Who Chooses? Who Loses? Culture, Institutions, and the Unequal Effects of School Choice,* pp. 118–137. Edited by Bruce Fuller and Richard Elmore. New York: Teachers College Press.

Wohlstetter, Priscilla, Roxane Smyer, and Susan Albers Mohrman. 1994. "New Boundaries for School-Based Management: The High Involvement Model." Paper presented at the Annual Meeting of the 1994 American Educational Research Association, New Orleans, April 4–8.

Wong, Kenneth, and Gail Sunderman. 1994. "Redesigning Accountability at the System Wide Level: The Politics of School Reform in Chicago." Paper presented at the Federal Reserve Bank of Chicago Symposium, Chicago, Ill.

Wood, Sarah (pseudonym), interview. 2002. Interview by author, Cleveland, Ohio, March 16.

# Index